The Grand Teton Reader

THE
GRAND
TETON
READER

EDITED BY ROBERT W. RIGHTER

THE UNIVERSITY OF UTAH PRESS
Salt Lake City

The Defiance House Man colophon is a registered trademark
of The University of Utah Press. It is based on a four-foot-tall
Ancient Puebloan pictograph (late PIII) near Glen Canyon, Utah.

LIBRARY OF CONGRESS CATALOGING-IN-PUBLICATION DATA

Names: Righter, Robert W., editor.
Title: The Grand Teton reader / edited by Robert W. Righter.
Description: Salt Lake City : The University of Utah Press, [2021] |
    Series: National Park Readers Series ; 5 | Includes bibliographical
    references. | Summary: "This collection of essays covers the long and
    varied history of Grand Teton National Park (GTNP) and the areas around
    its borders"—Provided by publisher.
Identifiers: LCCN 2020042494 (print) | LCCN 2020042495 (ebook) |
    ISBN 9781647690335 (paperback) | ISBN 9781647690328 (ebook)
Subjects: LCSH: Tales—Wyoming—Grand Teton National Park. | Indians of
    North America—Wyoming—Grand Teton National Park—Folklore. | Frontier
    and pioneer life—Wyoming—Grand Teton National Park—Folklore. |
    Mountaineers—Wyoming—Grand Teton National Park—Folklore. |
    Animals—Wyoming—Grand Teton National Park. | Nature
    conservation—Wyoming—History. | National parks and reserves—Wyoming.
    | American essays—21st century. | Grand Teton National Park
    (Wyo.)—Description and travel. | Jackson Hole (Wyo.)—Description and
    travel.
Classification: LCC F767.T3 G823 2021 (print) | LCC F767.T3 (ebook) |
    DDC 978.7/55—dc23
LC record available at https://lccn.loc.gov/2020042494
LC ebook record available at https://lccn.loc.gov/2020042495

Errata and further information on this and other titles available online at UofUpress.com

Printed and bound in the United States of America.

Dedicated to Trisha, Loy, Bonnie, and Ron

CONTENTS

Part V: The Mountains

Part VI: Inspiration from the Park

ACKNOWLEDGMENTS

Some of the entries in this collection first appeared in *A Teton Country Anthology*, which I edited for Roberts Rinehart in 1990. That was a long time ago, but I would still like to acknowledge those who helped make it possible: Leigh Ortenberger, David Love, Ken Diem, John Daugherty, Sharlene Milligan, Robert Rudd, Nancy Effinger, John Swartz, and Rick Rinehardt. Each in their own way contributed to the anthology and to our appreciation of the Teton Country's colorful history.

Now into the 21st Century, retired University of Utah Editor-in-Chief John Alley deserves thanks. He encouraged me to rethink and expand the readings for this much-beloved park. I appreciate his vision. Thanks also must go to Lance Newman, who gave very helpful editorial advice. For their interest and assistance in choosing entries, I thank Dan and Marlene Merrill and Sherry Smth. Finally, a heartfelt thanks to the authors who graciously contributed to this collection.

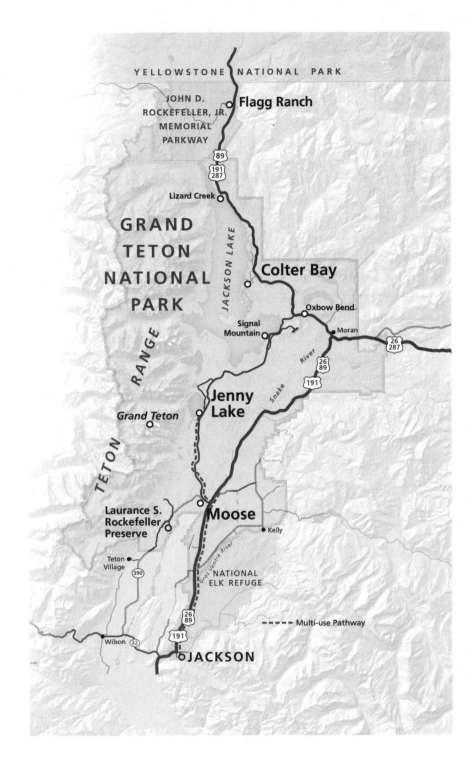

INTRODUCTION

In the summer of 2019, I volunteered to help out in Grand Teton National Park. For many years, I had considered repaying the park for all the good things it had done for me. Now was my chance. My first choice was to work at the Laurance S. Rockefeller Preserve. Luckily, that is where I was assigned. Among my tasks was to meet and greet people in the small parking lot, a lot designed to limit the number of cars in it and thus assure a quality experience. During busy summer days, visitors would often wait up to an hour for a parking space.

My job was to talk to, entertain, and prepare visitors until we could assign them a parking space. I expected tired and impatient tourists, disgruntled with the long wait. I expected irritated drivers or angry families demanding privileges I could not grant. But that was not my experience. Uniformly, people were of good spirits. If they had to wait, there was no other place they would rather be. I concluded that visitation to Grand Teton National Park could enhance the good qualities of human character—or at least modify disposition.

At first hesitant to approach visitors with a smile and a "welcome to the Laurance S. Rockefeller Preserve," I found that a friendly greeting engendered a like response. My summer job became fun and offered me a new view of a park I thought I knew.

I think tourists maintain an optimistic attitude since they are on vacation, but also because they are visiting one of America's most cherished parks. Grand Teton National Park features a combination of unforgettable mountains, abundant wildlife, thick forests, sagebrush-covered valleys—all bisected by the swift-flowing Snake River. Even common sagebrush can be a surprise. I encouraged guests to pick a sprig of sagebrush, roll it between their fingers, and put it to their noses. They were amazed at how a seemingly insignificant bush could produce such a delightful and refreshing fragrance.

Jackson Hole is a right-angle landscape. The level valley and the vertical
mountains astound the visitor and provide the visual drama of the park.
Courtesy National Park Service, Grand Teton National Park.

Sometimes these small discoveries delight, but ultimately the park
is a place of grandeur. Words fail many visitors in describing the natural
beauty before them. They fall back on their cameras to provide a reservoir
of memories. During the fall, the long-lensed camera buffs scour the park
for the perfect photo of a bull moose, a bugling elk, or a mother black bear
or grizzly bear devouring berries in preparation for a long winter. Of course,
not all visitors find satisfaction in photography. There is also the written
word. Hike the trails of Grand Teton and you are likely to find a solo journalist perched on a rock, scribbling thoughts on the splendor of a mountain scene or the Snake River and its rollicking tributaries. They record their
feelings and experiences. What they write may sometimes find its way into
print. With that thought in mind, what follows are thirty-five samplings
of such writings over time. They are my favorites. My hope is that these
selections will enlighten and inspire appreciation for this remarkable park.

Appreciation has been my own personal response to this place. As a
youngster, my parents introduced me to Yosemite and what John Muir

called the "Range of Light." In time, I found my way to the Wind River Range and the Tetons. Most of my backpacking was located in the Wind Rivers because Cody, my golden retriever, could accompany me. I looked longingly at the Tetons but could not envision an extended trip without my loyal companion.

When I accepted a history teaching position at the University of Wyoming, I developed a new fascination with the Tetons and Jackson Hole—what I soon called the aesthetic corner of the state. Over the years, this fascination resulted in my writing two books about the region and the building of a modest log cabin in the area, which my wife and I now make our permanent residence. I have had a love affair with the Tetons for many years. To a degree, my own path has followed that of Terry Tempest Williams, who writes of her "range of memory." The Tetons are the place where I am most at home. I am quick to add that I share this home with amazing wildlife and many people who feel passionately for this land.

The selection of essays that follow emerged from my own research and reading. Not all the essays are of the visitor/tourist genre. Many come from the pens of people who lived and worked before the park was created. They provide a varied view. For these residents, the magic and imagery of the Tetons may be underscored by the need to make a living, but no one is unaffected by where they live.

No one knows when the first human beings inhabited Jackson Hole, but measured by geologic time, their presence has been short, even fleeting. The valley remained unoccupied for many centuries, but the first Native Americans to reside in it likely settled on the shores of Jackson Lake perhaps ten thousand years ago. In northern Jackson Hole, hostile winters limited most Indian use of the land to the summer months. There are evidences of their occupation. Mountain climbers have seen and studied the "Enclosure," a stone ring created by humans near the crest of the Grand Teton. Both the Shoshone and Crow peoples claim an association to it, and it suggests that centuries ago the first human to summit the Grand Teton may have been a Native American.

I have included a tale from Laine Thom, a Shoshone-Bannock elder. He tells the story of the origins of the Yellowstone and Snake Rivers. It is a tale focusing on how Itsa-ppe, the wily coyote, created the Snake. The creativity and wry humor of this story makes us appreciate oral traditions associated with the Snake River as it wends its way through Jackson Hole toward the Pacific Ocean.

In the early nineteenth century, a few Euro-American adventurers looked in on Jackson Hole. They noted the terrain, but they did not gush over the mountains or the Snake River. It seems strange, but we must remember that a mountain range or a rushing river presented a barrier for a fur trapper, a miner, or any traveler. The Jackson Hole region had to be crossed, circumvented, or best avoided altogether. Therefore, few of these earliest people took pleasure in the country we treasure today.

Isolation delayed settlement. However, by 1885 a few Anglo-American homesteaders settled on land that eventually became part of Grand Teton National Park. They had farming in mind, but soon it became evident that most of the land was unsuited for agriculture. It was so rock strewn, as Struthers Burt put it, "even a badger won't dig in it." Yet the early settlers would not retreat without a fight. They faced a series of challenges, such as rocky soil, aridity, a short growing season, hungry elk consuming their haystacks, no irrigation water when they needed it, and little capital available to carry them through the rough times. The combination almost always dictated failure. It was a hard country, and the land simply wore out settlers. Joe Jones, whose writing is featured here, and his wife worked hard on their homestead and suffered terribly for very little return. Jones tried his best to succeed in a beautiful yet hostile environment. They finally moved to town. Today, the seasons are not much different. I have tried a garden of lettuce and snow peas, but a quick-moving hailstorm ended the experiment. Today, like many of my neighbors, I encourage the growth of indigenous trees, plants, and grasses.

While failure was common, a few settlers did manage to eke out a living by cultivating grain and hay, running cattle on the public lands, and guiding big game hunters in the fall months. They accepted the trade-off of rural hardship for exquisite nature. By 1920, a smattering of homesteaders had settled in northern Jackson Hole, primarily in the Mormon Row area. But most sold out to the Snake River Land Company when they had the chance. The Chambers family did not. Some years ago, I asked the elderly Roy Chambers if his view of the Tetons was inspirational to him. He turned his chiseled, wrinkled face to me as if to say, "that's a silly question." When I drive the Antelope Flats road today, I often think about how hard it would be to make a living here, and that landscapes of beauty do not necessarily put food on the table.

People with a different purpose, however, found the broad reaches of Jackson Hole more amenable. Wealthy sportsmen, such as British aristo-crat William Baillie-Grohman, loved the wildness of the valley as well as the hunting and fishing. Their exploitive attitudes, however, may surprise us. Such prominent and wealthy "conservationists" as Theodore Roosevelt, Owen Wister, George Bird Grinnell, Sir Rose Lambert Price, and Ernest Thompson Seton and his wife, Grace, were enthralled by the majesty of elk and other wildlife, yet they were intent on killing as much game as they could. Unthinkable today, they rarely refused a shot. Of course, some killed for food—such as the hunters for President Chester A. Arthur's party—but others killed for sport, leaving pounds of trout and heaps of meat to the benefit of the wolf and coyote populations.

As we might expect, intense hunting of elk, bear, moose, and prong-horns could not be sustained. Today, hunters still frequent northern Jack-son Hole and the park for a special elk hunt (called the Elk Reduction Program), but attitudes and regulations have eliminated the earlier carnage. Killing wildlife in the national park is illegal, and poaching, once a way of life for a few, is now despised. Thus, visitors and locals alike stalk wildlife with a camera, and they fish with barbless hooks and a philosophy of "catch and release." Both are equally challenging but more in keeping with the mission of the park.

This gentler rapport with nature is most evident in changing attitudes toward the landscape. New voices, mainly a contingent of artists, authors, and mountaineers, began to sing the praises of Jackson Hole, the Tetons, and the Rocky Mountain West. Today, that praise continues, enhanced by high-profile meetings, such as the Federal Reserve's annual meeting and the occasional visitation of presidents and first ladies. But, of course, the first notable visitations came from Eastern Americans. Their model for alpine inspiration had been the European Alps, but now their gaze turned west-ward, labeling the Greater Yellowstone region "The Switzerland of Amer-ica." The Rocky Mountains became a surrogate for the European Alps, and, as William O. Owen put it, the Grand Teton became the "Matterhorn of America."

Some adventurers were not content just to look at the mountains, sublime as they might be. They wanted to climb the peaks and to know the glacier-carved valleys and gorges. Who was the first white person to ascend the Grand Teton? We don't know for certain. The first successful mountaineer will always be in doubt. The state of Wyoming, however, has officially listed the Spaulding Party, led by Owen, with that honor. Since then, the Grand Teton and its adjacent peaks have become a destination for climbers worldwide. Paul Petzoldt and Glenn Exum showed the way, pioneering new routes and establishing the first climbing school. The reader will find that Paul and Glenn had a sense of humor as well, describing the struggle to "guide" two Labrador retriever dogs to the top of the Grand Teton.

The mountains have been a place of tragedies, heroics, and life-changing events. National Park Service climbing ranger Pete Sinclair reveals the drama of the 1967 "Grand Rescue" on the north face of the Grand. This rescue turned out as a proud moment, but that has not always been the case. My wife and I have witnessed such true-life dramas since our cabin is on the edge of the park between the airport and the mountains. In the summer months every week or two the yellow rescue helicopters sweep over our cabin. As I follow the flight from my deck, I know there is either a heartbreaking or happy story being played out in the mountains. The next day's newspaper will tell me which.

Today, I cannot imagine northern Jackson Hole as anything but a national park. But in the first half of the twentieth century the land was a battleground, one described by the writer Margaret Sanborn. Who would have control and ownership of this mountain terrain? Would it be private settlers and cattlemen? Most locals wished to continue harvesting the wealth of the valley. They were not immune to the scenic beauty of the land, but they did not wish to be restricted. If profitable, they wanted no limits in damming water, cutting timber, running cattle, taking an elk, or proving up a homestead. They opposed a national park, for it meant giving up the nineteenth-century lack of restrictions for the bewildering complexity of rules and bureaucracies.

On the other side, many individuals at both national and local levels believed that this special valley served a greater purpose than growing cattle for table steaks or lumber to build cabins. They found a man of similar views in John D. Rockefeller Jr. He provided both the financial resources and determination to make Grand Teton National Park possible. And yet the story is not only of philanthropy, but of locals who believed that Jackson Hole should not be exploited and carved up like most western land. It reminds me that when I lived in Dallas I cared little of the loss of open space in the city, but disturb a blade of grass in Grand Teton National Park and you have my attention.

Olaus and Mardy Murie also felt that way. They fought for what they believed, and they wrote about it in "Valley in Discord." To those of us who love the park, they are heroes, navigating the divisiveness of the community, meeting anger with the calming effect of their personalities, and finally in 1950 witnessing a hard-fought victory that culminated in the national park we have today.

Another influential advocate was the writer Struthers Burt. In 1911 Burt created the Bar BC, a successful dude ranch in northern Jackson Hole hugging the Snake River. Burt strongly favored a national park. I have often visited the ruins of the old Bar BC and reflected on Struthers Burt's commitment to the park. He was involved in a war of words and he even gave up ownership of the Bar BC to encourage support of the park. Without his dedication, and that of the Muries and a few other visionaries, Grand Teton National Park would have been nothing but an unrealized idea. Today, it is a great pleasure to see many of the Bar BC cabins restored by volunteer groups and interpreted by the National Park Service.

Understandably, Jackson Hole's attraction rests on the splendor of the perpendicular mountains, offset by the flat valley, and enhanced by abundant lakes and swift streams. It is a scene that never disappoints. No foothills separate the level valley and the peaks. I call it "a land of right angles." They leave one, as Fritiof Fryxell suggested, "likely to gaze silently upon them, conscious of the futility of speech." The mountains furnish the viewer a visual experience that philosophers have called sublime. Even a twelve-year-old girl understood the magic. Fanny Kemble Wister's description of the place and the freedom she experienced at the JY Ranch in 1911 makes one weep in appreciation.

In more recent decades, contemporary writers have carried on the literary tradition of Fanny Kemble Wister. Naturalist Bert Raynes describes with warmth and humor his observations of birds and wildlife in the park. Philosopher and climber Jack Turner introduces us to the remarkable pelicans soaring above the Grand Teton. Poet Lyn Dalebout brings her lyrical skills to the bears and landscape of the place she loves. Naturalist Frank C. Craighead Jr. is also conversant with the ursine world, but he provides sage advice on the continual progression of natural events in the park, noting where and when we can appreciate them. Terry Tempest Williams is nationally known as a nature writer and political advocate, and writes of the Teton mountains as her "range of memory." Paul Bruun is a legendary fisherman/guide who vigorously scribbles about fishing in our remarkable river where even if the fishing is "off," the adjacent mountains are always superb. Finally, environmental journalist and writer Todd Wilkinson contributes environmental advice on the Tetons and the Greater Yellowstone Ecosystem, asking the reader if we are "paying attention."

These essays speak to the beauty of mountains, rivers, and wildlife with the passion of Fanny Kemble. They also remind us of the role of human beings in preserving and appreciating what has become an iconic symbol of America. Millions of people, both nationally and internationally, visit Grand Teton National Park each year. They should know that what they see and admire is a paragon of natural forces, but also the design of men and women working toward a noble cause. Once seen, this landscape is seldom forgotten, and I hope that this mosaic of writings will prove it.

PART I

COMING INTO THE COUNTRY

THE BROKEN EARTH

Why the Tetons Are Grand (2000)

ROBERT B. SMITH (1938–) AND LEE J. SIEGEL (1953–)

Robert B. Smith is the preeminent geologist of Yellowstone National Park. He has written and spoken widely on the Yellowstone Caldera and what has happened and what may happen as a result of molten lava and water. He and his graduate students from the University of Utah continue to measure and document the geologic changes with the assistance of the National Park Service (NPS).

But Smith and his coauthor Lee J. Siegel have not ignored the Teton Range. In fact, Smith was raised in northern Jackson Hole where he beheld the Tetons every day. How could he not investigate their origins and movements? In time he would write of the Teton Fault, its slip rate and the earthquake occurrence rate. Eventually he built a cabin on the border of Grand Teton National Park where he spends much of his time today. One day I asked him if he had earthquake insurance. His answer was "yes."

The Smith/Siegel chapter, taken from their book Windows into the Earth: The Geologic Story of Yellowstone and Grand Teton National Parks *(2000), is the perfect opening essay for this work. Besides describing the origins of Jackson Hole, we are introduced to its lakes, the swift-flowing Snake River, and the natural features that make Jackson Hole and Grand Teton National Park such a special place.*

On a summer morning when the breeze blows cool, it is easy to realize the lakes and sagebrush-covered glacial plains of Wyoming's Jackson Hole sit at nearly 7,000 feet elevation. Yet the altitude of this gorgeous valley is diminished by the view to the west: The precipitous east front of the Teton Range towers above the valley floor, with 13,770-foot Grand Teton and other rugged, snowclad peaks catching the first golden rays of daybreak.

This is one of the most spectacular mountain vistas in America. Whether at chill dawn, in glistening light after a torrential afternoon thunderstorm, or during summer evenings when the sun descends behind the jagged Tetons, it is a view that brings solace and peace.

Yet the serene splendor of Grand Teton National Park belies a hidden fury. It is not volcanism, which is concealed beneath the gentle pine-covered Yellowstone Plateau to the north. Instead, this defiant topography was born of seismic disaster as the Teton fault repeatedly and violently broke the earth, producing a few thousand magnitude-7 to -7.5 earthquakes during the past 13 million years.

During each major jolt, Jackson Hole dropped downward and the Teton Range rose upward, increasing the vertical distance between the valley and the mountains by 3 to 6 feet and sometimes more. Now, after 13 million years of earthquakes, the tallest peaks tower almost 7,000 feet above the valley floor.

Actual movement on the fault has been even greater. Jackson hole dropped downward perhaps 16,000 feet during all those earthquakes. Rock eroded from the Teton Range and other mountains by streams and glaciers filled Jackson Hole with thousands of feet of sediment, disguising how much the valley sank.

Combine the uplift of the mountains and the sinking of Jackson Hole, and the best estimate—although still plagued by uncertainty—is that movement on the Teton fault has totaled 23,000 feet during the past 13 million years.

That is a tiny fraction of Earth's 4.6-billion-year history. Consider the effects of repeated episodes of mountain-building during eons before the Teton fault was born: The oldest rocks high in the Teton Range are 2.8-billion-year-old gneisses and schists and 2.4-billion-year-old granites. They have been lifted as much as 33,000 feet from their subterranean birth-places—more than the height of Mount Everest.

As impressive as that sounds, the power of the Teton fault is revealed by how quickly, in geologic time, it has lifted the mountains. Of the 33,000 feet or so of mountain-building uplift in 2.8 billion years, more than two-thirds of the movement happened only since the modern Teton fault became active 13 million years ago....

The seismic power of the Teton fault is not unique. Grand Teton National Park sits within the Intermountain Seismic Belt. The belt is a zone of weakness within the North American plate, one of the great, drifting slabs that make up Earth's crust and upper mantle.

The Rocky Mountains and Colorado Plateau sit east of the seismic belt. To the west is the Basin and Range Province, a region of the interior western United States that is being stretched apart. This stretching is responsible for creating the Teton, Wasatch, Hebgen Lake, and other powerful faults within the Intermountain Seismic Belt.

The belt is apparent on seismicity maps as a diffuse band defined by the epicenters of earthquakes, most of them small to moderate but also some of the strongest in U.S. history: the magnitude-7.5 Hebgen Lake disaster northwest of Yellowstone in 1959 and the 7.3 Borah Peak, Idaho, quake in 1983. The Hebgen Lake quake, centered only 55 miles northwest of the Teton Range, was the largest historic earthquake in the Rockies and the Intermountain Seismic Belt.

The Teton fault is a "normal" fault. Because the Earth is being stretched apart in the region, ground on one side of the fault moves down and away from ground on the other side during earthquakes. It is a different kind of fault than California's San Andreas, which is a "strike-slip" fault where ground on one side of the fault moves horizontally past ground on the other side. Normal faults like the Teton generated the Hebgen Lake and Borah Peak quakes. Violent ground shaking and rupturing of the landscape during those disasters indicate what lies in store for Grand Teton National Park when the Teton fault eventually lets loose—and for Salt Lake City when the Wasatch fault breaks.

The Teton fault first was described in the 1930s, but detailed studies did not begin until the 1970s, when there was wide recognition that it was capable of generating large earthquakes that could trigger landslides and avalanches, and threaten structures in the region, most significantly Jackson Lake Dam. If a major quake collapsed the dam, the upper 40 feet of water in this large lake would rush down the Snake River, flooding downstream inhabited areas such as Moose—the site of Grand Teton National Park head-quarters—and low-lying areas near Teton Village and the town of Wilson. Because of the threat, the dam was strengthened in the late 1980s.

There are large uncertainties in estimating how often big destructive quakes rip the Teton fault. However, an average of roughly once every couple thousand years is a good estimate. The last magnitude-7-plus quake happened sometime between 4,840 and 7,090 years ago. That suggests another seismic disaster in the Tetons—the first to be experienced by modern humans—is overdue.

Yet the 2,000-year "repeat time" for major quakes is only an estimate. And there is debate about the once-popular idea that "characteristic earthquakes" happen like clockwork on certain faults. Different kinds of faults—including the Teton and San Andreas—display evidence that clusters of several strong quakes can occur in a relatively short geologic time, followed by long, quiet periods with no earthquakes. So it is possible the Teton fault is now in such a slumber period, and the next major shake may be thousands of years in the future.

Whatever the uncertainty about the timing of the next big quake, there is little doubt it will happen. The Teton fault is "locked" and represents a "seismic gap"—a stretch of the Intermountain Seismic Belt deficient in quake activity in recent millennia. The quiet period must end, sooner or later, with a major quake that fills in the gap.

"Trois Tetons"

The Tetons were named by lonely French-Canadian beaver trappers in the late eighteenth century. They referred to Grand, Middle, and South Teton peaks as "Trois Tetons" or "three breasts." Nathaniel P. Langford—who explored Yellowstone in 1870 with Henry Washburn and military escort Lt. Gustavus Doane—said of the trappers: "He indeed must have been of a most susceptible nature and, I would fain believe, long a dweller amid these solitudes, who could trace in these cold and barren peaks any resemblance to the gentle bosom of a woman."

John Colter ventured into Jackson Hole shortly after leaving the Lewis and Clark expedition. He entered the valley on its east side and continued north into Yellowstone in late 1807—the first white man known to have visited the region. Many trappers visited Jackson Hole until beavers were trapped out and the fur trade collapsed in the late 1830s. It was left in solitude until the late 1800s, when geologists detoured from their exploration of Yellowstone and ostensibly made the first ascents of Grand Teton. Soon, pioneers began homesteading Jackson Hole—named for a fur trader, Davy Jackson—and established the town of Jackson, Wyoming.

Unlike Yellowstone, which was designated a national park a year after Ferdinand Hayden's 1871 expedition, it took decades of controversy to fully protect Grand Teton National Park, the "Switzerland of America." The Teton Range became part of a national forest in 1908 and much was designated Grand Teton National Park in 1929. Jackson Hole was excluded due to opposition by ranchers who feared for their livelihood and wanted freedom from government regulation. After John D. Rockefeller Jr. quietly bought several ranches and donated them to the government, the protected area was enlarged to include Jackson Hole and the north end of the Tetons in 1943. The park and monument were combined into Grand Teton National Park in 1950. The park encompasses the Teton fault, the Teton Range that rose along the fault and the valley of Jackson Hole, which dropped along the fault. The park owes its scenery and existence to an active fault.

Topography of the Tetons

Grand Teton National Park's landscape has been shaped by its active geology. The landscape reveals those processes: faulting, other earlier episode of mountain-building, and the relatively recent passage of huge glaciers.

The Teton Range extends 40 miles, from north to south, and is 15 miles wide east to west. Its spectacular eastern front is steep, gaining it world renown among mountaineers. From the loftiest peaks, the range drops eastward to Jackson Hole in only a few miles. In contrast, the western side of the Teton Range is a long, gentle slope, taking more than 10 miles to descend from the highest peaks west into Idaho. This striking lack of symmetry betrays the evolution of the Teton Range. It is evidence for the long-lived and still active Teton fault, which runs more than 40 miles from north to south in Jackson Hole along the eastern base of the range. The east front of the Teton Range runs along a fairly straight north-to-south line because the fault cleanly separates the mountains from Jackson Hole....

The valley of Jackson Hole is bounded by the precipitous Teton Range on the west and highlands on the east. The valley is up to 10 miles wide and 50 miles long, stretching from the north end of Jackson Lake southward beyond the city of Jackson, Wyoming. Jackson Hole is vegetated largely by sagebrush and grass flats, with some areas of cottonwood and aspen, and hills of glacial debris covered by pines and firs.

Imagine the steep east face of the Teton Range extending downward and eastward beneath Jackson Hole, like a big ramp slanted at an angle of between 45 and 60 degrees. This is the Teton fault. The fault intersects the ground surface at the east base of the Teton Range, then dips down and eastward beneath Jackson Hole, eventually reaching a depth of about 10 miles under the valley's east side.

During big earthquakes—jolts measuring 7 or more in magnitude—the valley dropped down and eastward along the ramp-like fault, tilting a bit westward in the process. Meanwhile, the mountains rose up and tilted westward. Over 13 million years, this activity created the abrupt east front of the Tetons and the gentle slope of the range's west side. The Teton Range is a westward-tilted block of rock bounded by the fault on its east side.

Each big earthquake on the Teton fault lifted the Teton Range an average of 3 to 6 feet upward relative to the land east of the fault, creating a small cliff—called a scarp—where the fault intersected and broke the ground surface. Over time, repeated quakes made the cliffs taller. Because glaciers resculpted the landscape until 14,000 years ago, only scarps younger than that are visible now. A prime example is the scarp above String Lake.

Of the total movement on the fault from the last 13 million years of earthquakes, Jackson Hole dropped roughly twice as far as the Teton Range rose. Erosion ate away at the mountains. Streams carried eroded rocks, gravel, and sand into the lakes and streams of Jackson Hole, filling the valley and making it relatively flat. This pattern has been observed on other normal faults, including those that produced the 1959 Hebgen Lake and 1983 Borah Peak quakes.

It is easy to visualize why the stretching of the Earth in the Teton region makes Jackson Hole sink lower along the fault during big quakes. It is harder to understand why the mountains rise. An analogy can help.

Imagine cutting a piece of lumber—a 2-inch-by-4-inch stud—in half. But instead of cutting straight down, cut downward at a 45-degree angle. This slope represents the Teton fault. Now put both pieces of wood in a tub of water and watch how they float. The piece of wood that is longer on top represents Jackson Hole. It floats lower in the water because it has more mass on top. The piece of wood that is longer on the bottom represents the Teton Range. It floats higher because there is more mass on the bottom, and that mass of wood is less dense than the water. In a similar manner, the Teton Range rises upward because the rocks that make up the roots of the mountain range are less dense than underlying rocks.

The lofty crest of the Teton Range is a cathedral of sharp pinnacles, including the highest peak, Grand Teton, at 13,770 feet. To its north is Mount Owen at 12,928 feet and Mount Moran at 12,605 feet. South of Grand Teton is 12,804-foot Middle Teton and 12,514-foot South Teton. This throne of peaks is cut by deep alpine canyons that drop eastward into Jackson Hole. They were carved by glaciation and stream erosion.

Year-round snow fills crevices and gullies at the top of the range, which has a dozen glaciers. These glaciers and their larger prehistoric predecessors have scoured and scraped the Tetons, sculpting the fine details of its ragged spires, horns, and precipices.

Faulted Earth, Flowing Waters

The Teton fault also shaped the topography of streams and lake basins, and thus influenced the flow of water. In most mountain ranges, the crest is the highest ridge and also delineates the drainage divide, with water flowing in opposite directions from the crest. Yet the high crest of the Teton Range is 2 to 3 miles east of the range's drainage divide and only a few miles west of Jackson Hole. Canyons rising from Jackson Hole cut through the crest and extend far west of it, so water falling west of the crest actually can flow downhill to the east. This odd effect is a direct result of the rapid uplift of the east face of the Tetons along the Teton fault. Streams on the precipitous east slope have greater power to erode than streams flowing more gently down the west slope. So the east-flowing streams cut canyons that are deeper and extend farther upstream to the west, encroaching on the west slope and diverting its drainage eastward.

Like the west slope of the Teton Range and the rock layers within it, Jackson Hole and the underlying rock layers also tilt gently westward. Most of the valley floor tilts less than 1 degree, which is not easily visible to the naked eye but can be measured by surveying instruments. Part of this tilt is due to debris that washed out of glaciers and is thicker in the middle of the valley than near the west side and the mountains. However, Jackson Hole's west side is lower than its east side primarily because the west side primarily because the west side is closest to the Teton Range and Teton fault. During big quakes, vertical movement was greatest near the fault, so the west side of Jackson Hole dropped more than the east side, tilting the valley floor and underlying sediment westward.

The effect of the tilting was to help create a low trough along the west side of Jackson Hole. Water still flows into the trough, helping to explain why a string of scenic lakes sits on the west side of Jackson Hole: Jackson, Leigh, Jenny, Bradley, and Taggart among them.

The Snake River originates in Yellowstone and flows south into the north end of 16-mile-long Jackson Lake. The river flows eastward out of the lake's east side, then turns south and southwest, leaving Jackson Hole at the valley's southern end. The ancestral Snake meandered back and forth across this valley, changing courses repeatedly over time and leaving a series of step-like terraces as evidence of ancient channels.

Streams flowing east out of the Teton Range normally would be expected to flow directly eastward into the Snake River. The lakes also would be expected to drain eastward into the Snake. Instead, the streams either flow southward once they enter Jackson Hole and later join the Snake, or they flow into the lakes, which then drain to the south via Cottonwood Creek. Why? For the same reason the lakes are where they are. The west side of Jackson Hole is lower than the east side because of the fault, and the streams and lakes cannot flow uphill to the east. Jackson Lake is an exception. It drains east toward the Snake River—and did so even before the dam raised the lake level—because tall ridges or "moraines" of glacial debris block the south end of the lake.

2

THE FIRSTCOMERS (1978)

ROBERT B. BETTS (1923–1989)

Robert B. Betts was an Easterner. He was from New York City to be specific. He went to Jackson Hole for a vacation. But like many people, he became enthralled with the forty-mile sun-draped peaks and pinnacles of the Teton Range. Year after year he went west to stay at the Triangle X dude ranch. Finally, he built a home. As is often the case, he had many summer visitors, escaping eastern heat and humidity and relishing in the intoxicating weather and landscape of Jackson Hole.

Being a hospitable host, Betts compiled a set of notes to inform his visitors. They grew into chapters, and then into a book of, as he put it, "primary forces and personalities." He was an excellent storyteller, able to entertain his reader.

His account of the "firstcomers" to Jackson Hole encompasses the qualities of a storyteller. Betts was neither an anthropologist nor a historian. He makes a few assertions that modern anthropologists may question. He does, however, present the big picture in a skillful and entertaining format. In this selection, taken from Along the Ramparts of the Tetons: The Saga of Jackson Hole, Wyoming *(1978), Betts succeeds in taking us back in time to a period without written records in which artifacts and memory provide us with what we know.*

While the story of the rocks in Jackson Hole is written in a legible script, the story of early man in the valley is not as easily deciphered. Because the Indians had no written language, the history of their ancient past is lost in the swirling mist of legends, and although archeologists and anthropologists have made revealing finds in recent years, the picture of Stone Age man's presence here is still somewhat blurred. But of this we can be sure: long before the glaciers on this hemisphere began their final retreat, hunting bands from Asia had crossed to Alaska over the Bering land bridge, had advanced with surprising swiftness down along high mountain valleys that served as narrow corridors through the shelf of ice then covering the upper part of the continent and, with spears in hand, were roaming the Great Plains and northern Rocky Mountains in pursuit of big game.

Pitting their not meager skills of survival against both the animals and elements of what was then truly the New World, the Early Hunters, as they are called, made their way into the region surrounding Jackson Hole by an early date. Across the Tetons, near American Falls in Idaho, bones of a bison belonging to a long-extinct species have been discovered under conditions suggesting that it may have been discovered under conditions suggesting that it may have been hunted down by men as far back as 30,000 years ago. Even closer to Jackson Hole, a cave in the Absaroka Range near what is now Yellowstone National Park was occupied by humans off and on for 9,000 years, with its many strata yielding weapons which gradually advanced from primitive stone points for spears to skillfully chipped arrowheads. Closer still, near the headwaters of the Gros Ventre River that flows into the valley from the east, and also at Astoria Hot Springs not far south of the valley, fluted stone points of a type dating back 11,000 years have been found, attesting to the fact that humans were in the vicinity by at least that time....

While the way of life of the firstcomers to Jackson Hole can be seen only in a half-light, they were human in the fullest sense of the word. They lived and roamed in small family units, were intelligent, spoke a language, used tools and had command of fire. They also possessed the most valuable of all traits in the struggle to survive: the ability to adapt. And it was good they did, because in the period following the end of the Ice Age more than one hundred species of mammals, including the horse, mysteriously died out in North America. With meat no longer plentiful, these people who had lived almost entirely on big game were forced to change their methods of gathering food. Gradually, they learned to supplement their more limited meat supply with roots, fish, nuts, wild berries and other growing things of the areas across which they ranged.

For thousands of years, the people of the high country found an hospitable summer habitat in Jackson Hole. Entering the valley in the spring and departing in the fall for more favorable winter hunting grounds, they adapted brilliantly to the local ecology, gathering blue camas from the meadows for food, fishing the streams for cutthroat trout, hunting in the higher elevations for bighorn sheep and obtaining obsidian from local deposits for chipping into weapons and tools—all the while observing ancient symbolic rituals that had been passed down to them over many generations. Then these people, who were probably speakers of the Athapaskan language, suddenly vanished, leaving behind no further traces of their presence in this land. What had happened is that a new and stronger people had arrived in the outlying regions.

In the sixteenth and seventeenth centuries, a great migration of Shoshonean-speaking people moved northeast from the Great Basin and eventually drove the Athapaskan-speaking people from their traditional winter hunting grounds. Overwhelmed by superior numbers and arms, the longtime residents of the high country moved well to the north into Canada, ostensibly leaving Jackson Hole for the summer use of the new arrivals. They also ostensibly let it for the summer use of the other now-familiar Indian nations of the northern Rockies who not long thereafter appeared and claimed tribal territories along a far-reaching perimeter mostly to the north and east of Jackson Hole. Surprisingly, however, instead of being visited and utilized by these various tribes, even in summer, Jackson Hole was virtually abandoned by the Indians for more than one hundred and fifty years before white men first came into the mountains. This avoidance of the valley by native Americans of any kind for such a long period time is a relatively recent finding, and it shatters a long-standing myth which has prevailed to this day about Jackson Hole.

When the first few white men ventured into the northern Rockies early in the nineteenth century, they encountered a number of major tribes encircling Jackson Hole. To the north in what is now Montana were the Blackfeet and the Gros Ventres, allies whose ferocity in battle made them the most hated and feared of all the tribes. To the northeast and east, from the Yellowstone River to the Wind River Basin, were the Crows, outstanding both as horsemen and horse thieves. Beginning in the Green River Basin to the southeast, the homeland of the Shoshonis (or Snakes) curved west below Jackson Hole through upper Utah, then ran north through eastern Idaho to a point roughly opposite the western boundary of Yellowstone Park. The Shoshonis shared the western section of this territory with the Bannocks, who were related to them and with whom they intermarried. Farther away in the northwest were the Flatheads, who did not flatten their heads, and the Nez Percés, who almost never pierced their noses.

All of these tribes had horses descended from those originally stolen from the Spanish by the Indians of the Southwest in earlier times, so they were able to range far outside their loosely defined territories in order to hunt and make war. Because of this mobility, it has long been assumed that the Indians of the northern Rockies were frequently visitors to Jackson Hole. In fact, over the years this assumption has persisted to the point where many now accept it as gospel that every summer and fall for centuries the tribes of the region, especially the Shoshonis, descended on the valley to enjoy festive reunions of the usually scattered hunting bands and to engage in great buffalo hunts. It is a pleasing picture which has grown to become part of the local lore regularly repeated to tourists, but unfortunately there is no evidence whatever to bear it out. Quite to the contrary, well-documented evidence compiled by Dr. Gary Wright, an anthropologist who has conducted extensive studies in the valley, shows that although more than three hundred archaeological sites have been uncovered in Jackson Hole, not one can be dated as having been occupied between the years 1640 and 1811—that is, between the time the Athapaskan-speaking people were driven north and a party sent out by John Jacob Astor to found a fur trading post on the Pacific Coast passed through....

This is not to say that Jackson Hole was a no-man's-land avoided entirely by Indians, for there were trails leading into it and out of it when the first white men arrived. But even in historic times, which began in the early nineteenth century when trappers who moved through the area kept journals, these trails were used by Indians less as a means to go into Jackson Hole than as a means to go through it. Although some Indians undoubtedly entered the valley now and then specifically to hunt, it served mainly as a corridor for parties traveling to other destinations for other purposes. The Gros Ventres, for instance, are reported to have passed through when they journeyed to visit their kinsmen to the south, the Arapahoes. In order to avoid the Crows, their enemies who lived to the east, the Gros Ventres are said to have entered the valley from the north and proceeded down along the foothills of the range which now bears their name. Journals of early trappers also refer to the transient presence of Flatheads in Jackson Hole, but in every instance they were either on their way to or from one of the annual fur trade rendezvous....

These various tribes of the northern Rockies were dispersed widely around Jackson Hole in the spring of 1804, when far to the east a series of events was set into motion which would forever alter the lives of all the western Indians. On May 14 of that year, near the frontier village of St. Louis, a small group of men started up the Missouri River to explore what was to them the unknown West. Although they thought of themselves only as soldiers carrying out a mission for their president, as things turned out they were much more than that. They were the advance guard of a people who had come late to North America, had built an energetic young nation out of its eastern wilderness and soon would burst across the Mississippi River all the way to the Pacific Ocean, claiming every last bit of this long-occupied land as their own. In the course of their westering, they would sweep the Indians aside like leaves in a storm.

THE ORIGIN OF THE SNAKE
AND YELLOWSTONE RIVERS (2018)

LAINE THOM (1952–)

We often forget that Native Americans inhabited the Jackson Hole area for hundreds of years, encamped along Jackson Lake or the Snake River. Over the centuries they created origin stories that have been handed down through oral traditions. One tribe much associated with Jackson Hole is the Northern Shoshone, with a land base located at Fort Hall, Idaho. It is the home of Laine Thom, a Shoshone elder who has written two books on Indian culture, travels widely, and serves as an NPS summer ranger in Grand Teton National Park.

Thom is very knowledgeable regarding Shoshone history and prehistory. He is a descendant of the Shoshone-Goshute Paiute tribes. In this entry, he brings us an intriguing story entitled "The Origin of the Snake and Yellowstone Rivers." It is a wonderful story told with wry humor. Thom believes the myth has "interesting parallels," particularly with the Two-Ocean Pass area.

Long ago there was no river in this part of the country. No Snake River ran through the land. During that time a man came up from the south. No one knew what kind of person he was, except that among the people he was always nosing around, always sticking his nose into everything.

He came through this country traveling north past the Tetons, and then went further north in what is now called the Yellowstone country. He looked around and there he found an old lady's camp. She had a big burden basket of fish in the water all kinds of fish and the man was hungry, so he said to her, "I am hungry, will you boil up some fish for me?"

"Yes, I will cook some for you," the old lady answered. "And don't bother my fish!" she warned, as she saw him looking into the burden basket. He did not obey her. While she was busy cooking, he kept nosing around, and with his feet he tipped the edge of the burden basket and spilled the water and the fish and the water spread all over.

The man ran fast, ahead of the water, and tried to stop it. He piled some rocks up high, in order to hold the water back, but the water broke his dam and rushed over the rocks. That is where the Upper Yellowstone Falls are now. The man ran ahead of the water again, and again he tried to stop the water. Four or five miles below Yellowstone Falls he build another pile of rocks, but that didn't hold the water back either, the rushing water broke that dam, that is where the Lower Yellowstone Falls are now today. The water kept on rushing and formed the Yellowstone River.

Then the man ran to the opposite side of the fish burden basket, to the other side of the water emptying from it. He built another dam where Idaho Falls are now. By the time he got there, the flood had become bigger and swifter. The man built a big dam, the water broke it and that is where American Falls are today.

The man rushed ahead and built two piles of rocks in the form of a half circle, one pile where Shoshone Falls are now and one where Twin Falls are now. I'll really stop the water this time he said to himself. But the water filled the dam, broke and rushed over the rocks in giant waterfalls.

The man ran ahead, down to near where Huntington, Oregon is today. There the valley narrows into a canyon. Here is where I'll stop the water he said between these high hills.

So he built a dam and walked along on top of it, singing and whistling. He was sure he stopped the water this time. He watched it coming toward him, sure that he would soon see it stop. It filled the dam, broke it, and rushed on down the canyon. With the rocks and the great flood of water, it gouged a deeper canyon, Hells Canyon it is called today. Just before the dam broke the man climbed up on top of the canyon wall.

"I give up!" he said as he watched the water rush through the gorge, "I won't build any more dams. They don't stop that water." After the river left Hells Canyon, it became wide again and very swift. The water went on down to the Bigger River and then down to the ocean, taking with it the big fish that spilled out of the old lady's burden basket. That is why we have only small fish up here. the salmon and sturgeon were carried on down the river to the ocean, and they have never been able to get back up here because of the water falls. Salmon used to come up as far as Twin Falls, a long time ago, but they don't come anymore. The big fish basket that the man tipped over is Yellowstone Lake. The water that spilled ran off in two different directions. Some of it made the Snake River, flowing into the Columbia River and the Pacific Ocean. Some of the water ran the other way and made the Yellowstone River, flowing into the Missouri and Mississippi Rivers and the Gulf of Mexico.

Who was the old lady with burden basket filled with water and fish? She was Sogo Pia–Mother Earth. Who was the man who wanted to see everything, who was always sticking his noise into everything? He was Itsa-ppe or Coyote.

UP THE WINDS, AND OVER THE TETONS (1860)

WILLIAM F. RAYNOLDS (1820–1894)

The first federal reconnaissance of the Jackson Hole country came in 1860. The Raynolds Expedition, led by Captain William F. Raynolds, intended to explore the Yellowstone Country, but at Union Pass guide Jim Bridger determined that a route to the north was impossible, blocked by heavy snow. They abandoned the Yellowstone plan. Instead, Raynolds followed the steep canyon of the Gros Ventre River into Jackson Hole.

Whereas the expedition avoided deep snow, they could not avoid the Snake River. They faced the spring runoff, which changed a large, swift river into a raging torrent. Finding a crossing on the braided river tested the resolve of Raynolds, Bridger, and the men. It took ingenuity and courage, time, and even death to cross the river. Once across, they continued west, topping Teton Pass with difficulty but no catastrophes. They never did explore Yellowstone, and Raynolds's accomplishments were soon overshadowed by the Civil War.

This selection comes from Raynolds's journal, published in Up the Winds and Over the Tetons: Journal Entries and Images from the 1860 Raynolds Expedition *(2012).*

Monday, June 11

Continued our route down the Gros Ventre fork. We are now on the regular Indian trail and the traveling is good tho the road is hilly for the first seven miles, as it passes over the spurs leading down to the river, there being no river bottom.

After traveling about 7 miles we reached the brow of a hill and looked down upon "Jackson's hole." It is a wide level valley extending up the river apparently to the foot of the main chain of Mountains and is bounded on the West by the Teton range, the east by the high spurs we have been traveling over. {Its approximate area is 100 square miles.} After the rugged Peaks we have been seeing for weeks just the sight was delightful. Snake River flows close to the Mountains on the West side of the valley, and we turned to the left crossing the Gros Ventre and continued our course so as, if possible, to reach the river at a point at which it might be forded, Bridger insisting it could not be done above. A bold butte standing just below the mouth of the fork had to be crossed before we reached the river, upon the banks of which we encamped having traveled twenty-five and ½ miles {the extraordinary distance being explained by the excellence of the road and the weather}.

Passing through Jackson's hole the traveling was so fine that no one realized how far we were going. The scene too helped to wile away the time. A small variety of Sun flower was in full bloom and covered large portions of the valley with their golden flowers which, in contrast with the green of the rest of the valley and the hill sides and the snow-clad summits of the Mountains, presented a picture not easily forgotten.

While passing through the hills soon after leaving camp, word was brought forward to me by Mr. Hutton that a small band of Indians were seen by himself and others watching our movements. As they ran when approached we conclude them to be a band of Blackfeet. And as they know they have been discovered and probably see us about as much as we do them, I only halted long enough to close up the train and move on. But to prevent their taking our animals, I have tonight doubled the guard.

As soon as we reached the river a search was made for a ford, but the prospect seems bad enough. The river is here divided into an almost innumerable number of channels and flows with the rapidity of a torrent. Some indians were encamped on the opposite bank who saw some of the party and came over to see us, swimming their horses to do so. They are a small band of Snakes—and seem as harmless as people can be. They were a good deal surprised when we told them we had seen other indians during the day and at once confirmed our suspicions of their being Blackfeet. They returned to their lodges after staying a very short time and begging a few plugs of tobacco.

Several hard showers today as usual.

Tuesday, June 12

Moved camp this morning down the river about two and a half miles to the indian crossing in hopes that we could make it available. As soon as we got into camp, Lance Corporal Lovett started to look at the ford. Seeing him starting I told him to go on as far as he could and let me know how it was. A few minutes after, I saw Lance Corporal Bradley following him. Within twenty minutes after, Lovett came back hollering that Bradley was drowned. All hands started at once to the rescue, but the deep channels and thick growth of brush prevented making any progress and, as soon as it was known that he had gone down in one of the swiftest currents, all hopes of saving him were abandoned. I however started parties to look for the body and the Indians coming into camp soon after started them by promising reward {for its recovery}. The river was carefully examined before the search was abandoned, but all is vain. {The calamity is deplorable, but it is one of those sad accidents for which blame attaches to no one.}

Other parties were out in the mean time looking for a crossing, and about noon word was brought that a point had been found at which it was thought possibly a raft might be used. Some of the men were set to work under Mr. Hutton to construct the raft {and completed it late in the afternoon. We shall try the experiment with it tomorrow}. Taking one man with me, I went to examine the river above. I wanted to look particularly above the mouth of the stream we had come down, which in commemoration of the sad event of the day I have concluded to call "Bradley's fork."

I passed up the river bottom some eight miles and found it to be some forty feet below the plain over which we traveled yesterday, and every where to consist of a black vegetable mold through which it would be next to impossible at this stage of the water to pass a train—to say nothing of the difficulty of crossing the river with such a bottom. I therefore returned to camp after having traveled some 30 miles in vain and determined to try the raft, which I found done, tomorrow. It rained hard again while I was out this after noon.

The river has now been examined over a distance of about 25 miles for a ford but without success.

Wednesday, June 13

Moved about half a mile so as to be near the point to take the raft. Stopped the train on the edge of the timber and took men over to first try the raft. The current was too rapid to turn it adrift, and on attempting to send it over, having it checked by a rope to shore, it [behaved] itself so badly that this plan had to be abandoned.

Before starting out I brought Bridger's talent into play by setting him to work with all the spare men to make a boat. When I returned I found they had made good progress and I ordered the train into camp where we were and set all hands to work to finish it. Out great difficulty is a covering. We have no sins, and I am compelled to use the Gutta Percha blankets bought of Mr. John River of N.Y. which like the tent, knapsacks, and all the articles purchased of him are so rotten as to be next to worthless. To protect it I am going to use a lodge skin that Bridger has, and have had every body I could spare, out gathering resin from the pine trees so as to prevent this from absorbing water. We have got a pretty fair looking boat nearly finished about 12½ feet long and [with a] 3½ [foot] beam. {It is remarkable for the fact that it is constructed entirely without nails or spikes, the framework being bound together with leather thongs.} If we can make our covering answer I hope, Providence permitting, to get across in time.

Three channels about 100 yards in width have to be crossed. Two of which a loaded horse can swim, and the 3rd is too deep and swift to swim between these channels. Unless we can find a better point the goods must be carried by hand. Some more indians visited us to whom I made a small present. This is the first day we have been on this side of the Mountains without rain.

Thursday, June 14

Our boat was ready to be launched about 9 AM. It then had to be carried over the Sloughs and Islands near a mile to the point of starting, putting 4 of our best swimmers in it and a small load of Indian goods.

The first channel was crossed in safety. Search was then made for a crossing beyond and a point situated at which the two remaining channels could be crossed at once. The goods and boat had to be packed by the 4 men. But the main shore was at length reached in safety and the boat packed to a point above from which the three channels could be avoided and the crossing made at once. After seeing the boat start on her return trip, I came back to camp. The men got in about 5 PM, too late to do any thing more this evening than to prepare for an early start tomorrow.

Our boat requires three men to manage her in this rapid current, which will only permit us to carry very small loads, so that time will be required. {I regret the delay but it is unavoidable.} The river is rising which will give us additional trouble.

Friday, June 15

Commenced by 5 AM to make our crossing. The goods had to be packed across Sloughs and Islands over a mile from camp, then put into the boat and loaded ¼ of a mile (by measurement) below the point of starting. The boat was then carried 700 paces upstream and then crossed to a point 200 paces below the point of departure. After carrying it over this space, it was ready for another load. Men were stationed to catch her and do the carrying and after getting all at their posts the round trip was accomplished in ¾ of an hour. The current is too swift to attempt sending anything over on the animals and all must be carried in the boat, even to halters and picket ropes.

The boat has made 17 trips today. But much still remains on the other shore. I crossed early in the day. Every thing is now on the beach ready for boating and two or three unsuccessful efforts have been made to cross the herd. The moment they strike the swift current they pull back, and no effort has succeeded as yet in making them swim across, and no one is willing to venture to lead them. The Sergeant with the guard have them in charge tonight. 15 persons all told are yet on the other shore and at least another day will be required to get all across.

Saturday, June 16

The men who were in the boat yesterday are so sore and sun burnt (having worked all day ready to swim at any trip) as hardly to be able to go to work this morning. They did not hold back however and I started them off with orders to cross the herd first. Lance Corporal Lovett volunteered to lead the way. The animals were now divided into 2 bands and [expertly] taken to where the first attempt was made with the boat, and where the river is divided into 3 channels. After much trouble the first band was finally made to follow Corporal Lovett, and got ashore in safety. And the second band also got across without accident, 'tho some of the animals swam and drifted a mile down stream. The men who had driven them to the crossing had now to be taken off with the boat after which she commenced her regular trips and brought over 10 more loads, landing everything on this shore but the cart which I have concluded to abandon as it is running too much of a risk to attempt to bring it.

Our things are badly scattered on the shore and some time will be required to gather them together. But I feel that we have been specifically blessed to have gotten over without accident. The main channel at this point is about 100 yards. Yet, as I have said the boat drifted ¼ a mile in crossing, and not withstanding an eddy about midway which was taken advantage of to paddle up and across the stream, the distance between landing was passed over in 2 minutes. This makes the current a full 7 miles per hour.

Sunday, June 17

A welcome day of rest after the labors of the past two days. Mr. Alexander {my foreman} volunteered to go for the cart, which he attempted to tow on a raft but had to abandon it in the stream. Much of the day was consumed in getting packs together and ready for starting tomorrow. Service at 9 PM, attended only by Dr. Hayden and George. Did not read a Sermon. Cut Nose, whom Bridger says is the hereditary chief of the Snakes, was in camp all day [and I] made him a small present. Some Indians brought some fine trout to camp that were bought by some of the men. I tried to buy for all the party but could not. Day warm and musquitoes very numerous. Yesterday a light snow storm. Changes enough surely to satisfy any one.

Our camp is now on the right or west bank of the Lewis or Snake river and about 10 miles southeast of the highest of the Tetons, the most noted landmarks in this region. They are basaltic peaks, rising not less than 5,000 feet above the level plain of Jackson's Hole, and are visible from a great distance from all directions.

Our route out of this valley will be to the westward and across the mountain chain of which they form a part, and which forms the western boundary of the valley we are now in.

5

THE ASCENT OF MOUNT HAYDEN (1873)

NATHANIEL LANGFORD (1832–1911)

Although the Greater Yellowstone region was known to many Indians and white trappers and miners, it was not until the 1870s that the region was systematically explored and publicized. No person was more instrumental in the effort than Nathaniel Langford. He was the leader of an expedition in 1870 to Yellowstone, an exploration that inspired Ferdinand V. Hayden to lead a scientific expedition in 1871. In 1872, Yellowstone National Park was created, with Langford as the first superintendent.

Hayden returned in 1872, instructing his trusted assistant James Stevenson to explore Jackson Hole and the Teton mountains. Nathaniel Langford accompanied the Stevenson party, as did William Henry Jackson, who photographed the landmark mountains for the first time. The following account of their explorations of the country south of the Yellowstone was prepared by Langford for Scribner's Magazine in 1873, and it centers on their climb of the Grand Teton, or Mount Hayden, as this exploration party named it. Although subsequent evidence indicates that Langford and Stevenson were unsuccessful in reaching the summit, this account nevertheless conveys the excitement and peril of mountain climbing with nothing more than a rope and raw nerve.

Our Ascending party, fourteen in number, being fully organized, we left camp at 10 o'clock, on the morning of the 28th July, and followed up the cañon nine miles, to the spot chosen for our temporary camp. Here we rested, and dined; after which Messrs. Adams and Taggart ascended a mountain on the left of the camp to a plateau, 3,000 feet above it, from which they were able to determine the general features of the route to the base of the Grand Teton. That peak rose majestically in the distance above a hundred smaller peaks, its sharp sides flecked with snow, and its bold gray summit half buried in fleecy clouds. It was indeed the lord of the empyrean. Pressing on toward it, they ascended a point of the plateau separated by an intervening chasm of nearly a thousand feet in depth from the elevation over which their pathway lay. The setting sun admonished them that they had barely time to return to camp before dark. They reached there in time to join the boys in a game of snow-balling, a singular amusement for the last days of July.

At half past four the next morning, the thermometer being 11° above zero, the party was aroused, and after partaking of a hearty breakfast, each man provided with an alpine staff, and a bacon sandwich for mid-day lunch, departed from camp, intent upon reaching the topmost summit of the loftiest Teton. The first two miles of the journey lay directly up the cañon, and over countless heaps of fallen trees. This tedious course of travel only terminated to give place to another, still more wearisome, through a ravine, and up a steep acclivity which we were enabled only to ascend by clinging to the points and angles of projecting rocks. Pausing at the summit to take breath, we saw lying between us and the first icy ridge a vast field of snow. Our aneroids showed that we were 9,000 feet above the ocean level—a height which entirely overlooked the walls of the cañon we had ascended, and took in an immense view of the surrounding country. Far as the eye could reach, looking north-ward, peak rose above peak, and range stretched beyond range, all glistening in the sunbeams like solid crystal. In the immediate vicinity of our position, the eye roamed over vast snow-fields, rocky chasms, straggling pine forests, and countless cascades.

The snow-field over which we next traveled, instead of the smoothness of a freshly-covered plain, was as irregular, as full of hummocks and billows as the rocks beneath it and the storms which for years had swept over it could possibly make it. It presented the appearance of an ocean frozen when the storm was at its height. Clambering over the first ridge, we traveled on in the direction of the second, which obstructed our view of the Tetons. Our route was over huge bowlders alternated with snow, and at this hour of the morning, before the sun had visited it, no traveling could be more unpleasant. We found our alpenstocks of infinite service, and we may thank them for the many falls we escaped upon the slippery surface, as well as for the comparative safety of many we made. Two miles of this kind of exercise brought us to the second ridge, which was composed of crumbling rock, and at least six hundred feet above the level of the field we had passed over. The view from this point was magnificent, but almost disheartening, from the increasing obstruction it presented to our progress. Another stretch of snow, rising to a sharp ridge, lay in front of us, at least five miles in length, across which, in our line of travel, was another upheaval of crumbling rock. On our right, a thousand feet below, was the open, blue Lake Cowan.

Resuming labor, some of our party crawled around the side of the gorge, preferring rather to cross over the snowy ridge on our left, than to descend the slippery side of elevation upon which we stood. Several projecting ledges of crumbling rock lay between them and the snow, from which, as they passed over them, detached masses rolled down the bank endangering the lives of all below. Mr. Beckler, by a sudden jump, barely escaped being crushed by a large rock, which whistled by him like an avalanche. As he jumped he fell, and rolled down upon an out-cropping bowlder, receiving an injury which disabled him. Others of the party slid down the ridge unharmed, and encountered fewer difficulties in their journey along its base than its sides. The snow in the long ridge was at least two hundred and fifty feet in depth, and apparently as solid as the granite it covered. After a walk of more than a mile upon its glassy surface, we made a long descent to the right, and passed over a lake about 600 yards long by 200 wide, covered with ice from twelve to fifteen feet thick. There was nothing about this frozen water to indicate that it had ever been open. The ice which bound it, as well as the snow surrounding, seemed eternal. So pure and clear was this frozen surface, that one could see, even at its greatest thickness, the water gurgling beneath. At the distance from which we first saw it, we supposed this lake lay at the very base of the Tetons, but after we passed over it, there still stretched between us and that point two miles of corrugated snow. Still receding and receding, those lofty peaks seemed to move before us like the Israelites' pillar of cloud, and had we not seen this last snow-field actually creeping up to the top, and into the recesses of that lofty crest, from which

The famous photographer William Henry Jackson snapped this photo of the
Stevenson/Langford party in 1872. Langford maintained that he climbed the
Grand Teton, but most authorities dispute his claim. US Archives and Records
Administration #516780.

the peaks shoot upward to the heavens, we should most willingly have
turned our faces campward from the present point of vision, and written
over the whole expedition, "Impossible."

There is no greater wonder in mountain scenery on this continent, than
the tendency it has to shorten distance to the eye and lengthen it to the feet.
A range of mountains apparently ten miles distant may be fifty miles away.
A plain, to all appearances as smooth as a floor, is often broken into deep
ravines, yawning chasms, and formidable foot-hills. Everything in distance
and surface is deceptive.

Beyond the lake we ascended the last rocky ridge, more precipitous than
the others, to take a last look at the dreary landscape.

We seemed to be in the midst of an arctic region. All around was snow
and rock and ice. Forward or backward everything was alike bleak, barren

and inhospitable; but our great labor was still unperformed. Encouraged by the certainty that we were upon the last of those great snow environments which lay at the feet of the mountains, we pushed onward to the base of the immense saddle between them. At this point several of the party, worn out with the day's exertions, and despairing of reaching the lofty summit which still towered five thousand feet in mockery above them, abandoned all further effort. Our kind surgeon, Dr. Reagles, had considerately accompanied us to the base of the ridge, provided with instruments and bandages in case of accident.

We lost no time in selecting from the numerous ravines that were made by the erosion of the friable rock from between the ascending granite ledges, such an one as we believed might be traversed to the top of the ridge without meeting lateral obstructions. Some of our party, mistaken in this, encountered when midway up the side a precipitous wall of granite, which made their return imperative. Five only of the company, after clambering over a snow-slide a thousand feet or more in width, reached the depression upon the right of the Grand Teton which we called "The Saddle." The ascent thus far had tested the endurance of all who made it. It was only difficult or dangerous to those who had selected the wrong passage through the ledges. We ate part of our luncheon while upon "The Saddle," which we reached about noon, and rested there a quarter of an hour beneath the shadow of the Great Teton. It seemed, as we looked up its erect sides, to challenge us to attempt its ascent. As we gazed upon the glaciers, the concavities, the precipices which now in more formidable aspect than ever presented themselves to us, we were almost ready to admit that the task we had undertaken was impossible to perform. The mountain side, from which the Saddle to the summit of the Grand Teton, arose at an angle of sixty degrees; broken by innumerable cavities and precipices.

Our leader, Captain Stevenson, had pushed on ahead, and when Messrs. Hamp, Spencer and the writer had reached "The Saddle," he was far up the mountain, lost to view in its intricacies. Our fears concerning him were allayed by occasionally seeing his footprints in the débris. Very soon after we commenced the ascent, we found ourselves clambering around projecting ledges of perpendicular rocks, inserting our fingers into crevices so far beyond us that we reached them with difficulty, and poising our weight upon shelves not exceeding two inches in width, jutting from the precipitous walls of gorges from fifty to three hundred feet in depth. This toilsome process, which severely tested our nerves, was occasionally interrupted by large banks of snow, which had lodged upon some of the projections or in the concavities of the mountain side,—in passing over the yielding surface of which we obtained tolerable foothold, unless, as was often the case, there was a groundwork of ice beneath. When this occurred, we found the climbing difficult and hazardous. In many places, the water from the melting snow had trickled through it, and congealed the lower surface. This, melting in turn, had worn long openings between the ice and the mountain side, from two to four feet or more. Great care was necessary to avoid slipping into these crevices. An occasional spur of rock or ice, connecting the ice-wall with the mountain, was all that held these patches of snow in their places. In Europe they would have been called glaciers. Distrustful as we all were of their permanency, we were taught, before our toil was ended, to wish there had been more of them. As a general thing, they were more easily surmounted than the bare rock precipices, though on one occasion they came near proving fatal to one of our party.

Mr. Hamp, fresh from his home in England, knew little of the properties of snow and ice, and at one of the critical points in our ascent, trusting too much to their support, slipped and fell. For a moment his destruction seemed inevitable, but with admirable dexterity he threw himself astride the icy ridge projecting from the mountain. Impelled by this movement, with one leg dangling in the crevice next to the mountain side, and the other sweeping the snow outside the glacier, he slid with fearful rapidity, at an angle of forty-five degrees, for the distance of fifty feet, falling headlong into a huge pile of soft snow, which prevented his descent of a thousand feet or more down the precipitous side of the mountain. I saw him fall, and supposed he would be dashed to pieces. A moment afterwards he crawled from the friendly snow-heap and rejoined us unharmed, and we all united in a round of laughter, as thankful as it was hearty. This did not quiet that tremulousness of the nerves, of which extreme and sudden danger is so frequent a cause, and underlying our joy there was still a feeling of terror which we could not shake off. Pressing carefully forward, we attained a recess in the rocks, six hundred feet below the summit, where we halted.

While resting here, far above us, we heard the loud shots of Captain Stevenson, which we answered. Soon he joined us, with the information that he had been arrested in his ascent, at a point two hundred feet above us, by an intervening rock, just too high for him to scale. It was perpendicular, and surmounted by a wide sheet of ice stretching upward towards the summit, and covered with snow. He had made several ineffectual efforts to reach the overhanging edge of the rock, and at one time lost his foothold, his entire weight coming upon his hands while he hung with his face to the wall. It was impossible without a leap to reach a standing place, and by loosening his hold without one he would drop several hundred feet down the mountain. Fortunately, there was a coating of ice and snow, which reached midway from his feet to his arms, and into this, by repeated kicks with the toe of his boot, he worked an indentation that afforded a poise for one foot. This enabled him to spring on one side to a narrow bench of rock, where he was safe.

We had periled life and limb to little purpose, if the small matter of five hundred feet was to prevent the accomplishment of our task. We determined, therefore, to ascend with Captain Stevenson, and make another effort to scale the rock. When I saw the perilous position from which he had escaped, I could not but regard his preservation as almost miraculous. In spite of nervous exhaustion, Mr. Hamp had persevered in the attempt to climb the mountain, but as all upward progress from this point was extremely hazardous, he and Mr. Spencer were persuaded to avail themselves of a foot-hold in the rocks, while Captain Stevenson and I made a last essay to reach the pinnacle.

A rope which I had brought with me, cast over a slight projection above our heads, enabled me to draw myself up so as to fix my hands in a crevice of the rock, and then, with my feet resting on the shoulders of Captain Stevenson, I easily clambered to the top. Letting the rope down to Captain Stevenson, he grasped it firmly, and by the aid of his staff soon worked his way to my side. The shelving expanse of ice, overlying the rocky surface at an angle of 70°, and fastened to it by slight arms of the same brittle material, now presented an obstacle apparently insurmountable. Beside the danger of incurring a slide which would insure a rapid descent to the base of the mountain, there was the other risk, that the frail fastenings which held the ice-sheet to the rocks might give way while we were crawling over it, and the whole field be carried with us down the terrible precipice. But the top was just before us, not three hundred feet away, and we preferred the risk to an abandonment of the task. Laying hold of the rocky points at the side of the ice-sheet, we broke with our feet in its surface a series of steps, up which we ascended, at an angle deflecting not more than twenty degrees from a vertical line, one hundred and seventy-five feet, to its topmost junction with the rock.

The peril to which this performance exposed us was now fully revealed, and had we seen it at the foot of the ice-sheet, the whole world would not have tempted us to the effort we had made. Why the entire mass of ice, yielding to our exertions, was not detached from its slender fastenings and hurled down the mountain is a mystery. On looking down through the space which separated it from the rock, I could see a half a dozen icy tentacles, all of small size, reaching from wall to wall. Seemingly the weight of a bird would have loosened the entire field. We felt, as we planted our feet on the solid mountain, that we had escaped a great peril—and quenching our thirst from one of the numerous little rivulets which trickled down the rock, set resolutely at work to clamber over the fragments and piles of granite which lay between us and the summit. This was more tedious than difficult, but we were amply rewarded when, at three o'clock P.M., after ten hours of the severest labor of my life, we stepped upon the highest point of the Grand Teton. Man measures his triumphs by the toil and exposure incurred in the attainment of them. We felt that we had achieved a victory, and that it was something for ourselves to know—a solitary satisfaction— that we were the first white men who had ever stood upon the spot we then occupied. Others might come after us, but to be the first where a hundred had failed was no braggart boast.

The several pinnacles of the Grand Teton seen from the valley seem of equal height, but the inequality in this respect was very apparent at the top. The main summit, separated by erosions from the surrounding knobs, embraced an irregular area of thirty by forty feet. Exposure to the winds kept it free from snow and ice, and its bald, denuded head was worn smooth by the elemental warfare waged around it. With the unshorn beams of a summer sun shining full upon us, we were obliged to don our overcoats for protection against the cold mountain breeze. Indeed, so light was the atmosphere, that our respiration from its frequency became almost burdensome, and we experienced, in no slight degree, how at such an elevation once could at a single exposure suffer the opposite intensities of heat and cold. Above the ice-belt, over which we had made such a perilous ascent, we saw in the débris the fresh track of that American Ibex, the mountain sheep,— the only animal known to clamber up the sides of our loftiest peaks. Floors also, of beauteous hue, and delicate fragrance, peeped through the snow, wherever a rocky jut had penetrated the icy surface.

On the top of an adjacent pinnacle, but little lower than the one we occupied, we found a circular enclosure, six feet in diameter, composed of granite slabs, set up endwise, about five feet in height. It was evidently intended, by whomsoever built, as a protection against the wind, and we were only too glad to avail ourselves of it while we finished our luncheon. On entering it we found ourselves a foot deep in the detritus, which had been worn by the canker of time from the surrounding walls. The great quantity of this substance bore evidence to the antiquity of the structure. Evidently the work of the Indians, it could not have been constructed less than a century ago, and it is not improbable that its age may reach back for many centuries. A period of time which human experience cannot calculate, was required to produce this wonderful disintegration of solid granite. It was the great wonder of our day's work, and proved that even the Indians, usually so incurious, had some time been influenced by the same spirit which had inspired us. No such curiosity, I imagine, affects the Indians of our day. The toil and exposure of a scramble up the Teton would daunt the bravest of them, if he should happen to possess energy enough to attempt it. Better men than any that now belong to the North Western tribes, must have ascended this mountain, and left this evidence of their visit: but what motive save that of the merest curiosity or a trial of skill could have caused the ascension, it would be impossible to determine.

Far away on the northern horizon, scarcely distinguishable from the clouds with which they are intermingled, we saw the Belt, Madison and Main Rocky ranges, from which long, lateral spurs stretch down on either side, and close up the immense amphitheater by uniting with the Malade Range on the south. Within this vast enclosure, and more immediately beneath us, we overlooked the valley of the Snake, the emerald surface of Pierre's Hole with its mountain surroundings, the dark defile leading into Jackson's Hole, and Jackson and De Lacy lakes, Madison Lake, the source of the Snake River,—Henry's Lake, the source of the North Fork, and afar off, beyond these, the cloud defined peaks of the Wind River mountains, and the peaks surrounding the great lake of the Yellowstone. Our elevation was so great that the valley beneath us, filled as it was with knobs cañon and foot-hills, had the appearance of a vast and level plain, stretching away to, and imperceptibly blending with the distant mountains.

We gazed upon the varied beauties of this wondrous panorama until reminded by the position of the sun that we had scarcely time to effect our descent, and return to camp before dark. Great caution was necessary while padding down the ice belt lest it should become detached, but it was our only passageway to the bottom, and we were greatly relieved when we reached in safety the cranny occupied by Hamp and Spencer. At this point Captain Stevenson separated from us, and was the first to reach the base of the mountain. We clambered over the rocks and precipices with all possible expedition, and stood in safety upon the saddle, just as the sun was setting.

The interval between sunset and evening in these high latitudes is very brief, and we had yet to descend the ridge. In our haste to accomplish this we elected a pathway between ledges too abrupt to scale, which led directly to a precipice, thirty-five feet in height, at the base of which was a mass of granite fragments and debris from three to four feet deep. We were now in a dilemma. Either we must pass the declivity or re-ascend the steep mountain side, five hundred feet or more, and select another passage. Crawling to the edge, I saw at a distance of twenty feet a jutting point, which would afford standing room for a single person, and about eight feet below it, a smaller projection, too sharp on the face for a safe foothold. Passing the rope alternately around the bodies of my comrades, I let them down the perpendicular wall to the base, then throwing the middle of the rope over a projecting crag, and seizing the two ends, I lowered myself to the narrow shelf first described, whence a well directed leap enabled me to poise myself on the smaller projection below, and gather for a final jump into a pile of debris, where my comrades stood. Our safe descent being thus accomplished, we had yet the snow-fields, ridges, and gorges to traverse, before we arrived in camp. Fatigued with the exercise of ascending and descending the Teton, the passage of these ridges was the most exhaustive effort of our lives. It was after nine o'clock, and very dark, when we first caught sight of our camp-fire, afar down the chasm. After a rough walk over prostrate trunks, through deep depressions, amid pine thickets, climbing bowlders, penetrating chapparal, wading streams,—at just thirty minutes past ten, when all our comrades had thought some serious and perhaps fatal accident had befallen us, we entered camp amid cordial greetings and shouts of delight. The joy of a re-union, after even so brief a separation, was as earnest and sincere as if we had been parted a year.

6

CAMPS IN THE TETON BASIN (1882)

WILLIAM A. BAILLIE-GROHMAN (1851–1921)

William A. Baillie-Grohman was another privileged Englishman who found spice in life through travel and often perilous adventure. Contrary to some, however, he carried out his adventures with little of the trappings of aristocracy. When he came to Jackson Hole in 1880, he was twenty-nine and in the prime of his life. Traveling light, he hunted in the Wind River range then continued north, entering Jackson Hole by way of the Gros Ventre River valley. As a mountaineer who climbed extensively in the Tyrol country of the Austrian Alps, Baillie-Grohman made frequent comparisons of the Teton country with European alpine scenery.

Above all, this blue blood reveled in the freedom of the West with its absence of artificiality so common in the society circles to which he was accustomed. Baillie-Grohman brought a hearty sense of adventure to his western escapade, and he had the ability to express that adventure and excitement in his prose. His account is not only eloquent, but it is an excellent expression of the hunter/naturalist/conservationist tradition that would eventually take hold in Jackson Hole.

This selection is taken from his book Camps in the Rockies *(1882), in which Baillie-Grohman reflected on the past but also the future. He understood that the elk (stags) would be replaced by a "huge cattle-yard," and that Native Americans would succumb to the ubiquitous stock raiser. But beyond his astute observations, this Englishman possessed a sense of humor. Fisherman and nonfisherman will enjoy his amusing account of his unique method of fishing at the outlet of Jenny Lake. Significant alteration from the English world of fly-fishing to that of the American West was the secret of his success!*

Game just then was very scarce; the Bighorn were still high up on the mountains, and Wapiti had not yet come into the Basin, so that we had been out of meat for one or two days; and the long face of my men when, on my return to camp from my first day's fishing, I informed them that I had sacrificed nearly all my hooks and part of my rod, put a hungry aspect on the matter, our "grub outfit" being then of the very lightest description. My pocket tool-box-a very essential commodity, as I found out, without which nobody ought to travel in those regions-had unfortunately been cached with some extra stores and the tent a week or so before, and hence we could not metamorphose horseshoe nails, of which we had some few with us, into fishhooks. But the instinct of practical self-help, so strongly developed by Western travel, came to the rescue, and by the end of a couple of hours' work, aided by the bright light of a huge camp-fire, we had completed three very deadly instruments. One was a landing net made of the top of a young pine-tree bent into a hoop, with an old flour sack laced to it with buckstring, half-a-dozen holes being cut in the canvas to let out the water. This was a triumph in itself; but what will the reader, who is probably an expert fisherman of long experience, say when he hears of the other two? I had just six hooks left, and the broken top pieces of my rod (I must plead ignorance of the technical name of the component parts of a rod) furnished the necessary thin thread wire to make two hooks out of six, by fastening three together, their points diverging grapnel fashion. The torn pieces of line were carefully twisted into a stout hawser, the strength of which we tested by fastening it to the collar of a Newfoundland pup, and lifting him clear from the ground.

The next day was a warm balmy September morning-not a cloud was to be seen in the sky of Alpine blueness. I returned to the same spot on the banks of the lake-the scene of the wholesale robbery of hooks on the preceding day, and on my way thither filled a small tin canister with "bugs" in the shape of remarkably live crickets, of large size and jet black colour, that could be found in thousands on the open barrens. In an hour I had landed about forty pounds of trout, mostly fish about two pounds in weight. All the larger fish—and I must have had at least three times the number on or near my hook—broke away; while the very large ones—of which I saw quite a number, and some of which must have scaled six pounds or seven pounds—snapped up the bait *en passant* in the most dexterous manner.

My favourite spot for the sport was, as I have said, at the outlet of one of the lakes (Jennie's Lake it is called on the latest Government Survey map), and the time an hour or so before sunset, when, after a long day on the rocks and in the dense timber, I would have returned to my old horse and got on my way back to camp. Highly fantastical, not to say demented, must I have appeared to an Old World angler, as, wading old Boreas into the water where creek and lake joined till it reached within a foot or so of the saddle, he would stand perfectly motionless till I had filled the two capacious Stalker's bags slung one on each side of him with the speckled beauties. Sitting well back in the saddle, with both legs dangling down on the same side, my rifle slung over my back—the landing net when not in use hung on one of my steed's ears, the only handy place for it—I plied my grapnel with neverfailing success. Fish after fish, with hardly a quarter of a minute between, would gobble up the bait, generally still alive, and if the fish was not of large dimensions, would be jerked out of the water, and safely ensconced in the folds of the flour sack.

As I have said, I usually began fishing "an hour by sun"—the trapper expression for an hour before sunset, and, with only one exception, I succeeded in filling the two bags with twenty-five pounds or so of fish (while proper tackle would have accomplished it in a quarter of an hour or twenty minutes) before the long shadows of the tall pine-trees growing down to within two or three feet of the water's edge would fall across the smooth, glassy surface of the tranquil mountain tarn. The sun once off the water, the fish would vanish as if by word of command, and I do not remember to have caught a single in the lake after sundown. Resuming my usual seat in the saddle—a signal well understood by trusty Boreas, and with a yelp of delight from the young Newfoundland, who, intensely interested in the whole proceedings, would sit, all attention, on the bank fifteen or twenty yards off, restrained only by my word from keeping up constant communication between me and the shore-I would turn my horse's head campward. Once, and only once, did serious disaster threaten me—it was when a more than commonly vigorous two-pounder snapped the threefold gut. But luck stood by me, and the second throw with my spare grapnel landed the very criminal, the hook still in his jaws.

Has the reader ever eaten salmon trout (for I believe this is the proper name of the fish I caught in the Teton Basin) fried in bear fat, with a bit of beaver's trail simmering alonside the pink mess? If he has not, I venture to say he knows not what makes a right royal dish.

7

PRESIDENT CHESTER ARTHUR'S JOURNEY THROUGH THE YELLOWSTONE NATIONAL PARK AND NORTHWESTERN WYOMING, 1883

THE ASSOCIATED PRESS

Many presidents of the United States have visited the Teton country, especially in recent years, but the first was Chester A. Arthur, who traversed the region in 1883 when it was a roadless wilderness. Arthur's purpose in embarking on a grand escapade in the wilderness is rather vague, but generally he wished to escape from Washington, regain his health, relax with friends, fish, confer with Indians of the region, and familiarize himself with a part of the United States that was little known to him or anyone else.

It fell to General Phil Sheridan to arrange a party of Indian guides, horse packers, and some seventy-five armed cavalry. Among the dignitaries were Robert Lincoln, Secretary of War; George Vest, U.S. Senator from Missouri; and John Schuyler, territorial governor of Montana.

At Green River, Wyoming, the entourage disembarked the Union Pacific Railroad and headed by spring wagons to the north. They passed South Pass City—not a city but an almost–abandoned town—and the deserted Camp Stambaugh. Soon they began the descent to the Wind River valley and the small town of Lander. There, the "Great Father" met with chiefs of the Arapaho and Shoshone tribes. The meeting was cordial and colorful, although little was accomplished save that Senator Vest was informed by the respective chiefs that the tribes were much opposed to the allotment of the reservation into 160-acre and 80-acre parcels.

North of the reservation, the party entered a virtual wilderness devoid of roads or telegraph wires. Communication was crude and reporters were banned. Without their own resources, the Associated Press and newspapers relied on daily dispatches that were probably written by Lieutenant Colonel Michael Sheridan, the general's nephew, and Lieutenant Colonel James Gregory. Although censored and sanitized, the dispatches nevertheless give the reader a good sense of the journey, if not all the newsworthy details. The following dispatches of August 16 to August 23, 1883, describe the party's descent down the Gros Ventre River and through Jackson Hole.

For those interested in more information on President Arthur's trip, please see Frank H. Goodyear's A President in Yellowstone *(University of Oklahoma Press, 2013).*

The Party:
CHESTER A. ARTHUR, President of the United States.
ROBERT T. LINCOLN, Secretary of War.
PHILIP H. SHERIDAN, Lieutenant General.
GEORGE G. VEST, United States Senator.
DAN G. ROLLINS, Surrogate of New York.
ANSON STAGER, Brigadier General, United States Volunteers.
JNO. SCHUYLER CROSBY, Governor of Montana.
M. V. SHERIDAN, Lieutenant Colonel and Military Secretary.
JAMES F. GREGORY, Lieutenant Colonel and Aide-de-Camp.
W. P. CLARK, Captain, Second Cavalry, Acting Aide-de-Camp.
W. H. FORWOOD, Surgeon, United States Army.
GEO. G. VEST, JR., Saint Louis, Missouri.

Escort:
TROOP G, FIFTH CAVALRY, CAPTAIN E. M. HAYES,
LIEUTENANT H. DEH. WAITE

CAMP TETON, *Aug.* 18, *via* FORT WASHASKIE, WYO., *Aug.* 20.— Promptly at 6:30 this morning we mounted our horses, and not without longing, lingering looks behind, rode away from Camp Arthur. Our course was in a westerly direction, along the north side of the Gros Ventre River. The air was clear and bracing, and the day as fine as any with which we have been favored since we set out from Fort Washakie. The trail was beset with few of those difficulties with which our fortnight's travels in the wilderness have made us so familiar. Indeed, in the absence of fallen timber, rocky side-hills and steep ascents and pitches, the ride would have seemed somewhat monotonous but for a single feature which actually glorified it. We had climbed to the summit of a long hill about five miles from Camp Arthur, when there suddenly burst upon our view a scene as grand and majestic as was ever witnessed. Below us, covered with grass and flowers, was a lovely valley many miles in extent, through which was threading its way the river on whose banks we had just encamped. Along the whole westerly edge of this valley, with no intervening foothills to obstruct the view, towered the magnificent Teton Mountains, their snowy summits piercing the air 13,000 feet above the sea level and 8,000 feet above the spot on which we stood in reverent admiration. It was the universal sentiment of the party that that sight alone would have fully repaid all the toils and perils of the march. We are encamped in the Teton basin on the bank of the Gros Ventre. The locality, aside from the splendid views of the mountains which it affords, is our least attractive camp. The river at this point has an excellent reputation as a trout stream, but the wind has been blowing at too many miles an hour to permit much success in angling. It has been powerful enough to break the ridge-pole of our mess tent, but fortunately not beyond repair.

To-morrow we shall resume our march and expect to make camp near the so-called Buffalo Fork of the Snake River.

CAMP HAMPTON, ON SNAKE RIVER, *Aug.* 20, *via* FORT WASHAKIE, *Aug.* 23.— The President's party reached this camp after traveling about eighteen miles along foothills between the Shoshone and Teton Mountains. The camp is named in honor of Senator Wade Hampton, who was expected to accompany the party. Its location is grand, being on the banks of the Snake River and facing the entire range of the Teton Mountains. Judge Rollins shot and brought in his first antelope. Nearly all the party are engaged to-day in angling for trout, the President and Senator Vest outstripping the rest, and vying for supremacy. Each landed a two and a half pound trout from the bluff facing the camp, which feats were witnessed by the entire command. Their catch for the day is much larger than on any day during the trip. At our last camp the temper of all the party was severely tried by the extremes of weather experienced. Hot weather in the middle of the day, and severe gales of wind throughout day and night, accompanied with blinding clouds of dust. Ice formed one-half inch thick on water buckets standing before the tents during the night. To-day the weather is clear and bracing, and all the party are in perfect health. Tomorrow's march will take us to near the southern boundary of the Yellowstone Park.

CAMP STRONG, WYO., *Aug.* 21, *via* Bozeman, MONT., *Aug.* 22.—Reveille call at 5 awoke us all from a refreshing sleep, though the ice in our buckets this morning was proof that three blankets had been none too many during the night for our comfort.

Half-past 6 found all the tents struck and packed on the mules, and the Presidential party in the saddle.

Our route to-day of thirty miles lay nearly northward over the foothills of the Shoshone Mountains, avoiding the marshy bottoms of the Snake River, which are very treacherous. It was a rough and rugged country, covered for nearly a quarter of the distance traveled by dense tracks of burned and fallen timber. At noon we reached a sparsely timbered knoll which commanded a view of Jackson's Lake, with the snow-covered Tetons rising from its shores in the background, which repaid us for our severe, hot and dusty march in the early part of the day.

The omniscient reporter who claims to be with us, and who has been purely a mythical personage since we left the railroad at Green River, carefully and considerately located the Secretary of War at Fort Washakie for an indefinite period after we had started on our present trip across the mountains, and as the Secretary had never been absent, it is a matter of much curiosity as to how the inventive genius of this fictitious correspondent would be able to restore him to us. As a matter of fact, Mr. Lincoln has been one of the keenest daily observers of the resources of the country through which we are passing, and is constantly and pleasantly reminding us of his presence.

This evening we are camping at the crossing of Snake River, which was named last year, by Gen. Sheridan, Camp Strong. Our tents are pitched on the banks of the stream in a grove of lofty pines. Trout are abundant, an opportunity the party are taking advantage of, for it is their last for fishing before reaching the Yellowstone region. The surroundings of this camp are beautiful and the opportunity for sport so good that the President has decided that we remain here another day.

CAMP LOGAN, LEWIS LAKE, *Aug.* 23, *via* LIVINGSTON, *Aug.* 25.—The white frost was still thick on the blades of grass, leaves, shrubs and plants, and glistened in the morning sunlight like diamond dust, and the mists and vapors rested close on the surface of the river as the Presidential party mounted at 6:45 a.m., and started out for the day's march. Last night was the coldest we have experienced, being 20 degrees Fahrenheit at 6 a.m., and in the mess tent the water which had been served a few moments before the party sat down for breakfast formed a beautiful network of ice on the inner surface of the glasses.

The trail was very crooked to-day, and led over a low range of mountains covered with pine forests. At intervals we found open, grassy parks, but the most of them were only a few acres in extent. About twelve miles out we came upon the lower falls of Lewis or Lake Fork, a dark gray gorge cut through solid walls of volcanic rock, its sides nearly perpendicular. About 600 feet below us the stream rushed and tumbled over its dark bed, broken white by its fretting. The upper falls, some six miles from the lower, we saw at a distance through an opening in the evergreen trees; it seemed to drop from out the dark foilage behind it like a flood of lace. Five miles further on we went into camp in a lovely open park at the head of Lewis Lake, the only spot on the shore which is not densely timbered.

The camp has been named Logan, in honor of the Senator, who was to have been one of the party, and whose unavoidable absence we have all regretted. Our tents look out on this beautiful sheet of water. The sound of the swirl of the waves on the beach mingles pleasantly with its twin sister sound, the soughing of the winds in the trees near by.

Along our line of march to-day we saw large quantities of Indian tea, diminutive species of evergreen whortleberries five to ten inches high, found only in timber and at an altitude of from 8,000 to 10,000 feet. The Indians are fond of the tea made from the dried leaves and stems of this plant, and I have been told by those who have drunk it that it forms a pleasant substitute for our own.

Yesterday we remained at Camp Strong, and its surroundings are worthy of more than a passing notice. A grassy bottom surrounded by mountains dad with evergreens, trees of all sizes from the young seedling up to mature age, scattered singly, grouped in dusters, or massed into dark forests. Our tents were pitched on the banks of Snake River, which here possesses all the attributes of a first-class trout stream. Clear, pure water rippling over pebbly bottoms, with here and there swift currents, eddies and deep holes. The President and Senator Vest, our two most expert fishermen, made the best of our stay, and scored the greatest victory yet achieved over the finny tribe.

At one cast the President landed three trout, weighing in the aggregate four and one-quarter pounds, and at each of some six other casts took two fine specimens. The President secured the greatest weight, the Senator the largest number, the total weight being 105 pounds. The sport is now about over. Senator Vest has caught the largest trout during the trip, it weighing three and one-half pounds.

Looking back over our course from Fort Washakie, where we first mounted our horses, abandoned wheeled vehicles, and took the Indian trail which has led us through some fertile valleys, across some bad lands, and over rugged mountains, many memories linger pleasantly in the mind of every member of the party. The hailstorm at Camp Crosby, the dust which sifted in our tents at Camp Teton, the trials of fallen timber, are lost and forgotten in the pleasant associations of the rest of the journey.

Picturesque Camp Lincoln, with its banks of snow lying placidly and slowly melting near the trail, and near the snow flowers, which had all the freshness of early spring, tender forgetme-nots, wild asters, buttercups, columbines, the latter with a delicate and scarcely perceptible shade of blue in its rich white, and for which many deem it the most beautiful of the wild flowers found in the Rocky Mountains, a carpeting of scarlet and blue and bold; added to this the White Mountain flox, nestling close to mother earth, and in such profusion as to suggest the idea that the hand of Nature had grasped some of her myriad stars and scattered them in wanton profusion on the grassy slopes of this romantic region.

Camp Arthur, grand beyond the power of pen to describe, located in a bend of the Gros Ventre River, and looking down upon it from the crest of the hill over which the trail led, we also got the first good view of the royal Tetons, or Titans, as they should be called. To the west forests of pine and spruce mantling the mountains. To the south and east clay and sand stone rising high in the sky, and rich red from its iron coloring, masked here and there by green foilage. The short, thick grass of the little valley furnished splendid grazing for our animals, and the trout, within twenty feet of the tents, made the immediate surroundings most delightful. Then the Teton basin, large as the state of Rhode Island, and covered at this season of the year with nutritious grasses, and profuse in evidences of being the winter grazing grounds of antelope, deer and elk. The near future must practically determine its value for stock purposes. Then Jackson's Lake, as we saw it from the crest of a high bluff on our line of march, a gigantic sapphire, its surface fretted and blown into white-caps by the winds which swept down over Mount Moran, and moanings lost themselves in the gloomy forests beyond.

Nature has indeed given a royal setting to this jewel, twelve miles long, three miles wide—on the east and north a fringe of quaking aspen and willow brush, on the west and south spruce and pines clothing the feet of the grand Tetons and scrambling up their sides until vegetation dies out. Above this the fissures and chasms of the grim, gray pile of rocks, filled with snowbanks, some of them 3,000 feet deep and of dazzling whiteness in the sun. Yes, the scenery along our route will furnish many pleasant memories in the years to come.

PART II

THE PROUD ADVENTURERS

THE SHOSHONE (1910)

ELIJAH NICHOLAS WILSON (1842–1915)

Elijah Nicholas "Nick" Wilson was a pioneer of Jackson Hole. In the 1890s, he led Mormon settlers over Teton Pass, at the base of which they established Wilson, named after Elijah. Today, Wilson is a small but thriving town.

But Elijah Wilson is perhaps best known for having lived with the Shoshone Indians in and around Jackson Hole. He had many adventures, and in his later years he regaled listeners with his adventures in the West. Howard Driggs, from the University of Utah, visited Wilson and heard many of his tales. Driggs eventually convinced Nick to put them on paper. With Driggs's help (Wilson had never spent a day of his life in formal school), Wilson published The White Indian Boy, or Uncle Nick Among the Shoshones *(1910), from which this section is taken. Driggs maintained that Wilson's adventures were all true, but one expects that Nick, as an accomplished storyteller, may have embellished here and there.*

The following story is how Nick became a hero among the Shoshone people. Alone on his horse, he came upon a Shoshone girl seriously injured by a bear attack. He managed to get her on his horse, and they rode back to the Indian camp. The grateful parents, who had assumed she was dead, and all the tribe praised Nick's bravery, and he was welcomed into a second home.

Well, after thinking the matter over, I decided it would be better for me to go back and face the music, let it be what it would. When I got near the camp, I met a lot of Indians that mother had sent to hunt me. When I saw them, I stopped and they came running up to me and said, "Yagaiki, we are hunting you." "What for?" I asked. They said that my mother had sent them, and they asked me if I had seen Washakie. They said that he was out hunting for me. When I asked them what the Indians would do to me, they said they would do nothing to me, that I had done just what anyone else would have done. I said I was afraid it was going to start another fight, but they laughed and said it would not. This made me feel much better. When I got to camp and mother saw me, she said, "Yagaiki, where have you been?" When I told her, she said I was the most foolish boy she ever saw for running off like that. "Well," I said, "I thought if I went away it might keep down another fight in camp." It was not long until Washakie came in, and he gave me a long talk. He said for me never to run off that way anymore, that when I got into trouble, to come to him and he would see that I was not hurt. I told him I had better go home, for I was always getting into trouble and making it hard for mother and him. He said he would not let me go home for that, but that I must be a little more careful, for I might have killed the boy if I had not stopped just when I did. He said a rope tied to a wild horse and around a boy's neck hasn't much fun in it for the boy. I told him I did not think about the rope being tied to the horse or I would not have done it, but the boy made me so mad I did not know what I was doing. I told him the boy was doing all he could to make the horse throw me off, and if he ever. did it again I would wring his blasted neck off. He told me the boy's neck was much skinned, and his father and mother felt very badly about it, but he would talk to them and try to fix it up. The other little boys that were with us said I did just right. Washakie had a long talk with the boy's parents and I heard no more about it, but I saw the boy going around with a greasy rag around his neck, and when he came around where I was, he would look very savagely at me.

The mosquitoes got so bad at this place that we had to move. We went east nearly to the Teton Peaks, where we found all kinds of game plentiful and the streams full of trout. We came to a beautiful valley with a river running north and south through the center of it. There was no timber growing on its banks, but there were great patches of willows from one to one and one-half miles wide extending for about twenty miles up and down the river. The white-tailed deer were plentiful among the willows.

I killed five while we were there and mother tanned the skins and made a suit of clothes for me out of their hides. There were also a number of moose killed among the willows.

Washakie told me that his tribe had a great fight with the Sioux Indians in this valley many years ago when he was a small boy, and that his people lost about two thousand of their best men. He took me all over the battle ground.

We stayed in this valley about 30 days and I started to breaking more colts. When I got up the first one after our racket, other said, "Leave your rope here." I told her that I could not do without it. "Well, don't use it on any more kids," she said. Everything passed off here very quietly except for two or three scares the Indians had when they thought the Crows were after them. If they saw a dust made by the wind, they would send out to see what caused it. They were like a band of sheep that had been run by wolves. Every little thing would scare them. It made me tired to see them so cowardly. I told Washakie that I did not think they would fight if they had a chance. I said, "When are you going to send more Indians out to steal the Crows' horses?" He said, "Why, do you want to go with them?" I said, "Not much, I have not lost any horses." "Well, we have," he said, "but I have nothing to do with that kind of business, the War Chief attends to all that. If the Crows do not come after us, we will send out a party against them after a while, but I do not know just when. We must, though, get back the horses we have lost, and do it before the snow comes." I asked him if he was going to winter here in this valley. "Oh, no, the snow falls too deep here. After the buffalo get fat and we get what meat we want for our winter use, we will go west, a long way off, to winter where no buffalo run, but where there are plenty of deer and antelope and fine fishing." He said that some of those fish were as long as I was.

The Indians killed a great many elk, deer, and moose, and the women had all they could do tanning the hides and drying the meat. Berries were getting ripe so we would go up in the mountains and gather them to dry. I had lots of fun going with mother to gather the berries. One day while we were up in a deep canyon, we found plenty of berries and were busy gathering them, when all at once we heard some awful screaming. Pretty soon here came a lot of squaws and papooses. "Wudutsi nia baititsi ke kudjawaia.

Wudutsi!" one said. That means, "A bear has killed my girl." I jumped onto my pinto, for I was riding him that day, and started up through the brush as fast as I could go. When I got a little way up the canyon, the brush was not quite so thick, and I could see a bear running up the hill. I went a little further and found the girl stretched out on the ground as if she were dead. Then I yelled as loud as I could for some of the Indians to come back, but they had all gone. I tried to lift her onto the horse, but she was too heavy for me, so I laid her down again. Then she asked for a drink. I took the cup she was picking berries in and gave her some water. I asked her if she felt better. She said, "Yes, where is my mother?" I said they all went down the canyon like a lot of scared sheep, and that they must be nearly home by this time. Seeing that she felt better, I took her by the arm and helped her up.

She was crying all the time and said her head and her side hurt her very much and that her arm hurt her, too. I asked her if she could ride. She said she would try, so I helped her on to the horse and led it about three miles until we got out of the canyon, then she said, "You get on behind, I think I can guide the horse." So I got on behind her, for we had to go about four miles yet to reach camp. When we got in sight of camp, we saw some Indians coming full tilt, and when we met them there was the greatest hubbub I ever heard. When we got to camp, her mother came running up and threw her arms around the girl and hugged and kissed her, and cried and went on like she was crazy. She would have hugged me, too, if I had been willing. She said I was a brave boy. Mother came up to me and said, "Yagaiki, I thought you had come down to camp ahead of me, or I never would have come without you." I said, "You were as scared as any of them." She said, "I know I was scared, but I never would have left you if I had known that you had not come out of the canyon."

That night the girl's mother and father came to our wickiup to see what I wanted for saving their daughter's life. I told them that I wanted nothing for doing what I ought to do. Her father said, "You are a good boy, and a brave boy, too." I asked her mother why she ran off, and left the girl behind in that way. "Well,"-she said, "I saw the bear knock her down and jump on her, and I thought she was dead, and that if I went up to her the bear would kill me, too; then there would be two of us dead." Her father said the way so many got killed by bears was because, if a bear caught one, others would run in and get killed. He said it was best if one got caught by a bear for the rest to run and get away while the bear was killing that one. I said that I did not like that way of doing, that I thought if a bear got hold of one, the rest should go after the bear and kill it, and that I would try to save anyone that got caught by a bear, even if I got killed myself. "I know you would, my brave boy. You have already shown what you would do," said my mother. Washakie said: "Don't brag on the boy too much or you will make him think he is a hero. Well, it was a brave act in the boy, and he will be more thought of by everybody in the tribe after this." Mother said that I would be one of the greatest war chiefs the tribe ever had when I got to be a man. She said she always knew there was something about me that was more than common. Washakie said, "Well, that is all right, let us go to sleep." The girl's mother told me that I could have her daughter for a wife when I got big enough, but I told her she could keep the girl for I did not want her. She said, "Maybe you will change your mind when you get older." The next day, I wanted mother and a lot more Indians to go up the same canyon to gather some more service berries. "No, sir," they said, "you don't get us up that place any more after berries." The thoughts of the bear scared them nearly to death. The Indians did not have much to do with bears, but if they came across one out of the brush in open ground, they would sometimes attack him.

One morning we saw two bears crossing the valley, and about fifty Indians on horses started after them. I ran and got Pinto, and when I came for my saddle mother said, "Where are you going?" "I am going to help kill those bears." "What bears?" "Those bears going yonder." "You are not." When Washakie told her to let me go, she consented, so I jumped on to the horse and started after the bears as fast as I could peg it. The Indians had headed them off from the timber and were popping arrows to them in good style. My horse was not a bit scared of them, so I ran up pretty close to one of the bears and put three arrows into his side. The Indians said, "Keep back, you little fool, that bear will tear you to pieces." But Mr. Bear was too full of arrows to tear much, for by this time you could hardly see him for arrows. He looked like a porcupine with the quills sticking out all over him. We soon killed the two bears, but the skins were so full of holes that they were not worth much, and the meat wasn't much good, either. That night they had a big dance around the two hides, and would have me join them and sing as loud as any of them, for they said I was the most daring one among them. One old Indian said, "The little fool don't know any better. If a bear ever got hold of him, he would not be so brave." Anyhow, they gave me the best hide. Mother tanned it and sewed up most of the holes, and it made a very good robe for me to sleep on.

Another small band of Indians came to our camp and the girl that hit me with the fishing pole was with them. After she saw that the Indians were so kind to me, and liked me so much, she wanted to make up with me. She came around several times before she said anything to me, but finally, one day, she came to where I was helping mother stake down a moose hide so it would dry, and said, "Yagaiki, I am sorry that I hit you that day with your fish pole." I said, "I am not." She said, "Why?" I said, "Because we had lots of fun that day." Mother said, "Yagaiki, why don't you make up with her?" I said I did not want to; that I would rather give her a few more kicks. "Kiss her, you mean boy," said my mother. Well, I didn't kiss her but I told her it was all right, that we would be friends again. She said, "Good! Come to our wickiup some day and play with me." "Not much," I said, "your mother will cut my head off with that big knife she has, if I go near her." "No, she will not hurt you. She is coming over to make it all right with your mother. She is very sorry for what we did to your folks, and so is my father." Well, everything was fixed up and we became pretty good friends after that.

By this time, we had gathered all the berries that grew along the foot hills, for the squaws were afraid to go up into the mountains after the bear excitement. They also went to work in dead earnest in tanning the elk and deer skins, and in drying meat for use during the coming winter. The Indians had quit hunting for elk and deer for they had all the skins that the women could get ready to take to some trading post where they could be swapped for red blankets and beads and other Indian goods. About every fall they would go to Salt Lake City to sell their buckskins and buffalo robes. Mother and Hanabi worked all day and away into the night to get their skins ready in time, and I helped them all I could. I took an old horse of mother's, went to the foothills and snaked down enough wood to last while we were there. I packed all the water for them, too, and no kid dared to call me a squaw, either.

Well, the time had come for us to start killing buffaloes for the winter supply of meat. We did not have to hunt them, either, for we could see them at any time, and in almost any direction. Many a time I would go with Washakie to see the Indians kill the buffaloes. Washakie only wanted five, and we soon got them; but it would take mother and Hanabi many days to tan their hides for market, and dry the meat for winter use.

GREAT GOD! I'VE JUST KILLED A BEAR (1958)

OWEN WISTER (1860–1938)

Owen Wister needs little introduction in Wyoming or the West. He is the author of The Virginian *(1900), a novel of cattlemen, cowboys, rustling, and romance set in the background of the vast mountains and grasslands of Wyoming. The book is considered the prototype for hundreds of western books and films to follow.*

It is not well known that Wister familiarized himself with Wyoming long before he sat down to write his classic novel. The well-heeled Philadelphian first arrived in 1885, following his graduation from Harvard. Each succeeding year the drudgery of law school was followed by an exhilarating summer in Wyoming where Wister gathered adventures and ideas.

The following selections include a brief note from his 1887 diary regarding a bear, and a lengthier one the following year, published in 1958 in Owen Wister Out West. *The latter rather humorously chronicles his adventures in finding Leigh and Jenny Lakes, and then hunting, fishing, and climbing nearby.*

Saturday, August 13

Great God! I've just killed a bear, and I'm writing this by his bloody carcass—6:30 A.M.

I looked down towards Jackson Hole and saw the ragged leavings of the thunder cloud prowling up the slopes of pine hills, beyond which the ice-sharp points of the Tetons glittered with snow and sunlight, and over the basin hung a brilliant golden cloud that swam in the rays, while all the other clouds were black or gray.

As I write [in the evening after killing the bear], we hear the ominous howl of some beast that would like to come into camp, and may before morning. The Ward-Dimmick hunting party that started from Washakie after us came and camped next door this evening. But they realize they are trespassing on our hunting field and are to move on tomorrow. Also there is a horse thief hanging about them and us. Altogether we are in good company with the bears, the catamount now howling, and the horse thief lurking about in an unoccupied manner. He sat by our fire tonight for about an hour without speaking a sentence or meeting anyone's eye. How we killed the bear I must record tomorrow, as it is ten (very late), and George and I get up at four to visit the bait. It is fearfully cold.

Tuesday, August 16, 8:30 P.M.

I return to Saturday's work. We went to bed Friday night, having settled that George and I with Tigie should visit the south bait in the morning. The weather was uncertain. Sometime during the night I waked and heard rain patting the canvas overhead steadily. Later I waked again in the dull gray and shivered and was sorry we were going to any bait at five in the morning. I went to sleep, hoping Tigie and West (who was to wake us and give us something to eat) would oversleep. But they didn't. My foot was pulled, and I rose and shivered into my cold greasy boots. We had some tea and bread and started.

The way was uphill at once, and in this altitude (the aneroid registers 8900 with a fall in the weather that probably would take 600 off the reading of the barometer) breathing is a desultory operation, and a rifle becomes wonderfully heavy in five minutes. But it was necessary to follow Tigie like his shadow. I tried to make as little noise as he did, slipping by jagged rotten boughs, letting his shoulder go an inch from them and stepping over the twigs that lay thick in the timber. His moccasins slipped over them with never a crack. Luckily the rain had wet the ground enough for the twigs to be pliant; so our boots made much less noise than they would after a dry night.

Owen Wister, author of *The Virginian*, loved hunting in Jackson Hole. He stayed at the Bar BC dude ranch, but he and his family eventually built a substantial cabin (in the photograph) on their homestead. Collection of the Jackson Hole Historical Society and Museum, 1958.1540.001.

And so we went over the grass and under the trees till we came to a gulch where a little stream flowed, and Tigie pointed among the trees where the bait was, though it was too far among the thickets to see. We became more silent and snaky as we circled beyond the place to come down on it under cover. Just then the sun rose feebly into a very light blue sky and sent some useless rays across the tops of the pine trees behind us. Now we peered over some brushwood at the bait. It hung there alone, and as we searched its neighborhood a squirrel burst into scolding directly beside us. After the sudden start it gave me, coming in the middle of such a tense silence, I could have flayed that squirrel alive. He would have suggested danger to any moderately intelligent bear. Also some of the gray carrion crow birds that swarm in this country began to talk and caw. So we came up close to the bait and saw it had been torn and mangled by big jaws recently. The other piece near it, but just inside the timber, was untouched. Tigies said that at sunset the bear would return and so should we. We returned our steps somewhat wearily and found breakfast hot.

Owen Wister (*top right*) pours a drink for his guide while on an 1880's hunting trip in northern Jackson Hole. Collection of the Jackson Hole Historical Society and Museum, 1958.2438.001.

As we were finishing it, Tigie, who had gone to get the horses into camp, suddenly appeared over the rise to the northeast of camp beckoning violently from his horse. I grabbed my rifle and rushed across our bathroom and pantry (viz., a stoney little hole in the thread of water on which we are camped) and up through the wet brush to him. "Bear! Bear!" he said. "Jump up here. Go. Quick." He had seen a bear crossing on the edge of the timber some three hundred years beyond. So I jumped on the bare rump of his horse and sat there behind Tigie, my rifle in one hand, the other on his shoulder. Away he started, trotting and galloping. My horror was that I should slide off somewhere with a crash and ruin the whole thing. For the way we went was over anything that happened to be in the straight line that Tigie made for the gulch that we had lately left. Down across the stones of dry water channels, up their banks perpendicularly, under limbs of trees bending right and left to avoid them. I have never taken such a ride. Then we came across the gulch a good deal above the bait, and the feeling of hush came down hard on me.

Tigie whispered, "Over there, way over, down." I saw nothing but a wide grass clearing and pines beyond, but I got down among the sparse trees and so did Tigie. Then we crept forward. Tigie put me up front, and as I looked over my shoulder at him for directions I caught the horse's eye as he found himself alone, left behind watching after us with anxious self-control.

Then again Tigie said, "There," and crouched against the grass.

I looked across some three hundred yards to the edge of the pines and saw the bear leisurely sauntering along. I had wondered how it would be with me when this moment should come, and now found myself simply submerged in staring—no excitement, at best no shaking of any nerves, but only my eyes misted on that big beast as he rolled along by the edge of the wood. He looked brown and gray, and his gestures were those of a good-natured old gentleman taking a little morning air for health's sake. Now he would wag his head, then gaze at the landscape judicially, then pause at a rotten trunk on the ground, or sit up with it between his paws looking for insects on the damp underside.

"Quick," said Tigie behind me. "He comes then—so-so," pointing the course the bear would come along.

I hurried forward nearly parallel to the bear's march and sat behind a good wide tree, Tigie at my side. The sun was now bright as I looked across the intervening grass. The bear arrived at where the line of woodland curved down more in my direction, rounding off the end of the lawn some hundred yards ahead of where I sat holding my rifle and wondering when it would begin to be unsteady in my grip. Slowly the bear came down, admiring the weather and pulling his rotten logs. Then he passed behind a tree that stood in the middle of the open. I looked at Tigie, who nodded. Then I ran forward out on the grass, and the bear's head came out from the further side of my tree. I shifted my course so that he and I were like the opposite spokes of a wheel of which the tree was the center, only I neared the tree as quickly as I could. Each time the bear's snout showed to the right of it, I edged to the left correspondingly. When I got under its branches, I stood up full height (for I had been mincing along in a very hunched up position), and the bear walked out into full view on the other side. He saw me and stopped short. Well, my hand's steady after all, I said to myself, as I looked at him along my rifle barrel. I remembered how the brown hair on his shoulder looked thick. I heard my rifle crack and saw him fall at once on his head with a slanting kind of rush and near enough for me to see the dirt scatter a little from his claws.

"Shoot, shoot!" screamed Tigie from behind. I did as I was bid, but I was loath to do it—that first lucky shot had been enough. He tried to get up twice, and before he was half way up his feet they rolled up under him and he tumbled in a heap each time, head downwards. But I shot.

"Shoot! shoot!" said Tigie, running out from his tree, and he worked his arms as if he held the lever of the Winchester himself. I felt like a murderer as I pumped the bullets into the poor old gentleman who swayed about on the grass, utterly gone. My last shot went through part of the skull and down into his throat almost to the shoulder, where I afterwards found its flattened remains. We turned him over and rode back to camp, where I found the betting was three to one against my having hit anything.

Here begins Western trip the third—may I someday write the thirtieth with as much zest! We have been going most of two days now. Yesterday morning, George Norman and Bob Simes met each other at Jersey City and met me at Philadelphia.

Sunday Morning, July 29, 1888, Headwaters of Wind River

We came here up the narrowing valley, past old man Clark and his domicile, the last inhabitant we shall see. Bobby missed an antelope. I missed a big gander with my rifle, but luckily Paul and George got the young ones by chasing them. They were very good at supper. Here Wind River leads up into the timber and is gone. This meadow is the last one. Ahead of us the woods close in. Above to the right is a glorious fortress of rock half a mile long—hundreds of feet above the highest timber—and broken into battlements and turrets by the hundred, with a big stone man sitting at one end watching the valley. The sun shines along this whole line, leaving the crevices filled with a pale blue floating colour while the buttresses stand out brown-yellow in the daylight. There's another fortress to the left and a long regular line of wall joining the two, with a green timbered hill rising in front of it—and so Wind River begins its journey.

Wednesday Afternoon, August 8

This camp we came to on Sunday, and we had to work to get here. First I will correct a slight error. Our last camp on the Snake just below Crawford's shack was not six miles away from the Tetons but fifteen at least, as every one of this party can now testify through painful experience. The atmosphere in this country is like all other mountain atmosphere—tricky. After a sharp rain last Saturday evening, Bobby and I set out for the geese which Paul had seen in a slue of the river just above. It was too late. Moreover, had we shot any, a boat would have been necessary to get at them, for a large belt of willow swamp makes approach to their feeding ground impossible. But what was tantalizing was the sight of five sand-hill crane roosting on one leg along a sand island, hopelessly out of reach. I never eat a bird I thought better than the sand-hill crane we had on the Snake a year ago. May have been self and stomach, but think it was the bird. Bobby and I returned to camp, drenched through with the marsh, and found George had caught some dubious looking fish, whose taste at breakfast was more dubious still.

On Sunday morning George and I consulted the maps and found out just where we wished to go and just where we are now camped—but no thanks to the natives for that. The trouble that morning was twofold; Paul LeRose was having an old man's fit of crustiness (owing to his insides, I think), and he had never been or heard of where we wanted to go. He told us in husky and forbidding tones that he did not know the country west of the Snake. When we made a diffident allusion to two lakes that lay south of Jackson Lake, under the Tetons (we did not dare to call them their United States map Christian names, since the bare idea of a map gives Paul acute nervous trouble), Paul said he had never heard that there were any lakes there. This was his method of denying their existence. Then, how to cross the Snake at this place? Well, we told him to go and find a crossing at once, and in the meantime George and I went up a hill to survey our route but learned nothing in particular except that the prickly pear will penetrate a moccasin. After a while we packed and got away, a crossing of course being found within a mile.

Monday, August 13

Why all the horses did not break each a leg or two, I cannot explain. I never was in a worse place. Long wet grass and weeds completely hid the scaffolding of rotting and rotten pine trunks that lay across this piece of marsh, and the ground was so boggy that often your horse lurched up to his shoulders in it and the frantically plunged forward and fell against the hidden timber. At the edge of this where trees began and the land suddenly rose steep, we became securely netted. Spikey trunks pointed down the hill, and had to be jumped over from loose stones to loose stones. Any pack horse with pretence to originality of mind chose a separate trail for himself and after following it a while, halted at a good distance off from the rest of us. My horse nearly fell backwards with me, so I hurried off of him into the oozy patch of mud. Getting over this piece of our road (certainly our road, for nobody ever used it before, and nobody will ever use it again) took an hour, and it was not much more than three hundred yards we traveled from the beginning of the swamp to clear going. There we followed up the Snake River, which flows nearly due east here before bending south to Buffalo Fork. Presently it spread into the beginning of Jackson Lake, and still we kept along shore.

The lakes we were aiming for, we were pretty sure, lay south of our direction to some degree anyhow, but Paul, the crusty, continued his way in the van. I spoke to George, but George said we were going properly, and to a certain extent he was right. We were aiming generally for anywhere along the two little lakes west of the river, and had we continued as we were going, we should finally have come out (or rather scraped under and climbed through) on the northeast shore of the north lake. That route would have increased our experience of timber if we have not already enough for a liberal Wyoming education.

I gradually grew nearly as crusty as Paul—and kept riding to the south of the outfit, which Paul observed clearly enough but never turned a hair. At last we came to a fork and turned southwest, after having gone round two bays the lake made, instead of cutting south of them and so saving time, trouble, and temper. Dick Washakie's derision of Old Paul waked up now, for he said, "What a ridiculous trail we are taking." Dick, whole breed of Indian, has continual amusement out of Paul, half-breed and white man, as near as he can do it. Paul declines to speak anything but English to the Indians and affects to be without their instinct for trail-finding. But he claims a special white gift of his own for that Art. So Paul took us south, but not enough, and always into needless and very vile timber. So we came to the fork again and told him to keep out of the timber in the sagebursh, and he did.

All this time the great Teton range had declined to come nearer though we had been making for it since starting. At length we did make some impression on distance, for when you looked up the valleys between the peaks, you could distinguish particular trees from the mass and see the water moving down. Paul had now got to riding about due south, though we had pointed out to him a sinking of the pine woods, just at the foot of the two most southern mountains, which held out promises of a lake or of water at any rate.

As we passed a thinner share in the timber to our right which looked as if it might get us near the mountains pretty clear of tree-trunks, I suggested going through that way to George, who agreed. Paul ventilated some wrath. "Why did you tell me to keep out of timber if you want to go right among it?" I diffidently said that I thought it looked thinner—and then added that of course I didn't know the ways of the country very well and if he thought that would take us into bad timber, we'd not go. "No, you chose that way and you shall go," snarled ancient Paul, and in we went. Then I think he thought he'd box me up—for he said, "I don't know which way you want to go. You ride in front now." So I did, and very fortunately I had hit on a pretty good pass between thick woods—and we all got through without entanglement. George's horse cut up—dashed him against a tree and banged his jaw—but nothing really serious. I steered as well as I could for the dip in the woods below the range, and we came out on a big sage park. Paul has ceased to be crusty and rode alongside talking affably on many topics. Then I rode ahead some way to a ridge to look over if possible, but woods stood in the way. It had been very hot for many hours, and nobody had had any water or food.

As I stood on the ridge, I heard far off coming from the dip a faint and sustained roar. When Paul came up, I made him listen. He said it sounded like water, and we went on. He had been very sceptical about lakes and water over here all day, and presently it returned to him. We went up a ridge over which we expected to find ourselves close to mountains and water, and then in front stretched a big yellow waste of sage and cobble stones as wide and flat and dry as the ones we had just crossed. On the farther side of it a belt of pines, and then the mountains rose at once.

"Well, we shall see camp without water tonight," said Paul with a cackle of triumph, though not a joyful one.

"Listen again," I said. The roar was just as sustained as before and much louder.

"Oh, that's the mountain wind," said Paul.

Then Bobby came by and said that George said the lakes must be east of us now—there could be no room for them in front. Till this I had kept unshaken faith in lakes and water ahead, but now I passed a bad quarter of an hour during which Dick came by hilariously repeating, "No water! Camp tonight—no water!" and West looked at the belt of pines and saw no cottonwood, which led him to join the chorus.

But where, I thought, in creation is a big mountain range 20 miles long and 13,000 feet high with snow in giant patches and green valleys and no water at all at the bottom? Possible in the moon—but on this planet, no-where. The situation grew strained, for we seemed now about two hundred yards [from] the rise of the Tetons. Dick rode ahead and came back laughing. "All right," he said. And so we came to a big rushing stream which slipped out of a placid shallow spread above and went into the woods below, foaming down rocks, perfectly clear and not cold. Next day we found one lake ten minutes ride above us and the other lake fifteen minutes walk below us, and water enough to drown yourself in or to float a fleet in—of canoes anyhow. The lake below us is the best of the two—very deep and jammed with trout. I'll detail here the resources of this camp. Of the following fauna and flora all have been killed, seen, or eaten by one of the party: black currants, raspberries, strawberries, red and blue huckleberries (the red new to me, and very sweet) trout, duck, mink, otter, porcupine, beaver, fox, ante-lope, blacktail deer, elk, moose, and an unknown black quadruped seen by Bobby and not likely to be anybody's dog.

Our camp could hardly be better, and we struck exactly the best place along this water system—below and above us is too much timber and too little pasture. On Monday, winning the matching, I hunted with Paul north—in timber all the time. Late in the day had a good shot at an elk and hit him. He fell down and kicked, and so like a fool when he got up and stood vaguely looking about, I concluded one shot enough and did not fire again. He had not fallen at once but sank down slowly. Well, he got away, and Paul was justly enraged. So was I, but luckily he and Dick found him an hour or so later, and we eat him. I should have probably found him myself; but Paul was so disgusted that with that and his affectation of not being an Indian he lost the elk's trail and got us all snarled up away off—and so we came home.

I don't yet claim to have the hunting training enough to follow a trail with unless there's more blood than this bore—but my economy of shots on this occasion was the act of a chump. Bobby went out with Dick, and maybe he saw a moose. Paul saw one with me, but the moose had the wind of us and left the country.

Next day, Tuesday, Bobby went with Paul, George with Dick. The latter saw not even a fresh track (to the south). Bobby unluckily missed about five animals, including all the venison species in the neighborhood. West and I struggled up the mountain range and found a lake perched about three hundred feet above us and game trail so thick that in spots it smelt like cow stables. Sounds Wes tern and romantic this—but quite true. We also found the mountain as mountains usually are, higher than when seen from the bottom. Going up took us four hours. Very steep all the way—first grass, then rocks, and lastly snow and shale. We did not get to any peak but up to a collar between over which we could look into a wild country below-and blue mountains far beyond in Idaho. The view of the basin on this side has given me a permanent and very accurate idea of the whole country here. On the way down we saw two otter. Next day our account of this ascent sent George, Bobby, and Dick up. They took much longer—having all day—and reached West and myself and afternoon tea on the lake up the hill. Next day, Thursday, we concentrated forces on young trout and netted some two hundred—making a whitebait effect of them that was quite taking. I sat with my legs bare in the water on logs too long in the morning and therefore suffered horribly from sunburn. Fishing for big trout in the afternoon I fell in to my waist and neglected to do anything about it. So got slowly and surely chilled and then sick.

On Saturday, I went off alone to see if any trail could be found over into Idaho between the Grand Teton and the next to the north, opposite which we are. But one way round the lake I did nothing but empale my poor horse in the timber, luckily not deep, and the other way round I found also impracticable by reason of timber into which I did not penetrate. On this ride I spent a long time crawling over the baking cobble stones and trying to screen my carcass from three antelope behind sultry clumps of sagebrush. The antelope grazed on, suspicious but not alarmed, and slowly grazed their way to a position where nothing but pancake could have approached them unobserved. So I gave up and came into camp weary and my sickness not gone but worse apparently. This day two mink came tearing into camp together, all among the pots and kettles while all but I were at dinner. They were proposing marriage on the spot—and therefore ignored all other things. Result—she escaped, his skin hangs on a tree. Paul has trapped a fine beaver.

10

AN ELK-HUNT AT TWO-OCEAN PASS (1892)

THEODORE ROOSEVELT (1858–1919)

Theodore Roosevelt's conservation accomplishments are legendary. He established six times more national forests than any other president. He signed national parks bills into law and made liberal use of the Antiquities Act of 1906 to establish national monuments. Almost all of these land withdrawals were in the American West. Those who use and appreciate the public lands and parks owe Roosevelt much for his wise stewardship.

Unlike Chester A. Arthur, President Roosevelt was intimately acquainted with the West. He wrote its history, Winning of the West, *in four volumes, and for a time owned a ranch in the Badlands of North Dakota. Above all, he hunted big game throughout the mountains and plains. Almost a compulsive writer, he often wrote of his adventures for the more prestigious magazines of his day, such as* Scribner's *or* Century Magazine. *The following, published in* Century Magazine, *is an 1892 account of a hunting expedition in the Teton Wilderness area, then known as the Thoroughfare region, comprising the Continental Divide, and separating Jackson Hole from Yellowstone and the Atlantic drainage from that of the Pacific. Today it is an officially designated wilderness area and is still famed for its beauty and superb hunting.*

ONE FALL with my ranch-partner Ferguson, I made an elk-hunt in northwestern Wyoming among the Shoshone Mountains, where they join the Hoodoo and Absoraka ranges. There is no more beautiful game-country in the United States. It is a parkland, where glades, meadows, and high mountain pastures break the evergreen forest: a forest which is open compared to the tangled density of the woodland farther north. It is a high, cold region of many lakes and clear, rushing streams. The steep mountains are generally of the rounded form so often seen in the ranges of the Cordilleras of the United States; but the Hoodoos, or Goblins, are carved in fantastic and extraordinary shapes; while the Tetons, a group of isolated rock peaks, show a striking boldness in their lofty outlines.

This was one of the pleasantest hunts I ever made. As always in the mountains, save where the country is so rough and so densely wooded that one must go afoot, we had a pack-train; and we took a more complete outfit than we had ever before taken on such a hunt, and so traveled in much comfort....

We went over mountain passes, with ranges of scalped peaks on each hand; we skirted the edges of lovely lakes, and of streams with boulder-strewn beds; we plunged into depths of somber woodland, broken by wet prairies. It was a picturesque sight to see the loaded pack-train stringing across one of these high mountain meadows, the motley-colored line of ponies winding round the marshy spots through the bright green grass, while beyond rose the dark line of frowning forest, with lofty peaks towering in the background. Some of the meadows were beautiful with many flowers—goldenrod, purple aster, bluebells, white immortelles, and here and there masses of blood-red Indian pinks. In the park-country, on the edges of the evergreen forest, were groves of delicate quaking-aspen, the trees often growing to a considerable height; their tremulous leaves were already changing to bright green and yellow, occasionally with a reddish blush. In the Rocky Mountains the aspens are almost the only deciduous trees, their foliage offering a pleasant relief to the eye after the monotony of the unending pine and spruce woods, which afford so striking a contrast to the hard-wood forest east of the Mississippi.

For two days our journey was uneventful, save that we came on the camp of a squaw-man, one Beaver Dick, an old mountain hunter, living in a skin tepee, where dwelt his comely Indian wife and half-breed children. He had quite a herd of horses, many of them mares and colts; they had evidently been well treated, and came up to us fearlessly.

The morning of the third day of our journey was gray and lowering. Gusts of rain blew in my face as I rode at the head of the train. It still lacked an hour of noon, as we were plodding up a valley, beside a rapid brook running through narrow willowflats, with the dark forest crowding down on each hand from the low foot-hills of the mountains. Suddenly the call of a bull elk came echoing down through the wet woodland on our right, beyond the brook, seemingly less than half a mile off, and was answered by a faint, far-off call from a rival on the mountain beyond. Instantly halting the train, Woody and I slipped off, our horses, crossed the brook, and started to still-hunt for the first bull.

In this place the forest was composed of western tamarack; the large, tall tress stood well apart, and there was much down timber, but the ground was covered with deep, wet moss, over which we trod silently. The elk was traveling up-wind, but slowly, stopping continually to paw the ground and to thrash the bushes with his antlers. He was very noisy, challenging every minute or two, being doubtless much excited by the neighborhood of his rival on the mountain. We followed, Woody leading, guided by the incessant calling.

It was very exciting as we crept toward the great bull, and the challenge sounded nearer and nearer. While we were still at some distance the pealing notes were like those of a bugle, delivered in two bars, first rising, then abruptly falling; as we drew nearer they took on a harsh, squealing sound. Each call made our veins thrill; it sounded like the cry of some huge beast of prey. At last we heard the roar of the challenge not eighty yards off. Stealing forward three or four rods, I saw the tips of the horns through a mass of dead timber and young growth, and slipped to one side to get a clean shot. Seeing us, but not making out what we were, and full of fierce and insolent excitement, the wapiti bull stepped boldly toward us with a stately, swinging gait. Then he stood motionless, facing us, barely fifty yards away, his handsome twelve-tined antlers tossed aloft, as he held his head with the lordly grace of his kind. I fired into his chest, and as he turned I raced forward and shot him in the flank; but the second bullet was not needed, for the first wound was mortal, and he fell before going fifty yards.

The dead elk lay among the young evergreens. The huge, shapely body was set on legs that were as strong as steel rods, and yet slender, clean, and smooth; they were in color a beautiful dark brown, contrasting well with the yellowish of the body. The neck and throat were garnished with a mane of long hair; the symmetry of the great horns set off the fine, delicate lines of the noble head. He had been wallowing, as elk are fond of doing, and the dried mud clung in patches to his flank; a stab in the haunch showed that he had been overcome in battle by some master bull, who had turned him out of the herd.

We cut off the head, and bore it down to the train. The horses crowded together, snorting, with their ears pricked forward, as they smelled the blood. We also took the loins with us, as we were out of meat, though bull elk in the rutting season is not very good. The rain had changed to a steady downpour when we again got under way. Two or three miles further we pitched camp in a clump of pines on a hillock in the bottom of the valley, starting hot fires of pitchy stumps before the tents, to dry our wet things.

Next day opened with fog and cold rain. The drenched packanimals, when driven into camp, stood mopingly, with drooping heads and arched backs; they groaned and grunted as the loads were placed on their backs and the cinches tightened, the packers bracing one foot against the pack to get a purchase as they hauled in on the lash-rope. A stormy morning is a trial to temper: the packs are wet and heavy, and the cold makes the work even more than usually hard on the hands. By ten we broke camp. It needs between two and three hours to break camp and to get such a train properly packed; once started, our day's journey was from six to eight hours long, making no halt. We started up a steep, pine-clad mountainside, broken by cliffs. My hunting-shoes, though comfortable, were old and thin, and let the water through like a sieve. On the top of the first plateau, where black-spruce groves were strewn across the grassy surface, we saw a band of elk, cows and calves, trotting off through the rain. Then we plunged down into a deep valley, and, crossing it, a hard climb took us to the top of a great bare table-land, bleak and wind-swept. We passed little alpine lakes, fringed with scattering dwarf evergreens. Snow lay in drifts on the north sides of gullies; a cutting wind blew the icy rain in our faces. For two or ·three hours we traveled toward the farther edge of the table-land. In one place a spike-bull elk stood half a mile off in the open; he traveled to and fro, watching us.

As we neared the edge the storm lulled, and pale, watery sunshine gleamed through the rifts in the low-scudding clouds. At last our horses stood on the brink of a bold cliff. Deep down beneath our feet lay the wild and lonely valley of Two-Ocean Pass, walled in on each hand by rugged mountain-chains, their flanks scarred and gashed by precipice and chasm. Beyond, in a wilderness of jagged and barren peaks, stretched the Shoshones. At the middle point of the pass two streams welled down from each side. At first each flowed in but one bed, but soon divided into two; each of the twin branches then joined the like branch of the brook opposite, and swept one to the east and one to the west, on their long journey to the two great oceans. They ran as rapid brooks, through wet meadows and willow-flats, the eastern to the Yellowstone, the western to the Snake....

As evening fell, we reached the bottom, and pitched camp in a beautiful point of open pine forest thrust out into the meadow. There we found good shelter and plenty of wood, water, and grass; we built a huge fire and put up our tents, scattering them in likely places among the pines, which grew far apart and without undergrowth. We dried our steaming clothes, and ate a hearty supper of elk-meat; then we turned into our beds, warm and dry, and slept soundly under the canvas, while all night long the storm roared without.

Next morning dawned clear and cold, the sky a glorious blue. Woody and I started out to hunt over the great table-land, and led our stout horses up the mountain-side by elk-trails so bad that they had to climb like goats. All these elk-trails have one striking peculiarity: they lead through thick timber, but every now and then send off short, well-worn branches to some cliffedge or jutting crag, commanding a view far and wide over the country beneath. Elk love to stand on these lookout points, and scan the valleys and mountains round about.

Blue grouse rose from beside our path; Clarke's crows flew past us, with a hollow, flapping sound, or lighted in the pinetops, calling and flirting their tails; the gray-clad whisky-jacks, with multitudinous. cries, hopped and fluttered near us. Snowshoe rabbits scuttled away, the great furry feet which give them their name already turning white. At last we came out on the great plateau, seamed with deep, narrow ravines. Reaches of pasture alternated with groves and open forests of varying size. Almost immediately we heard the bugle of a bull elk, and saw a big band of cows and calves on the other side of the valley. There were three bulls with them, one very large, and we tried to creep up on them; but the wind was baffling, and spoiled our stalk. So we returned to our horses, mounted them, and rode a mile farther, toward a large open wood on a hillside. When within two hundred yards we heard directly ahead the bugle of a bull, and pulled up short. In a moment I saw him walking through an open glade; he had not seen us. The slight breeze brought us his scent. Elk have a strong characteristic smell; it is usually sweet, like that of a herd of Alderney cows, but in old bulls, while rutting, it is rank, pungent, and lasting. We stood motionless till the bull was out of sight, then stole to the wood, tied our horses, and trotted after him. He was traveling fast, occasionally calling, whereupon others in the neighborhood would answer. Evidently he had been driven out of some herd by the master bull.

He went faster than we did, and while we were vainly trying to overtake him we heard another very loud and sonorous challenge to our left. It came from a ridge-crest at the edge of the woods, among some scattered clumps of the northern nut-pine, or piñon, a queer conifer, growing very high on the mountains, its multiforked trunk and wide-spreading branches giving it the rounded top and, at a distance, the general look of an oak rather than a pine. We at once walked toward the ridge, up-wind. In a minute or two, to our chagrin, we stumbled on an outlying spike-bull, evidently kept on the outskirts of the herd by the master bull. I thought it would alarm all the rest; but, as we stood motionless, it could not see clearly what we were. It stood, ran, stood again, gazed at us, and trotted slowly off. We hurried forward as fast as we dared, and with too little care, for we suddenly came in view of two cows. As they raised their heads to look, Woody squatted down where he was, to keep their attention fixed, while I cautiously tried to slip off to one side unobserved. Favored by the neutral tint of my buckskin hunting-shirt, with which my shoes, leggings, and soft hat matched, I succeeded. As soon as I was out of sight, I ran hard and came up to a hillock crested with piñons, behind which I judged I should find the herd. As I approached the crest, their strong, sweet smell smote my nostrils. In another moment I saw the tips of a pair of mighty antlers, and I peered over the crest with my rifle at the ready. Thirty yards off, behind a clump of piñons, stood a huge bull, his head thrown back as he rubbed his shoulders with his horns. There were several cows around him, and one saw me immediately, and took alarm.

I fired into the bull's shoulder, inflicting a mortal wound; but he went off, and I raced after him at top speed, firing twice into his flank; then he stopped, very sick, and I broke his neck with a fourth bullet....

The elk I thus slew was a giant. His body was the size of the steer's, and his antlers, though not unusually long, were very massive and heavy. He lay in a glade, on the edge of a great cliff. Standing on its brink, we overlooked a most beautiful country, the home of all homes for the elk: a wilderness of mountains, the immense evergreen forest broken by park and glade, by meadow and pasture, by bare hillside and barren table-land. Some five miles off lay the sheet of water known to the old hunters as Spotted Lake; two or three shallow, sedgy places, and spots of geyser formation made pale green blotches on its wind-rippled surface. Far to the southwest, in daring beauty and majesty, the grand domes and lofty spires of the Teton shot into the blue sky. Too sheer for the snow to rest on their sides, it yet filled the rents in their rough flanks, and lay deep between the towering pinnacles of dark rock.

A SUMMER ON THE ROCKIES (1898)

MAJOR SIR ROSE LAMBERT PRICE (1837–1899)

Major Sir Rose Lambert Price was born of English nobility, and in some respects he was as pretentious as his name. With inherited wealth he was free to roam the globe sightseeing, hunting, and observing the cultures of unfamiliar peoples.

He had so enjoyed his Nebraska hunting adventure in 1875 that when General John Coppinger invited him to return in 1898, Price welcomed the opportunity. Why not for the general specialized in combining a wilderness experience with all the amenities of civilization? Coppinger saw to it that Price was pampered by his adjutant the moment he disembarked in New York City. Under such circumstances, traveling in America was quite tolerable.

Once in Teton country, Price joined Dr. Seward Webb's party at his hunting camp a little north of Jackson Lake. In a sense, Webb represented American royalty, for he had married Eliza Osgood Vanderbilt, daughter of Cornelius Vanderbilt. He had plenty of money and believed that it ought to be used to alleviate any hardships for his guests. The chef, Price noted, kept them "a very long way from starvation." A Black trooper in the Ninth Cavalry proved "a capital servant." Champagne was served every night, while 150 men, 113 horses, and 164 mules guaranteed that the seven or so hunters need not be inconvenienced by work.

Before meeting the Webb party, Price, General Coppinger, and a substantial Army contingent made their way up the Wind River from Fort Washakie. They reached the Continental Divide by way of Union Pass and then enjoyed a pleasant descent down the Gros Ventre River. Price's account begins as the party enters Jackson Hole.

Once in Jackson Hole, life was good for Price. He joined a more comfortable camp, the weather was not too hot, and the hunting was superb. This selection is taken from Price's book A Summer on the Rockies *(1898).*

A few miles further through the wooded valley of the Snake River brought us to a succession of large grass-covered flats, and on a small backwater of the main river we found our new camp, with the U.S. flag floating gaily in its midst. The two outfits now joined forces, and we all became the guests of Dr. Seward Webb.

The camp, for a hunting party, was an unusually large one, and consisted of 150 men, 113 horses, and 164 mules. The first item embraced the "guns," officers, non-commissioned officers, troopers, civilian employés, enlisted teamsters, packers, Indians, and civilian servants. The tents formed three sides of a large square, with the escort wagons and spring hunting wagons in the centre. The site, though not anything like as convenient or well-chosen as our camp on Buffalo Fork, was picturesque in the extreme. On one side the Tetons rose in all their majesty, the Snake River running at their base. A break in them, more resembling a chasm than the entrance to a trail, fronted our position, and afforded the only way of penetrating an apparently impregnable position that led to the ground, where the local hunters assured us we should find mountain sheep.

On the opposite side a succession of lower mountains, covered with all the variegated foilage of autumnal tints, stretched away until some five and thirty or forty miles off they met the still higher range, where Bat and Emmet had hunted for a mountain sheep.

To our north lay the wooded rising country included in the timber reservation attached to the Yellowstone National Park; and to the south the grand alluvial plains of Jackson's Hole, which run for over forty miles on each side of the Snake River, and form the great winter feeding ground for all the elk and antelope for more than a hundred miles on each side of it. The winters in the Park are so severe, all the deer in it are driven by starvation from the sanctuary which it affords on to these plains, where they can be slaughtered literally by thousands.

Hunting guide Ben Sheffield liked to advertise his hunters' success in northern Jackson Hole. Courtesy National Park Service, Grand Teton National Park.

An effort is being made by some people interested in the preservation of wild animals, to induce the government to add a considerable portion of these winter feeding grounds to the National Park. I hope most sincerely they may succeed, for if they do not it will only be a matter of time for the elk to follow the buffalo and disappear off the face of creation. The Doctor's party consisted of five guns: Dr. Seward Webb, Messrs. Creighton and Louis Webb, Purdy, and Bird. As only Emmet and myself hunted from the General's outfit it brought the guns up to seven, or perhaps I should say rifles, as being certainly the more correct expression.

Of our creature comforts while in camp the Doctor took the greatest possible care. A *chef*, with a couple of assistants, kept us a very long way from starvation, and champagne every night for those who liked it was at any rate a beverage not often to be found in a camping outfit near Jackson's Hole. It was very luxurious and very jolly, but "all hands" were far more intent on hunting than on either eating or drinking, and we were all more or less away on detached hunting parties for days or weeks at a time, when neither *chef* nor champagne was included in our commissariat.

The Doctor started off, with Bat Garnier and Beaver Dick as hunters, the day after we arrived in camp, to look for sheep up the gorge penetrating the Tetons. Years ago I have got sheep on quite comfortable ground, and with very little difficulty; but now they are only to be found on, and in, the most uncompromising places; and the Tetons, rugged, bare, and in places utterly inaccessible, form a very typical ground for these rapidly disappearing animals. Beaver Dick, who had a ranche in the neighbourhood, had, with the assistance of his Indian wife (who was quite as good a hunter as himself) located a band of sheep in the Tetons. The Doctor had "blood in his eye," and was keen on the *ovis montana*. I did not see him again for a fortnight, but I believe he got four of them, and one carried a very good head.

Emmet had a mysterious adventure with one which allowed him to get within twenty yards, and then disappeared like a dissolving view. It quite scared Tigee, the Shoshone hunter, who, though a pious-minded Indian, and not given to habitual profanity, declared it was the devil, and seemed quite relieved when he got clear of the locality.

On the 16th of September the wagons we had brought from Fort Washakie were started back empty under the charge of a non-commissioned officer, on the return journey, the General fearing that if they delayed here longer they might get obstructed by snow when crossing the Divide. The weather was lovely, but we had sharp frosts in the early morning, and the water left in a basin one night in my tent was in the morning frozen solid. The entire party were at this time away in different directions from the main camp; some singly, some by twos. There was any amount of transport for whoever required it. Ten, twenty, thirty mules if necessary, with their aparajoes and packers, were always in immediate readiness for whoever required them, with cook, tent, and as much food and drink as suited the individual requirements of the gentleman, or gentlemen, forming the party. Nothing could have been better managed or complete.

The hunting radius was generally from twenty to forty miles from permanent camp, so that there was any amount of ground for everyone without the slightest bit of crowding or interfering with one another. With regard to game one could hardly go wrong. It was everywhere. The only difficulty was in getting *good* heads, but of elk there was any quantity.

12

ONE NEVER TIRES OF GAZING AT THE GRAND RANGE (1884)

GEORGE BIRD GRINNELL (1849–1938)

George Bird Grinnell personified the broad interests and active life of educated, wealthy men of the late nineteenth century. Often concurrently, his career embraced big game hunting, ranching, ethnology, editing, and writing. Furthermore, his knowledge of geology and the natural sciences marked him as one of the nation's first conservationists concerned with the rampant waste of natural resources. From his position as editor of Forest and Stream, *he crusaded against the wanton destruction of wildlife and habitat.*

During his long life, Grinnell journeyed often to the West, although he preferred to live in New York City. His first western adventure was in 1870, when as a Yale student he accompanied Othniel Marsh on a paleontology trip to the Badlands. It was the beginning of his long love affair with the wilderness of the West.

The following selection is from Grinnell's unpublished diary, written in the field in 1884. He accompanied Arnold Hague, a geologist officially employed to survey Yellowstone's geological wonders and enlarge the earlier work of the Hayden surveys. In their wanderings Hague and Grinnell journeyed south of Yellowstone and into the northern Jackson Hole country.

Occasionally, Grinnell's diary is difficult to decipher, and sometimes it is devoid of punctuation. Some editing has been necessary, but it is hoped that nothing has been subtracted from Grinnell's obvious delight with his surroundings.

September 3, 1884. I started before the pack train this morning intending to try to kill some meat. I crossed the Snake River and rode into the timber pushing up the hill as fast as possible. Down timber and marshy spots made my progress rather slow. The character of the vegetation here is entirely different from that on the other side of the divide. The mountain side, among the green timber, is covered with a thick undergrowth of plants from three to ten feet high. Willows grow along very little creeks and in every depression and ravine. All this shows the greater moisture of the western slope of the mountains. Often it was difficult to force one's horse through the underbrush.

At length, after some hard climbing, I reached the upper edge of the timber; timber which had once extended to the summit of the mountain but had long ago been destroyed by fire. By zigzagging my horse up the steep slope and winding about the low ridges that run out from it, I, at length, reached the summit of a high mountain from which a superb view could be had. The Red Mountain Range cut off the view, but to the northeast the broad valley of the Snake River lay spread out with its winding silver ribbon of a stream. To the southwest was Jackson's lake, a shining sheet of beautiful water dotted with pine-clad islets. Beyond and above the lake rose the superb mass of the Teton Range. From this point almost the whole range was in view: Moran, a gigantic pile with two or three glacier-like masses of ice on its northern face, and then to the southward two or three smaller mountains. Still further south the towering pinnacles of the Three Tetons shoot skyward, reminding one of the Matterhorn. Along the eastern side of Jackson's lake there are extensive park-like meadow lands and then to the eastward are spread low bare ridges over which the fire has swept, now covered with fallen timber. To the southwest or east lies a massive range of mountains which seem low only by comparison with the wonderful height of the Tetons, and in which lies the Continental Divide....

I kept along the side of the hill where it was pretty steep and below me to the left was a wide valley in which there was some green timber. I was riding along looking down in the valley when suddenly my eye caught sight of an animal standing in an open spot, tail toward me. For an instant I thought it was a horse and the idea flashed through my mind that there was a camp down there. Then the animal turned its head and I saw that it was an elk. In a moment I was off my horse and had moved him back into a little clump of pines where he would be fairly hidden, for the white animal would soon catch the eye of the game. Then divesting myself of my spurs I crept back to the ridge. There were two or three elk in the open, a bull and one or two old cows. A number of others could be seen farther off among the timber. I could have killed one or two of them for they were only about 100 yards away, but if I did so, I could only carry the sirloin with me for I had twenty-five miles to go and I did not care to load my horse with meat and wall.

So I waited about in the hope that a calf or a yearling would show itself. While I waited the elk became uneasy. They would run twenty or thirty yards and then stop and look about them. Just then the pinto got lonely and made a noise. The band started and all plunged into the timbers. I could hear them for quite a distance, making the sticks crash as they trotted through the forest and then I saw them climb the steep hill near the head of the ravine....

For several miles further I kept to the bare burnt hills, seeing a few recent elk tracks, but no more game. Then I came down to the meadows at the head of Jackson's lake and, striking the trail, pushed on after the pack train. In the afternoon I passed a half breed and a boy who were going into the park. The country is perfectly lovely and one never tires of grazing at the grand range toward which we are going. The mountains are so high that they seem close at hand, yet they never seem to come any closer all through the day's march. They are masses of granite almost ivory in hue with gray here and there. They are little blackened by groves of pine timbers or whitened by patches of snow. They are so steep, however, that it is only in the ravines that the snow can cling to them. Elsewhere it slips off or is blown away by the wind. The ice masses on the north side of Moran appear to be true glaciers, though this could only be certainly determined by an examination of the water that flow out from beneath them.

A prominent feature of Moran which today came into view is a nearly vertical dike of dark rock moving up the side of a granite face where the rock has been cut away. The dike must be 100 feet wide, and reaches from the summit of the mountain down under a snow mass and then rock at its foot and then appears again on the mountain side below and in a direct line with the upper part of the dike. Just south of the snow and the debris appears a dark mass which looks like a part of the dike broken and pushed to one side.

No good view of Jackson's lake is had after leaving the meadows near its head for the trail passes mostly through the lowlands and the shores of the lake are covered with timber. Later in the afternoon we turned away from the lake to cut across to the bend of the Snake River. The country is wet with small lakes and meadows. The timber is very fine, much larger than that seen on the other side of the divide. Some of the pines and firs bring from eighteen inches to two feet in diameter....

A little after passing Buffalo Fork I ran across a buck antelope on the Snake River bottom but got no shot at him. The camp is opposite Mt. Moran and the whole superb Teton Range is seen to the best possible advantage. Fishing good here.

September 4, 1884. Thursday. Yesterday afternoon I saw quite a number of white swans on the Snake River and in little ponds and lakes near at hand. The prospector and his partner, who are camped near us, killed one out of a flock of eight.

Hague and I started about 10 o'clock to go over to Leighs lake and get a nearer view of the Teton Range. We forded the stream in which the water was about halfway up to the horses backs, and then attempted to make our way over to the bluffs. We found a brown marsh overgrown with willows and intersected in all directions by muddy sloughs in which a horse might readily enough sink out of sight. It took us two hours of hard work to make our way northward to a point where we could ride out without difficulty onto the hard prairie....

Reaching the bluffs, we rode over toward the range. The country is curiously carved and sculptured by glacial actions and everywhere are to be seen moraine deposits of great extent. The drift is mainly quartzite granite and serpentine with some volcanic rock. Long ridges composed wholly of this drift run out for a distance from the foot of the range and are now bare of timber for the most part, though on some of them the fire has spared many of the pines, and young quaking aspen timber grows on almost all of them. On the main river terrace—the highest one on the west side—are a number of groups of gorgeous timber stands and single trees left standing by themselves. This is very curious. This terrace is essentially a flat plain though occasionally traversed by ancient waterways a few feet below the general surface of the plain and from 100 yards to one half mile broad. In one place on this plain is left an oval mound, regular in shape, its longer axis at right angle to that of the range. It is perhaps three hundred yards in length, and is, I presume, morainal in character. Quite a number of antelope were seen on this plain but they were very wild and there was no opportunity to get a shot at them....

Keeping onto the northwest we passed over a number of the burned ridges hoping to see Jackson's lake, which there runs in close to the foot of Mt. Moran, but we were unsuccessful. Then, turning southwest, we began to look for Leighs lake. Riding over the burnt hills in this direction we saw a great quantity of elk tracks and trails; some made the night before and some since day light. There was no doubt in my mind but that the ridge here was full of trees.

Having passed over a number of ridges we at length reached one a little higher than the rest from which we had a fine view of the south of Jackson's lake. It winds and twists about among its points and islands and sends out long narrow finger-like bays into the hills in a curious way. Hague said that it only needed a few more points to make it look like the Japanese islands. After looking for a while at this and the grand old mountains and searching the hills for elk, we rode off again to the southwest. In a little while we saw Leighs lake from a hilltop, a pretty sheet of water flowing by an outlet to the south into the Snake River. Here we sat down on the hillside and studied the Tetons again before turning back toward camp. One of the most impressive features about them is their nakedness. They are so utterly bare that it adds to their majesty....

On the way home we saw some antelope, and I shot at a running bunch, shooting a little too high. Passing the end of a burnt hill, a blacktail doe jumped out of the brush and ran across in front of us. I jumped off my horse to shoot, but as I did so she went down into a depression and when I was ready I could only see her ears. She ran off down the ravine....

September 5, 1884. Friday. The storm which had been threatening so long broke upon us last night and today it is raining hard. We did not move, but had breakfast at camp. The rain, sometimes mingled with snow, came down with a persistent drip. Stewart and I and the major rigged up a capital shelter and we ate our breakfast very comfortably in a dry place....

The packers went fishing but came in without having had a bite. About 3 o'clock I set up my rod and went up the river from camp. I had only about an hour and a half to fish, as dinner was promised at 4:30 or five. I began casting at the tail of a riffle below which the water was swift and deep. After a few casts I caught a small trout and then a larger one—perhaps weighing half or three quarters of a pound. They were strong, vigorous fish and their eager way of taking the fly was very pleasant to see.

I followed them down the swift water, and had made a long cast out toward the middle of the stream when a huge fish rose to my tail fly, a brown hackle, but missed it. I cast again over the same spot but this time moved my fly more slowly. He rose again and I struck at just the right moment and had him fast. For a moment he seemed too much astonished to do anything, but he soon recovered himself and then ensued the grandest fight that I have ever had with a trout. He threw himself out of water, then struggled under it, throwing himself over and over as if trying to break the line by twisting it. Then followed furious shaking and tugging, and a long, swift, strong, rush. Then another series of shakes and tugs. It took me twenty-four minutes by the watch to land him. I think it was the most exciting struggle I ever took in part in....

PART III

SEEING AND SETTLING THE COUNTRY

13

OUTFIT AND ADVICE FOR THE-WOMAN-WHO-GOES-HUNTING-WITH-HER-HUSBAND (1900)

GRACE GALLATIN SETON-THOMPSON (1872–1959)

Grace Gallatin Seton-Thompson, a proper Victorian lady, preferred to summer in Europe rather than the American West. However, when she married Ernest Seton-Thompson in 1896, her holidays changed. Her new husband was a well-established painter, writer, and lecturer. His topics included the American Indian, wilderness, hunting animals, and nature. He found his material in the American West. Thus in 1898 Grace followed "Nimrod," as she called her hunter/husband, to Jackson Hole.

Grace's account of her adventures is delightful, taken from her book A Woman Tenderfoot (1900). She is always up to the task. As she says, one must "keep your nerve, grasp it firmly, and look at it closely." The following excerpts tell of her crossing the Snake River during spring runoff, and her elk hunt, both of which surely tested her nerve.

Another day of dust and long hard miles over gradually rising hills, with the huge mass of the Tetons looming ever nearer, and the next day we climbed the Teton Pass.

There is nothing extraordinary about climbing the Teton Pass—to tell about. We just went up, and then we went down. It took six half a day to draw us up the last mile—some twenty thousand seconds of conviction on my part (unexpressed, of course; see side talk) that the next second would find us dashed to everlasting splinters. And it took ten minutes to get us down!

Of the two, I preferred going. If you have ever climbed a grease pole during Fourth of July festivities in your grandmother's village, you will understand.

When we got to the bottom there was something different. Our driver informed us that in two hours we should be eating dinner at the ranch house in Jackson's Hole, where we expected to stop for a while to recuperate from the past year's hard grind and the past two weeks of travel. This was good news, as it was then five o'clock and our midday meal had been light—despite the abundance of coffee, soggy potatoes, salt pork, wafer slices of meat swimming in grease, and evaporated apricots wherein some nice red ants were banqueting.

"We'll just cross the Snake River, and then it'll be plain sailing," he said. Perhaps it was so. I was inexperienced in the West. This was what followed:

Closing the door on the memory of my recent perilous passage, I prepared to be calm inwardly, as I like to think I was outwardly. The Snake River is so named because for every mile it goes ahead it retreats half way alongside to see how well it has been done. I mention this as a pleasing instance of a name that really describes the thing named. But this is after knowledge.

About half past five, we came to a rolling tumbling yellow stream where the road stopped abruptly with a horrid drop into water that covered the hubs of the wheels. The current was strong, and the horses had to struggle hard to gain the opposite bank. I began to thank my patron saint that the Snake River was crossed.

Crossed? Oh, no! A narrow strip of pebbly road, and the high willows suddenly parted to disclose another stream like the last, but a little deeper, a little wider, a little worse. We crossed it. I made no comments.

At the third stream the horses rebelled. There are many things four horses can do on the edge of a wicked looking river to make it uncomfortable, but at last they had to go in, plunging madly, and dragging the wagon into the stream nearly broadside, which made at least one in the party consider the frailty of human contrivances when matched against a raging flood.

Soon there was another stream. I shall not describe it. When we eventually got through it, the driver stopped his horses to rest, wiped his brow,

Crossing the Snake River at Menor's Ferry at Moose offered the only way to cross the river until 1926. Courtesy National Park Service, Grand Teton National Park.

went around the wagon and pulled a few ropes tighter, cut a willow stick and mended his broken whip, gave a hitch to his trousers, and remarked as he started the horses:

"Now, when we get through the Snake River on here a piece, we'll be all right."

"I thought we had been crossing it for the past hour," I was feminine enough to gasp.

"Oh, yes, them's forks of it; but the main stream's on ahead, and it's mighty treacherous, too," was the calm reply.

When we reached the Snake River, there was no doubt that the others were mere forks. Fortunately, Joe Miller and his two sons live on the opposite bank, and make a living by helping people escape destruction from the mighty waters. Two men waved us back from the place where our driver was lashing his horses into the rushing current, and guided us down stream some distance. One of them said:

"This yere ford changes every week, but I reckon you might try here."
We did.

Had my hair been of the dramatic kind that realises situations, it would
have turned white in the next ten minutes. The water was over the horses'
backs immediately, the wagon box was afloat, and we were being borne
rapidly downstream in the boiling seething flood, when the wheels struck
a shingly bar which gave the horses a chance to half swing, half plunge.
The two men, who were on horseback, each seized one of the leaders, and
kept his head pointed for a cut in the bank, the only place where we could
get out.

Everything in the wagon was afloat. A leather case with a forty-dollar
fishing rod stowed snugly inside slipped quietly downstream. I rescued
my camera from the same fate just in time. Overshoes, wraps, field glasses,
guns were suddenly endowed with motion. Another moment and we
should surely have sunk, when the horses, by a supreme effort, managed to
scramble on to the bank, but were too exhausted to draw more than half
of the wagon after them, so that it was practically on end in the water, our
outfit submerged, of course, and ourselves reclining as gracefully as possible
on the backs of the seats.

Had anything given away then, there might have been a tragedy. The
two men immediately fastened a rope to the tongue of the wagon, and
each winding an end around the pommel of his saddle, set his cow pony
pulling. Our horses made another effort, and up we came out of the water,
wet, storm tossed, but calm. Oh, yes—calm!

After that, earth had no terrors for me; the worst road that we could
bump over was but an incident. I was not surprised that it grew dark very
soon, and that we blundered on and on for hours in the night until the
near wheeler just lay down in the dirt, a dark spot in the dark road, and our
driver, after coming back from a tour of inspection on foot, looked worried.
I mildly asked if we would soon cross Snake River, but his reply was an
admission that he was lost. There was nothing visible but the twinkling
stars and a dim outline of the grim Tetons. The prospect was excellent for
passing the rest of the night where we were, famished, freezing, and so tired
I could hardly speak....

Then I heard a noise and listened eagerly. The driver said it was a coyote howling up on the mountain. At last voices did come to me from out of the blackness, and Nimrod returned with a man and a fresh horse. The man was no other than the owner of the house for which we were searching, and in ten minutes I was drying myself by his fireplace, while his hastily aroused wife was preparing a midnight supper for us.

To this day, I am sure that driver's worst nightmare is when he lives over again the time when he took a tenderfoot and his wife into Jackson's Hole, and, but for the tenderfoot, would have made them stay overnight, wet, famished, frozen, within a stone's throw of the very house for which they were looking.

"If you want to see elk, you just follow up the road till you strike a trail on the left, up over that hog's back, and that will bring you in a mile or so on to a grassy flat, and in two or three miles more you come to a lake back in the mountains."

Mrs. Cummings, the speakers, was no ordinary woman of Western make. She had been imported from the East by her husband of three years before. She had been 'forelady in a corset factory,' when matrimony had enticed her away, and the thought that walked beside her as she baked, and washed, and fed the calves, was that someday she would go 'back East.' And this in spite of the fact that for those parts she was very comfortable.

Her log house was the largest in the country, barring Captain Jones's, her nearest neighbor, ten miles up at Jackson's Lake, and his was a hotel. Hers could boast of six rooms and two clothes' closets. The ceilings were white muslin to shut off the rafters, the sitting room had wall-paper and a rag carpet, and in one corner was the post-office....

The sun was just dropping behind the great Tetons, massed in front of us across the valley. We sat on our horses motionless, looking at the peaceful and majestic scene, when out from the shadows on the sandy flats far below us came a dark shadow, and then leisurely another and another. They were elk, two bulls and a doe, grazing placidly in a little meadow surrounded by trees.

We kept as still as statues.

The Cunningham Homestead has a stunning setting, but surviving the winters in northern Jackson Hole required stamina and courage. Collection of the Jackson Hole Historical Society and Museum, 2003.0050.007.

Nimrod said, "There is your chance."

"Yes," I echoed, "here is my chance."

We waited until they passed into the trees again. Then we dismounted. Nimrod handed me the rifle, saying:

"There are seven shots in it. I will stay behind with the horses."

I took the gun without a word and crept down the mountain side, keeping under cover as much as possible. The sunset quiet surrounded me; the deadly quiet of but one idea—to creep upon that elk and kill him—possessed me. That gradual painful drawing nearer to my prey seemed a lifetime. I was conscious of nothing to the right, or to the left of me, only of what I was going to do. There were pine woods and scrub brush and more woods. Then, suddenly, I saw him standing by the river about to drink. I crawled nearer until I was within one hundred and fifty yards of him, when at the snapping of a twig he raised his head with its crown of branching horn. He saw nothing, so turned again to drink.

Now was the time. I crawled a few feet nearer and raised the deadly weapon. The stag turned partly away from me. In another moment he would be gone. I sighted along the metal barrel and a terrible bang went booming through the dim secluded spot. The elk raised his proud, antlered head and looked in my direction. Another shot tore through the air. Without another move the animal dropped where he stood. He lay as still as the stones beside him, and all was quiet again in the twilight.

I sat on the ground where I was and made no attempt to go near him. So that was all. One instant a magnificent breathing thing, the next—nothing.

Death had been so sudden. I had no regret; I had no triumph—just a sort of wonder at what I had done—a surprise that the breath of life could be taken away so easily.

Meanwhile, Nimrod had become alarmed at the long silence, and, tying the horses, had followed me down the mountain. He was nearly down when he heard the shots, and now came rushing up.

"I have done it," I said in a dull tone, pointing at the dark, quiet object on the bank.

"You surely have."

Nimrod paced the distance—it was one hundred and thirty-five yards—as we went up to the elk. How beautiful his coat was, glossy and shaded in browns, and those great horns—eleven points—that did not seem so big now to my eyes.

Nimrod examined the carcass.

"You are an apt pupil," he said. "You put a bullet through his heart and another through his brain."

"Yes," I said; "he never knew what killed him." But I felt no glory in the achievement.

14

THE DIARY OF A DUDE-WRANGLER (1924)

STRUTHERS BURT (1882–1954)

Dude ranching was the first activity within Grand Teton National Park that drew numbers of tourists. The most significant proponent was Struthers Burt. Burt partnered with Louis Joy to establish the JY Ranch in 1909, the first in Jackson Hole. He soon parted ways with Joy to establish the Bar BC ranch in 1911. He and his new partner, Horace Carncross, were very successful and managed a thriving business until the 1930s. Burt had the advantage of a Princeton education and eastern refinement, combined with an immense love of the West and its people. His clients returned year after year.

Struthers Burt also had a good sense of the future. He understood that protection of the beauty of Jackson Hole was essential to his business and represented the highest and best use of the country. He also understood that the National Park Service could best accomplish his conservation goals. He fought for the park idea, and it can be argued that without Burt's commitment, there would be no Grand Teton National Park today.

Burt was also a nationally known author. He wrote at least a half dozen books, while his wife, Katherine, produced a dozen novels. They brought a literary flair to the isolated world of Jackson Hole. Perhaps Burt's most successful and entertaining work was The Diary of a Dude-Wrangler *(1924). In the following excerpts, Burt explains the uniqueness of the "industry," the difficulties of the environment, picking a ranch site, and how to be a success.*

A dude-ranch is not a summer hotel, nor is it a summer boarding-house, much as it may seem like one or the other to the ignorant. Physically it is an ordinary ranch amplified, in some sections of the country the buildings made out of logs, in others, out of adobe, or frame, or even brick. There is usually a large central ranch-house containing sitting-rooms, a dining-room, kitchens, storehouses, and so on, and, scattered about the grounds, smaller cabins or houses, holding from one to four people, used as sleeping-quarters. There is also invariably a great variety of other buildings, ice-houses, saddle-sheds, blacksmith-shops, camp storehouses, frequently a store and post-office, and almost always an extra-large cabin that can be used for dancing. And as a rule, unless the ranch is an old ranch turned into a dude-ranch, the dude-wrangler has picked his location for its beauty and, if he is a wise dude-wrangler, has so disposed his buildings through the trees that there is no effect of crowding or of size. You must do your best, even on a place where from fifty to over a hundred people are gathered together, not to destroy the impression of wildness and isolation.

And spiritually as well a dude-ranch is very far removed from either a summer hotel or a summer boarding-house. Unaware as dudes may be of this fact, there is a social and moral and actual responsibility unlike any responsibility attached to the job of being an hotelkeeper. That is what, in some ways, makes the dude-business a very pleasant business and, in other ways, a very trying one. You have, you see, upon your hands a number of people most of whom are in an entirely new and rather bewildering environment. It is not sufficient merely to give them rooms and baths and then turn them loose; it is necessary to entertain them, or see that they are entertained, and to instruct them in a strange and wild and, if not properly handled, fairly dangerous country. You give them horses and teach them to ride, you beg and argue with them not to over-ride, you outfit them and send them out on pack-trips, you flirt occasionally, if you have to, with some of the younger, or, as you get older, youngish ones, and you try to prevent some of the still younger ones from breaking up discipline by flirting with your cowboys, you tell innumerable stories, so that at times your voice becomes hoarse and your mind wanders, and you answer an infinite number of questions.

It is a large patriarchal life in which at moments you feel you are the father of an unruly family and, at other moments, especially when you are asked, as you are every hour or so, about the weather, that someone has mistaken you for a minor deity.

As to discipline, we fluctuate, as do most dude-ranches, between beautiful young cowpunchers who attract the eye and whom we keep until they become thoroughly useless and 'trashy', and by no means beautiful old men, losing with the latter atmosphere and putting up with being told just what to do, for the sake of work accomplished. The happiest combination, perhaps, is a beautiful young cowpuncher with a young and jealous wife. I am speaking, of course, only of certain positions; others require by their very nature mature men. On the whole of our discipline, however especially lately, has been excellent, and the summers recently have been busy and cheery ones devoid for the most part of the added duty of chaperonage.

Yet this chaperonage, even when needed, was never such a serious task. The younger generation of the East is abundantly well able to take care of itself and the average cowpuncher is on the whole a pretty upstanding fellow, with a fundamental decency and a vast amount of common sense. Of all sections of the country, mothers need be least afraid of the Far West. Moreover, one of the charming qualities of the Far Westerner is his sense of loyalty—a feudal sense—to the outfit he happens at the moment to be working for. He is extremely jealous, even to the point of fighting, of its honor and dignity and good name. He foregoes even the, on the whole, innocent pleasures of flirtation if he thinks it is injuring "his outfit's" reputation.

That this loyalty is transferred immediately in case a man leaves one ranch to the next were he gets a job makes it even more interesting. It is the result of isolation and a close-knit communal life.

But you can see that dude-wrangling is somewhat like a gigantic game of chess and that the dude-wrangler must be on the alert from the moment his guests open their eyes in the morning to the sleepy twittering of birds to the moment they close them at any odd hour of the night.

He must cajole the obstreperous, encourage the shy, restrain the too active, propel the lazy, and, at times, gently snub the impertinent. He must know just what each person is doing on that particular day, whether he or

Dude rancher Struthers Burt at the Bar BC, circa 1925. Burt and his wife Katherine were successful hosts. However, their strong support of the national park idea may have been their greatest accomplishment. Collection of the Jackson Hole Historical Society and Museum, 2008.0038.067.

she is going fishing or shooting or mountain climbing or just riding, and if he finds a person, or a group of people, at loose ends he must insinuate into the bored mind, or minds, the idea of a new and delightful trip or occupation. Also he must be a solvent between antagonistic personalities.

Try as you may, careful as you may be in your selection, you cannot hope to get together fifty or more people of all ages and characteristics from all corners of the country, even from all corners of the globe, and expect them to adore each other universally. But the dude-wrangler must see that they are at least polite to each other, for they are in a peculiar position, they— out of their usual surroundings, against a new background—are caught together in a little eddy of lonely life, and they are more or less dependent upon each other. And lonely eddies of life, although they are the pleasantest spots in the world, can also be very dangerous if gossip is not looked after.

Nor do the dude-wrangler's duties end, as I have already indicated, when most other honest men's labors cease—except the dairy farmer's—and that is at night. Again and again when he is tired from riding all day, or from manual work, or when he is wet from rain, or sleepy, he must conquer his natural instincts and 'be about.' He has to listen to a great deal. Something about high altitudes, something about dislocation of environment, the patriarchal position a dude-wrangler possesses, makes his guests confidential and him a father confessor. People, ladies especially, tell him things they wouldn't tell ordinarily. The greatest personal dangers that the dude-wrangler incurs are the dangers of becoming at too early an age gentle world-weary and, at too early an age, anecdotal.

Furthermore—and here is the inner secret of it all—the dude-wrangler must do these things—'wrangle' his dudes in all their bewildering complexity—without letting them for a moment know that he is doing so. A salient characteristic of the human mind, and very naturally, seems to be a dislike of being herded, with an unconscious desire none the less to have it done; people hate to be directed, but they get excessively angry if they aren't. The best way to direct them, therefore, either in dude-wrangling or the ordinary relations of life, is to let them think each new idea is their own. A fellow dude-wrangler, a magnificent specimen physically, told me he lost about thirty pounds a summer directing people without letting them know he was doing it.

I have been describing the perfect dude-wrangler, and there is, of course, no such creature; but there are rather a lot of them who are qualifying for some sort of busy and executive and story-telling sort of sainthood.

On the top of these multifarious social and spiritual duties the dude-wrangler has the ordinary duties of the man who undertakes to feed and bed a number of his fellow human beings, feeding and bedding them in an isolated country, far from the railway, where, as a rule, nothing grows in profusion, not even eggs, and no delicate thing grows at all, and where more of his outfit—except in outdoor matters—is to begin with untrained. The dude-wrangler is a ranch-owner, a cowman, a horseman, a guide, a wholesale chambermaid, a cook, and storekeeper rolled into one....

IX
A New Partnership

We had an infinitesimal capital, the doctor and myself—a couple of thousand dollars each, my share of it borrowed, and he was almost totally ignorant of conditions, while I, although not so ignorant, was handicapped by the frequently disastrous impetuousness of youth. Or is it disastrous? I don't know. Sometimes it is necessary. Without it youth would frequently get nowhere. Had the doctor and I appreciated what we were doing, perhaps we would have done nothing at all. And that would have been a pity, for we would have missed a considerable amount of success, a vast amount of happiness, and an experience which has been invaluable. As it was, we set out in the most nonchalant manner possible to burden ourselves with debt, depending on the business of the following summer for recompense. What would have happened had no tourist appeared I shudder to think.

By the time I had finally decided that my former partnership was on the point of dissolution and the doctor had decided to abandon the East and become a Westerner, the year was approaching its fall and we had only about two and a half months in which to make our plans and look about us. We appreciated the necessity for continuity in the business. It would not do to allow a season to lapse, not only for the psychological value of not going into abeyance for any length of time, but also because, having so little capital, it was imperative, as I have said, to take in some returns as speedily as possible. But this meant that with the best of luck—an early spring, and all the materials on hand, and labor easy to obtain and hold, in a country where material is always scarce and labor always hard to obtain and hold—we would only have two months, May and June, to get ready in. in that time, out of sage-brush and deadfall, we would have to create a home for fifteen Easter people and the five or six Westerners needed to take care of them, and not only a home for the former but a comfortable and artistic one as well, a very different matter from starting an ordinary ranch. Moreover, having taken care of the interiors of our guests and the interiors of our cabins, we would have to turn our attention to the outside world and see that there were cows to milk and horses to ride and other horses to the hauling and farm work. In short, we had to build a small town in the wilderness, complete and self-sustaining in every detail.

Such a task might seem impossible unless you bear in mind the aston-ishingly short time it takes experts to build a log-house and the genius of the Westerner for turning his hand to anything. Our fireplaces were built by a man who had never built a fireplace before in his life and the rocks with which he had to work were the worst that can be imagined—slipper cobble-stones and unshaped granite. The same man who one day is laying logs, the next can manufacture the pleasantest kind of an easy chair or a dining-room table. We made excellent chairs out of two by two lumber and elk hides and are using them still; we made chairs and beds out of willows and alder and stripped aspens and pine poles. And the most beautiful furniture in the world, of course, is home-made, as the most beautiful houses in the world are, on the whole, unless really great architects are employed, those built from necessity not artifice. Nothing is lovelier and fits more perfectly into the background from which it came than a Western log-cabin, and nothing is more comfortable. In the summer it is cool, in the winter it is warm. Its walls inside are restful to the eye, taking on a mellow ruddy patina as they get older. Moreover, they form the best of settings for anything you choose to put upon them. There is something of magic about the inevitable correctness of simplicity and usefulness.

In regard to the things we could not make, I conceived the brilliant idea, if I say it myself, of reading from beginning to end the huge catalogues of two of the largest mail-order houses...'Western Bibles,' the irreverent call them...and checking off what we needed from adzes to zithers. In this way nothing was overlooked, although possibly a good deal was ordered we did not really need. These catalogues are ingenious. Little pictures accompany the text. And as a result, you get into the habit of sending for various objects just to see if they are as useful and as pretty as the pictures make them out to be. By the time the winter was over I could repeat those catalogues backward....

As a matter of fact, we never did use a zither on the ranch or order one, although we have had imported from time to time plenty of ukuleles and guitars and have always had down in the bunk-house a plethora of mouth-organs, that most typical of cowboy musical instruments....

But, to return to the task on hand, here, specifically, was what we had to build and assemble by July 1 of the following summer.... We had decided that we would take only fifteen people and for some reason, why I don't know, it never occurred to us for a moment that we wouldn't have those fifteen people, although it was not until the last few weeks before they actually arrived that we were sure of any one of them.... We would have to have at least seven small sleeping-cabins, fourteen by sixteen, with fire-places, four bunkhouses, a couple of storehouse, a meat-house, corrals and necessary fencing, a well, and a large central cabin, the last with a kitchen, a dining-room, a sitting-room, and two or more smaller rooms for writing and card-playing. Those were not the days of bridge, but even then we had to make some provision for people who can find nothing better to do at night but follow suit. Nowadays with bridge and the added complication of Mah-Jong—an extraordinarily spreading—we use every unoccupied cabin on the ranch and probably eventually will have to put up a mess-tent some-where out in the sage-brush.

We built for fifteen people—we have been enlarging ever since. This is what we have to-day: forty-five buildings, ranging from single room and double room sleeping-cabins through cabins designed for all kinds of use, to the central cabin with its two dining-rooms, its kitchen, its two big sitting-rooms and its two smaller rooms, a cabin ninety feet long one way and sixty feet long the other way. We have a blacksmith-shop, a garage, a saddle-shed, a granary, a camp storehouse, three ordinary storehouses, a root-cellar, an office, an ice-house, an outfit dining-room, five bunkhouses, a store a laundry, four houses in which live the partners and the upper ranch foreman, and a dance-hall, or recreation-hall, or whatever you choose to call it. We have eighty saddle-ponies, two work teams, ten cows, sixty saddles with their paraphernalia of bridles, blankets, and so on, complete camping outfits for about twenty people, a motor-bus, a smaller car, and an incredible amount of diversified supplies. We must be in a position to replace anything at a moment's notice. I cannot tell you how many sheets and blankets and quilts and things like that are stored away. These, I am glad to say, are in charge of a person delegated to keep track of them.

Furthermore, to this Indian village of an upper ranch, we have added recently two more ranches, a lower ranch which is a stock-ranch and which has an outfit and life of its own, and another ranch which we use as a boys' camp and as headquarters for pack-trips for boys.

These additional ranches have added two more partners, two more fore-men, about twenty more employees, half a hundred more buildings, con-siderably over a thousand acres, and more than a hundred horses, counting saddle and pack and work horses. It is interesting to reflect that the whole thing started twelve years ago from practically no capital and directly—with the exception of the stock-ranch—from sage-brush. The dude-business is the only business I know of in the world, certainly the only business in the West, where such a thing would be possible, and even at that we would have gone along considerably quicker and have made a net profit considerably earlier had we had sufficient capital to begin with. As it was, for years we put back into the business every cent we made and, having often to build hastily, lost money by this haste and by having to amplify and rebuild at our leisure.

We did not know in the beginning that the dude-business is something like the old-fashioned game of 'idiot's delight,' you no sooner get one thumb on top than you have to get the other on top of it. We found that fifteen tourists were not enough—the overhead charges ate up the profits. We tried twenty-five, thirty, forty, eventually we discovered that you could run fifty people with just about the same outfit with which you could run thirty, and we also discovered the simple fact that a dude-ranch that takes only five tourists can be made profitable because you can run it as an ordinary ranch and make little extra provision, but that from five up to fifty tourists there is no stopping.

Having once discovered these facts, we seemed never to be able to build quickly enough to keep up with the demand. I have nightmarish recollections of trying to get the builders out of a cabin just before its first occupants were due to appear over the bench. And the oddness of human nature was never better exemplified than by our difficulty in meeting the demand. Whatever limit we set we had always more applications than we could handle, the surplus showing a surprising evenness of ratio to the limit. Any place that limits its capacity seems to be the one place to which most people want to go.

The doctor and I utilized the last two months of that final summer at the lake ranch hunting for a ranch of our own. It would have been easy enough to buy a ranch, but there was no site already occupied that exactly suited our purposes. We decided eventually that we would have to take up government land. Almost every day we would get on our horses and ride until sundown, exploring out-of-the-way corners of the valley. We argued and fought endlessly. We have done that ever since, but always with infinite mutual respect and forbearance. The doctor is a conservative man and sees the worst side of things first; I am just the other way about. Sometimes we have fought for days over a five-foot jog in a fence. But this combination of opposing qualities makes for a good partnership. Frequently in the end our final half-and-half conclusion is not so far from being right. While we were hunting for a ranch our respective characteristics were uppermost. We would no sooner find a likely spot than one or the other would discover a dozen objections.

There are so many more things to be taken into consideration when you are choosing a dude-ranch than when you are merely choosing an ordinary ranch—and heaven knows, even with an ordinary ranch there are a score of factors that require the use of experience and common sense—soil, the lay of the land, prevailing winds, timber for winter shelter of stock, nearness to range, water rights, nearness to building material, neighbors, five or six other considerations, but with a dude-ranch all these factors have to be governed by and adjusted to the factors of beauty of situation, a certain amount of isolation, opportunities for fishing and shooting and other sports, and the close proximity to points of interest. Even mosquitoes have to be considered. A ranch along a stream where a river wind blows is much less likely to be troubled by mosquitoes than a ranch back from a stream or in thick woods.

At last, after many weeks of search, of delighted discovery and ultimate disappointment, the doctor and I found the place we were looking for. It was not perfect, but as nearly so for our purpose as any piece of land could be. It lay on three benches sloping down to the river; the first bench had no agricultural value at all; the second not very much; and the final flat beside the river, although it contained rich soil, was so stony and cut up with numerous little draws that irrigating would be peculiarly difficult. All this was emphasized later on. The whole place, moreover, was covered with sage-brush—supposed to be a good sign of its growing capacity but a dreadful thing to clear off—and on the lowest flat, where we would want to put our houses, the sage-brush was of the giant variety that reaches up to a man's neck, and there was dead-fall piled like jackstraws. A grim task was ahead of us.

Yet, on the other hand, aspens and pine-trees grew in a half-moon at the base of a bench and were beautifully parked out in the open, and to the south were the beginnings of a meadow, and to the west was a magnificent view of the Tetons, not over two miles away. While further off the south, blue in the distance, closing the valley, was a gorgeous horizon of rolling mountains, and to the east, fifteen miles or so distant, the green containing walls of the Grovont Range. The whole landscape, except to the north, spread out before you. On your left hand, bounding the flat on that side, was the Snake River, very useful in the fishing season, and along the Tetons, within riding distance, was a series of forested sapphire lakes. Ducks and geese were plentiful, the latter along the river and the former both on the river and in some near-by sloughs. But there was no water on the place except at its southern end; we would have to dig a well and bring our irrigation ditch over three miles. All in all, though, a lovely hidden spot.

The doctor and I, after we had made up our minds, used to ride up two or three times a week to what was to be our ranch and dismounting on one of the upper benches, lie on our stomachs in the warm sunlight and roll cigarettes and dream of what we were going to do.

Strange, I can still feel the warmth on the back of my neck, and I have no sense of time. I might have been doing this yesterday. It is odd when you look back and place yourself in a situation that happened twelve years ago. The site we had chosen was eight miles north of the ranch we were then on, in what, until we built, was totally unsettled country, and as we looked down on this untroubled stretch of sage-brush, we did not know how many feet before long were to cross it, and we had no idea how many things—some of them tragic—were to happen to us there.

Pretty soon, however, the opportunity for dreaming ended, for the autumn came and on top of it a record winter.

The winter started, I remember, the second day of November. I recollect the date well because, unfortunately, it was the date on which I had arranged to go out to the nearest good-sized town in order to see a lawyer and definitely wind up my affairs with my former partner. Usually in our country the winter does not really settle down until around the middle of

December, and I recall one Christmas Day when our guests rode up to the ranch on horses, but the year of which I speak the snow started the day I left, and it continued to snow for a week, and the snow never again left the ground until the spring. I was outside several days and by the time I was ready to come back The Pass was blocked and we were the first team to start breaking it open. Following the initial storm came weeks of iron-cold weather. The elk poured down from the hills to their all-too-scant winter feeding-grounds just north of the nearest town a month or two before they were due, and the world seemed suspended in a glimmering gray net of frigidity where the only color was the blood-red of the sunsets.

15

RIVERS, RANCHES, AND RESERVATIONS (1929)

Henry Van Dyke (1852–1933)

It is only natural that we include a piece on fly-fishing the Snake River. Grand Teton National Park is known for its mountains but also this very scenic river. Visiting in the 1920s, Henry Van Dyke gives us a lively piece in The Travel Diary of An Angler *(1929). His journal "set down a few notes of things seen and caught." The "things" were trout, and he fished extensively throughout the Yellowstone ecosystem. In August 1921, Van Dyke came to the Snake River, which he described as "a big river of big trout." He stayed with Struthers Burt at the Bar BC where he could effortlessly cast a line.*

It was on the 14th of August that I first visited this ranch, and on the morning of the 15th I went down to where the clear Cottenwood stream flows into the turbid flood of the main river. There was a long pool where the line of junction between the two currents was plainly traced. Along this line, on either side of it and swinging back and forth between it, I cast my flies—large ones, now, a "dark Montreal" and a "Professor," or a "brown tackle" and a "coachman," dressed on No. 6 hooks. After the too-eager small trout were thinned off a little and returned unhurt to the stream the big fellows began. Before luncheon that pool yielded ten fish, of which the largest weighed a plump five pounds, and the total weight was fifteen pounds. The "dark Montreal" was the favorite fly, and the "Professor" came next.

These fish were all the native trout of the Rocky Mountain "black-spotted" or "red-throat" variety. The small and medium-sized ones (say up to two pounds) are very silvery-scaled and have a rainbow tint on the gill-covers down the middle of the body. The larger ones are darker, greenish on the back and golden on the sides. The black spots are smaller and less distinct. But the shape of the fish is the same—clean-cut and graceful with broad, angled tail and powerful fins, a body formed for speed in swift waters.

I have come back to the ranch for a second visit and find the river now much lower and the fishing better. Many of the channels into which it was parceled and divided have gone dry, and the others, which can now be easily waded (thigh deep), have disclosed new pools. The best are those which are close to main current and the swiftest water, into which the fish always rush when hooked. They pull vigorously and fight to a finish. Not a day have I angled without taking at least one trout of between three and four pounds weight and several others of from one to three pounds. The casting, for the most part, is open, and a long line is needed. A couple of hours in the morning or in the evening will give a man all he wants (or ought to take) of this royal sport.

Through these hours he has only to lift his eyes from the lovely curves of the flowing water to behold the most entrancing mountain view in our country—the pinnacles and spires of the Tetons and the buttressed bulk of Mount Moran—the Grand Teton 13,700 feet high, a giant finger of bare rock lifted into the deep sapphire sky. In the morning light these mountains seem to recede so their distance of four or five miles looks like ten or twelve. But when the sun has set in glory behind their spear-crested battlement they seem to move forward, draw swiftly nearer in the dusk, almost to bend over you like mighty sentinels of the night, beneath whose shadow the orange lights of the ranch begin to gleam from the first terrace above the river.

This is a "dude-ranch." The terms needs explanation to Fifth Avenue. A "dude" is a person who comes from a city—New York, San Francisco, Springfield, Chicago, Peoria, Philadelphia or any other sophisticated place—to tackle the rude delights of life in the wild West before it vanishes. A "dude-ranch" is an establishment where these people are lodged in log cabins, fed on hearty fare, provided with cowponies and pack horses and let loose, under the guidance of cowpunchers and old hunters, to find on mountain trails and by flowing streams those elements of a complete education which college, society and business have failed to give them. With some of them it fails. Their minds are too fat and soggy and gritty with prejudices. They are invincibly super-civilized. But most of the "dudes" take to the better life like hen-hatched ducks to water. The women array themselves in riding breeches, blue overalls, pearl-colored sweaters, leather coats and other vagarious attire. The men wear high boots, flapping hats, jingling spurs, flannel shirts and neckerchiefs of flagrant hues. They ride and climb and fish, and when the season opens they will hunt. The cowpunchers and horse-wranglers are good companions—self-reliant, daring, courteous, fun-loving and sober-minded. When the day's play-work is ended, and the scattered company has come in from forest, stream and hill, they stretch out on skins of elk and bear around the blazing fire of logs on the broad stone hearth and sing or tell stories or discuss the structure of the universe in general, and Jackson's Hole in particular.

There are perhaps a dozen ranches of this kind within riding distance. The partners in this one are a physician, an aviator-ace and a well-known writer of short stories and poems. They have another ranch where they range cattle and horses some twenty miles down the valley. My old friend and pupil, the writer, is firm (almost fierce) in his conviction that the wild West has not disappeared nor even changed essentially.

"It is the same old thing," he says, "or rather the same everlasting new thing that it was when you were out in the Bad Lands in 1879, or Roosevelt at Medora a few years later. Of course there is a little less of it in size, but is not really different in quality. Look at these cowpunchers and guides of ours. Haven't they got the same old traits of courage and good humor and reticence and frankness and long patience and sport temper under certain kinds of provocation? Don't they pick out a "bad man" by the same old marks, and hold a "tin horn" in the same admiring distrust? Why, only two years ago there was a real little cattle-war not twenty miles from here: and two men were killed for grazing their stock on a range that a slick old "bad man" claimed, though he didn't own it.

"Of course, the coming of the automobile legions has made a difference. There are three roads to Moran already, and next year there will be a fourth—through the Hoback Cañon. The "sage brushers" pass through in hordes. They clutter up the country a little, but they can't really change it. They can't break off the Tetons and carry them away. Jackson's Hole isn't a mining country nor a farming country. It is a cattle country and a game country and an admiration country. That is the way God made it, and that way we want to keep it."

Talk like this inevitably leads us to a discussion of the proposal to extend the boundary of the Yellowstone Park southeast and south. On this question my friend Burt feels that Jackson's Hole is "between the devil and the deep sea." To leave the country as it is, under the Forest Reserve, exposes it more or less to the slow invasion of land sharks and water grabbers, who want to dam lakes and get leaseholds on places of wild beauty and otherwise spoil the region. That would be the devil. But to include the country in the National Park and put it under control of the Department of the Interior would necessarily circumscribe some of its present liberties and subject it to park regulations. On the other hand, it would give a surer protection against despoilment and the extermination of the game.

Most of the sensible people with whom I have talked out here—including those fine representatives of Wyoming, Governor Carey and Senator Kendrick—prefer the "deep sea" to the devil. They favor the park extension on principle and differ only in regard to details. They know that Jackson's Hole (where snow fell this Summer on July 4 and Sept. 4) can hardly be turned into an agricultural paradise like Central Idaho. The season is too short and the ground too stony. Therefore they want to keep the country for tourists, game and cattle. The only question is how to run the boundary lines and to reconcile the different interests.

With a little common sense it can be done. The main objects of the extension are two: to include the Thorofare Plateau as a game sanctuary and the source of the Yellowstone River, and to take in the Teton Range as a magnificent region of mountain scenery. This can easily be accomplished without injury to anybody. Run the new boundary line south by east from Pinnacle Mountain in the Absaroka Range, including Kingfisher and Yount's Peak. Then turn westerly and follow the divide between Buffalo Fork and Pacific Creek, thus leaving the old cattle ranchers on the Buffalo undisturbed. Take in "Two Ocean" and "Emma Matilda" Lakes, but pass north of the village of Moran. Then cross Jackson Lake to the west shore and follow southward, taking in to a line half a mile east of the shore of Leigh, Jenny, String, Bradley and Taggart Lakes, and perhaps the upper end of Phelps lake at the foot of Death Cañon. Then swing to the west and north, including all the Tetons and rejoining the present park line at the southwest corner.

Such an extension as this, which I have roughly outline, would take nothing away from anybody deserving of consideration. Private holdings could be acquired by compensation. The State of Wyoming would be greatly benefited in several ways. The southern avenues of approach to the Yellowstone would be developed and sane touring and camping would be promoted. Above all, a glorious addition—the Teton Mountains and lakes—would be included and safeguarded among the nation's heirlooms of beauty.

16

JACKSON HOLE, WYOMING (1958)

FANNY KEMBLE WISTER (1902–1992)

Shortly after the turn of the twentieth century, Jackson Hole was discovered by a select group of wealthy easterners. They first came to hunt big game but soon discovered the pleasures of spending a summer in the wild and remote valley. The dude ranch business was born, featuring a sophisticated primitivist way of life far from the city crowds and summer humidity.

One of the most famous easterners to frequent Jackson Hole was Owen Wister. He loved the West and spent many summers in Wyoming and Montana. Wister kept coming back, and he could usually be found at the JY Ranch on Phelps Lake, the first dude ranch in the valley. In the summer of 1911, he brought his daughter, Fanny. She treasured her summer months at the ranch, experiencing a freedom not available in her city life. Fanny's love of the valley, the mountains, and the state of Wyoming is evident in this introduction to her father's diaries, published in Owen Wister Out West *(1958).*

In 1911 my parents took us, their four oldest children, to Jackson Hole, Wyoming, for the summer. First we camped through Yellowstone Park. We had two teams of horses; one wagon was a buckboard with three rows of seats for us, and the other was a wagon for our camp outfit. There were two drivers and a cook. We camped beside the geysers, where the men made the campfire, put up our tents, and sometimes sang "Turkey in the Straw," with words of their own, while cooking supper. Everybody in the West seemed to have *The Virginian*, and as soon as they heard my father's name would

Young Frances Kemble Wister loved her life of summer
freedom at the JY Ranch. Frances Kemble Wister Photofile,
American Heritage Center, University of Wyoming.

speak to him about it. The guides talked endlessly to him, asking him questions about the old West. It took about a week to get through Yellowstone,
and then we drove into Jackson Hole. When we reached the Snake River,
we crossed it on Meaner's Ferry, a flat barge pulled across the turbulent
deep river on a cable by Mr. Meaner. We paid, I think, fifty cents a team to
Mr. Meaner, who had a white beard and lived alone in his log cabin by the
river and ran the ferry by himself.

Mr. Meaner had the only vegetable garden in Jackson Hole, and during
the rest of the summer we would often ride to call on him and buy his
fresh peas—the only fresh vegetables we had. We stayed for three months
at the JY Ranch on Phelps Lake, the first dude ranch in Jackson Hole. We
four children had a log cabin to ourselves, and our parents had a cabin of
their own next to us. Our wooden bunks were filled with pine boughs and
covered with the gray blankets that we slept between. Every morning a
bucket of hot water was brought to the cabin door by a filthy old man who,
we thought, had something permanently wrong with his jaw. At the end

Dude ranch outing in northern Jackson Hole. Collection of the Jackson Hole Historical Society and Museum, 1991.3734.001.

of our stay this turned out to be a quid of tobacco that he had kept in his mouth in the same place for months.

The corral the horses spent the day in was across the outlet of the lake from our cabin. Every morning the old wrangler on the ranch rounded up the horses, turned loose overnight to graze, and drove them back over the hill into the corral. Many of the horses wore bells around their necks at night so that by hearing a bell the wrangler would know where to look for the horse. The delicious clanging of these variously toned bells as the horses galloped into the corral woke us up each day. The old wrangler filled us with awe and admiration. We hung around him as much as possible, for we knew he was the real thing. He wore high-heeled boots and leather chaps; the handkerchief around his neck was held by drawing the two ends together through a piece of ham bone. He seldom took off his ten-gallon hat. He could do fancy roping that none of us could learn and from outside the corral could rope whichever horse he chose while they were all madly galloping round and round. Often the horse he caught would be too man-shy to let him come near it. Then he would hand me the heavy bridle embossed in silver with Mexican wheelbit and ask me to bridle the horse for him. At last my destiny was fulfilled. With careful carelessness, I walked slowly into the corral.

We ate in the dining-room cabin, next to the kitchen cabin where a cockney English cook converted by the Mormons was in charge. She had a wooden trough filled by a bucket to wash the tin plates and cups in. She had a young daughter about our age at whom she would fly into terrible noisy rages, screaming at her, "I'll knock your blooming 'ead against the blooming wall." Knowing by her tone that "blooming" was a swear word, we could not comprehend it when the words to our Sunday school hymn next winter at home said the "the blooming earth," which everybody sang with pious looks. Food at the ranch was often scanty, being driven 104 miles by team over the mountains from St. Anthony, Idaho. We had many canned tomatoes; and on days when a steer was shot for beef, we would have some of it for supper that night. The rest of it would hang, covered with a bloody canvas, from a tree until we and the flies had eaten it up. We ate dried, smoked, salted bear meat (like dark brown leather) from the year before; fresh elk too tough to chew, shot when the big-game season opened in September; trout caught by my father, who was skilled dry-fly fisherman. We frequently found dead flies between the flap-jacks at breakfast, and we drank condensed milk.

We all tried to learn dry-fly fishing from my father, but only the oldest of us succeeded. Mostly we rode, I bareback for miles each day. Fording Snake River, loping through the sagebrush with no trail, we went into the foothills as far as our laboring horses could climb. We were not too young to be stunned with admiration by the Tetons, and we loved the acres of wild flowers growing up their slopes—the tremulous Harebell blue and fragile, the Indian Paintbrush bright red, and the pale, elegant Columbine. We were not awed by the wilderness, feeling that the Grand Teton was our own mountain and the most wonderful mountain in the world, and the Snake River the fastest, longest river in America. We could ride all day and never get past the Tetons. When we returned to the ranch in the late afternoon, we would ride up the brief slope and suddenly Phelps Lake would appear in front of us. The mountains encircling it rose abruptly from the water,

Local photographer Harrison Crandall enjoyed taking his family and guests camping at Lake Solitude. Courtesy National Park Service, Grand Teton National Park.

with Death Canyon at the far end. Often as we hitched our horses to the rail at the main cabin a cow pony was being lassoed in the corral. There was activity at the ranch; our parents were there. It was good to be back.

Once at the JY a so-called chicken hawk was shot by some enthusiast. We never knew who, and the hawk was thrown for dead on the woodpile where we picked him up intending to add his skin to our collection, which consisted mostly of pack rats whose skins had already turned white for the winter. When we found the hawk still alive, glaring in helpless, savage rage at us, we took him to our parents' cabin and gave him to our father. He found out that the bird's wings were not broken and said that he was not a chicken hawk but a mouse hawk, much more rare, which would never have preyed on the flock of about a dozen chickens at the ranch. My father explained that hawks were unusually strong and that he would try to nurse this one back to health by feeding him raw meat and keeping him for us in his cabin. We agreed that if the bird got well he should go free, for hawks can never be tamed. So, many times a day my father fed raw meat to the hawk, which perched resentfully on his wrist, digging the claws into his skin, watching us hostilely while eating. The bird never became friendly, and one day while we were all there he suddenly without effort soared into the air from my father's wrist and disappeared.

We stayed at Jackson hole until the snow came in late September. The first elk had been shot. We rode far up into the foothills to watch it being skinned and saw the bullets flattened against its shoulder blade. The pack horses were laden with the carcass and led down the mountain.

At last we had to return East. We could not stand the thought of leaving. What—sleep in a real bed again and see trolley cars? How frightful! No more smell of sagebrush, no more rushing Snake River, no more Grand Teton. Why did we have to go back?

To get to St. Anthony, Idaho, we drove 104 miles on a single-track dirt road all the way, fording the Snake River and crossing the mountain pass. We spent four nights in roadhouses, the only place for travelers to sleep. The first one, the Lee Road House, was still in Jackson Hole. There the walls were papered with ancient yellow newspapers. Then came Canyon Creek, where arriving in the dark we made a treacherous descent down the steep road to a villainous-looking group of cabins and one barn beside a narrow, roaring river at the bottom of a black canyon. Here I slept behind a curtain on the landing of the stairs. The next day we reached Driggs, a town of one street. It had boardwalks for sidewalks, false fronts on some of the houses to make them look as if they were two stories high, and saloons with half-length swinging doors at the corners. All the roadhouses lacked plumbing, and at all of them we ate at long tables covered with white oil-cloth. We used to eat from enameled plates and cups, tin forks and spoons, and we sat on backless benches, talking to the other transients. When we got to Victor, we saw some real two-story houses. The last stop of our journey was St. Anthony, where we boarded the train.

In 1912 we returned to Jackson Hole. We were back with a ranch of our own, for my father had bought 160 acres, and we could not drive fast enough to get to it. When we came to the stone marking the boundary between Idaho and Wyoming, we yelled with joy. Every rock, every sage bush, every aspen tree was different and better because it grew in Wyoming. The landscape changed radically. There was no such other state. With condescension we had looked at Utah, Montana, Idaho, but here at last was Wyoming.

That year we brought our youngest brother, who was then three, and our German governess to look after him—surely the first German governess to set foot in Jackson Hole. We also brought our negro houseman from home, who attracted the attention of Westerners who had never seen a colored man. We brought him to help us build our cabin and to cook for us. We were going to live on *our* ranch.

We also brought with us from home our pet black and white Japanese waltzing mouse in a round "butter tin" with wire handle and tight-fitting cover with holes punched in it for air. Her name was Psyche, which we knew to be "Greek Goddess of Beauty" but pronounced by us "Peeshee." I suppose our parents, who gave us permission to take her on our long journey, never knew what her name really was. Peeshee spent the summer waltzing in Jackson Hole.

We stayed at the JY while building our two-story cabin. The whole family worked, and I can remember no outside help at all. Our ranch was on a sagebrush plain not far from the JY, and we moved in before the cabin was finished.

In October, with hideous reluctance, we had to start East; the weather was cold, and there had been snow. To keep Peeshee warm on the long drive, we took turns holding her in her tin on our laps in the buckboard, but by the end of the day somehow we had all had enough of her. Then my father, who was riding, took her as it began to get dark and much colder. He put on the top of the pommel of his Mexican saddle a hot-water bag; on the top of the hot-water bag he balanced Peeshee in her tin. I cannot now imagine how he got the hot water, but Peeshee survived the trip.

Thinking back forty years to our summers in Wyoming, I see that going West in 1885 made my father. Taking us to undomesticated Jackson Hole linked us to his youth, making us in spirit next of kin to the country of his choice.

17

VITAL LAUGHTER (1954)

FRANCES JUDGE

Frances Judge spent her childhood in Jackson Hole, and like Fanny Wister, she has a positive remembrance of the experience. However, although the setting was the same, Judge's situation was different. While Wister recalls the delightful freedom of life on a dude ranch, Judge writes of life on a hardscrabble homestead. It was a work-filled, insecure world they endured, but one they would not trade. For all the travail, Judge's grandparents found the valley a paradise, dominated by work yet ruled by laughter and love.

This story, which appeared in The Atlantic Monthly *in 1954, is of "Gram" and "Gramps," 1892 pioneers to the valley. Their experiences and their zest for the hard-ranching life of Jackson Hole, whether fighting winter, isolation, or mosquitoes, gives a wonderfully accurate portrayal of many pioneer settlers in the valley. The physical remains of their labor has largely disappeared, but the glorious setting remains. It was a good life that Gram lived: one filled with children, hard work, self-sufficiency, and always "vital laughter."*

"I don't know who they are," Gram would say, "but I wish they were in hell." And she'd put the binoculars back on the sill of the kitchen window and study for a while, with the naked eye, the potential visitors coming along the road that wound down Uhl Hill, through fields, and along our willow lane.

When Gram felt the need of people beyond the ranch, she dropped everything and took off, down country, on horseback or with team and

118

buggy or, if it were winter, on skis that Gramp had made for her. She pre-ferred going to people rather than having them come to her. It was annoying to have guests come to the ranch; they knocked her routine into a cocked hat; they upset her spontaneous plans. But she never suffered from a guilty conscience over upsetting the plans of others. Yet ranchers were glad to see her arrive, if for no other reason than to hear her laugh. She was the only person we three children knew who could laugh a mile. More than once we had heard her laugh move, full and clear, across the wild, wild fields.

She had known sorrow and uncertainty before she came to Jackson Hole. Here she found her heaven and no one was going to make it hell for her if she could help it.

In 1896, when Gram met and married Gramp—a powerful, handsome Dutchman with a quick limp—he was already established on 160 acres in the upper reaches of the Jackson Hole valley in Wyoming. Gramp—John Shive—took up the land, by squatter's right, about 1892. Since no man could outwork him and few even keep up with him, by the time he married Gram and found himself with a ten-year-old stepdaughter, he was doing as well, in ranching, as could be expected in this high valley in the 1890s.

Gram was thirty-nine years old when she married Gramp. She was not beautiful—never had been; she wasn't even pretty. Her body was short, sturdy, compact, and nail-hard. Her ankles were thick. She was high-chested, flat-breasted. Her face was full, her skin well broken into wrinkles. Her nose was short and round—an unusual nose, unlike anyone else's. Her pre-maturely gray hair came to a widow's peak on a high forehead. Her eyes were large, wide apart, intelligent, mischievous, and a lovely gentian blue.

Her coarsened skin and her white hair made her seem, upon first ap-pearance, much older than Gramp (she was four years his senior), but not for long. Her high spirit, vitality, and rough gaiety could match those of anyone of any age. Because she did things other women did not do, and didn't give a damn, she was envied.

Her childhood had been free but not happy. She grew up in a harum-scarum fashion in the gold camp of Bannack, Montana. She was given the name of Lucy Priscilla, but it was second choice. Since she was born on the eighth of May, her mother wanted to call her Eighthy May, but fortunately her father put his foot down.

That she learned to read is a wonder; she never went beyond the first few grades, and life around her was too interesting and too full of work to be varied with reading. Yet she read well, spelled well, and wrote a pleasing hand. But her English sounded as though it had been chopped with an ax, and always sailed out on a high, harsh voice.

In her teens she was inveigled into marriage by an old man. They had two children: a son that died in infancy, and a daughter, Frances—Fannie. The old, old man could not support his family, so Gram divorced him and hired herself out as a ranch hand. She labored in the hayfields and even broke saddle and work horses as a man might do; in fact, not all men could do such work.

When Fannie was six or seven years old, Gram remarried. Her second husband, James Nesbitt, was a young, meticulous, good-looking Irishman. Because he owned a "photographic studio" in Dillon, Montana, he was known as an "artist." His hair lay beautifully curled on his high forehead and he played in the "city" band. With Jim for a husband Lucy Priscilla—Lou—lived, for a few years, the life of a lady—she who was in the habitat of riding horseback over the folded hills around Dillon, herding cattle, chasing wild horses, killing rattlesnakes, cursing the prickly pear, loving the smell of sage, open fields, and log barns. This new life must have been stifling, but she probably would have forced herself to remain in fancy harness for the sake of her two daughters, Fannie and little Carrie Maybelle, if her husband had not been a drunkard. When Carrie was three and Fannie thirteen, she divorced Jim Nesbitt and took pride in hating him and whiskey the rest of her long life.

So she was twice widowed—by choice and probably good sense.

She worked her way through hard years. And always with her was the sorrow of Fannie's chronic ill health. A year or two after the girl's marriage Fannie died—a tragic invalid. Gram dispelled her sorrow through heavy work; she scattered her grief over the fields and through the mountains—Fannie had been a gentle, lovely girl. Gram all but fought her heartache with her two fists.

At last, being adventuresome, she made her way to the wild, remote Jackson Hole country. Here with John Shive she found her paradise. They and the West were young together, rough and unbounded. Where the rivers of this valley came from and ran to was no concern of Gram's. Who first saw them and the Teton Mountains meant nothing. She knew no curiosity about their past. The rivers and the mountains were here; wasn't that enough? Life began in this valley with her and Gramp, not beyond. The wind and the rain against her and the sun on her head—that was important. And work and laughter. She never lived in the past; there was no name among her ancestors that she pickled, guarded, and talked about with starched pride. She was not even inquisitive about Gramp's ancestors or his past.

They were simple people, Gram and Gramp. Their original buildings, clustered at the far side of the west field, were entirely utilitarian. But when Gramp built his first house, he saw to it that one window opened to the Teton Range. Later he built Gram a bay window from photographer's glass plates discarded by her. This window swept into view her feeble flower garden that was choked by what nature flung into the yard. The garden was enclosed by an elkhorn fence. The antlers had been hilariously and laboriously gathered by Gram and Mother—Carrie—during those first years in Jackson Hole, when Mother was a child. The two would travel horseback up through open wild meadows into the hills back of the ranch, taking Topsy with them—a mare who would stand perfectly still while being piled high with antlers. After two or three had been roped to a packsaddle, the rest would interlock and cling one to another—a great bleached network of arms.

All the old buildings wore sod roofs. In the spring they were green with foxtail.

And each spring the old house was papered inside with interesting material. Gram would make a trip down country with team and buggy, gathering magazines and newspapers. She was hardly home when they were slapped on the walls, which was always disappointing and frustrating to Mother, who was thirsty for knowledge; she always hoped for a little time to read before the magazines became a part of the house. But Gram could never see the necessity of learning through reading. However, she would condescend to hand the sheets right side up so that Mother could get a page of a story here, a column of an article there. And she gleaned, through opera glasses given her by a dude, what the ceiling had to offer.

But in time the old house was ready to fall in on them, so they were willing to move. Gramp always said, "Wear out the old before using the new." Literally this had been done.

In all the rest of Jackson Hole there was nothing quite so elegant as the new two-story buildings—the Big House and the Little House—built by my father with all of Gram and Gramp's savings and thousands of dollars more. The houses stood on a bare knoll backed by sage-covered hills that rose into mountains and a wilderness of aspen and pine. The knoll commanded a sweeping view of fields cut by the Buffalo River; a view of many-ridged mountains. And jagging the western skyline were the pinnacles of the Teton Range, standing without foothills, as though they had sprung up overnight. Dad was proud of these buildings he had designed and built. But to Gram and Gramp these buildings were no more pleasant than were the old ones in the west field with the elkhorn fence, the bachelor-buttons and weeds in the yard, and hop vines climbing the house logs.

Work was the one significant thing in ranch life. Gram, having the strength of a horse, expected the same strength of everyone else. Everyone had to work. To get ahead of what? Perhaps Mother Nature, perhaps Gram. Gramp was the only one who could keep ahead of both from spring until fall, through winter, and back to spring again.

Spring! It never came until May. March would be filled with wind, sunshine, snow flurries, and melting icicles—and worry over lack of hay for the stock. April meant hot sun, cold wind, deep snow, more worry over hay, and a restlessness and a longing for spring. It was hell underfoot, as Gram said. The snow was dejected, dirty, porous. One foot went through the crust, the other stayed on top. Damn!

Gram was one of the main reasons we never missed the outside world during those slow months of late winter. Though she ruled us with an exacting hand and tongue and made us do our share of work, she could never hold from us her laughter or her spontaneous fun, and she never tried.

She would come in from outside work looking like the "ragged end of hard times" and pour a cup of coffee. Always the spoon stood in her cup ready to gouge an eye. If Mother and we children were at work in the house, she made our work light with her clowning. She would put down her coffee cup, jump up on a chair, and crow like a rooster or roar like a lion, her eyes big, round, and startlingly blue. Sometimes she drew her skirts tight between her legs and stood on her head for us, against the wall. She could never master this feat without a wall to fall against. We'd howl with laughter and beg, "Do it again, Gram! Do it some more!" If, in our delight, one of us tried to kiss her, she would either hiss like a snake or open her mouth wide so that we'd come within an ace of falling in. She'd say, "You're a bunch of little warriors," and then she'd pretend to swear at us in Chinese, "Afleeuumbaya-a...a-eunna-combaya-a...." We never knew whether she made up the Chinese words or had in her childhood heard them in the Montana mining camp. If Gramp happened to be in the kitchen, his face would turn red with his silent laughter. He always enjoyed her raucity.

At table she was funny too. When we had uncooked cabbage at a meal, one or all of us would say, "Oh, be a rabbit, Gram; eat like a rabbit, please!" If she was in the proper mood, she would draw in her cheeks, leaving her lips pinched until they stood up and down, and then she would rabbit-chew. We would sit with our mouths hanging open and watch the cabbage disappear like magic.

Gram's musical entertainment usually came in the evening during that brief period between late chores and early bed. Once in a while she sang for us in Chinese and played her own weird accompaniment on the fiddle. When she played something other than her Chinese specialty, Mother chorded for her on the piano (a small grand that Dad bought Mother when we children were babies), but the accompaniment would be drowned out. When Gram sat at the piano, she played with such gusto that I'm sure the strings vibrated for the rest of the night. Whenever we attended a party at Moran or the Elk schoolhouse or at some ranch, Gram played the banjo or fiddle and called a square dance at the same time, one foot pounding the floor. When she chose the banjo, she always used a nickel as a pick because it made more noise than her fingers could make. Her playing was out of tune, but there was such zip to it no one could keep his feet still. As she said herself, she could play to beat hens a pecking. If she caught the eye of one of us, she would wink as much as to say, "Pretty good, ain't it.?" She'd end a fiddling tune suddenly on a bass note as though she had run amuck and struck something head-on. Once in a great while she played a slow waltz such as "Over the Waves" and it would sound so sorrowful that I would fill with tears. It is probably a good thing her playing was no better than it was or I couldn't have stood it!

When happy, Gram was happy all over; she whistled, laughed, and yelled. When she was mad, she was mad all over. When she was sick, she was sick all over—and funny too. She would groan, "I'm going to die. Yes, I'm going to die. Oh, my God, why can't I die?"

She gave herself such drastic treatment for any and all ailments that it is a tribute to her constitution that she lived to be eighty. Once she put a bit of lye into an aching tooth; the pain almost took off her head—and ours too. She gradually lost her hearing in one ear because she put oil into it that was too hot for the sensitive drum. But Gram, always making the most of any situation, slept with the deaf ear up so as not to be disturbed with night sounds. And her partial deafness brought pleasure to the rest of us in a roundabout way. She would laugh hilariously over amusing things some drab person said to her; someone whom the rest of us had never heard emit a clever word. She would repeat the remarks and we'd all laugh. We finally realized that Gram was laughing over what she *thought* the person said; she never knew that *she* was the clever one.

Once a cow she was milking kicked her in the face, breaking her nose. Gramp and Mother did what they could to repair the damage with the help of a can of Denver Mud. But when the nose was swollen as big as a washtub (it felt that big to Gram), a bee stung her on the chin, swelling it to meet the nose. She looked so tragically funny that no one could keep from laughing. Gram couldn't laugh—there wasn't any place on her face for laughing—but she was a good sport even though she suffered so loud that she could be heard all over the ranch.

One March, when the crusted snow was dangerously glistening, she was struck with snow blindness after a long ski trip. Willingly she took a severe cure, since it was her own idea. Rocks were heated very hot and placed in a tin tub on the floor; Gram was seated on a low chair beside the tub with a heavy blanket thrown over her, tub, and rocks. Slowly sugar was sprinkled on the boulders, sending up a stinging smoke, making the eyes water and burn. Gram wailed and laughed under the blanket, but she lived through the cure. How could her eyes remain their lovely blue?

Gram loved horses. Her love for them was fearless, aggressive, and often took the form of open hostility. Now and again, when she drove a team, the team ran away. Gram would brace her short, thick legs, curse and yell at the horses, and enjoy herself immensely. When she rode Nemo, Mother's dainty chestnut sorrel, the mare ran away, scattering Gram's hairpins over field or hill. However, Nemo never ran away with Mother. She rode the mare with a martingale and checkrein, but Gram couldn't be bothered with a checkrein—she never wore one herself.

Not only could she break horses to ride, but she could also shoe them. However, Gramp never allowed her to do so. He was such a silent man I never knew whether he thought it was unladylike or that Gram might do some damage to the horse.

When Nig died—the co-star of her top buggy team, Nig and Hix—his death brought grief in high comedy. Gram found him dead in the barn one early spring morning; he had gradually waste away with some horse disease. We all heard her crying as she returned to the kitchen. She didn't want to show weakness, so in the middle of her tears she laughed to herself. She leaned over the stove and actually dripped tears into the huge can of garbage she was heating for the chickens. "Oh, my God, how'll I get on without Nig?" She threw her apron over her face, sat on the arm of a chair, and wailed. Then she laughed for being such a fool over a horse. We gathered around her in sympathy and laughed too, to ease her embarrassment. Ruff, my younger brother, suggested sympathetically that Nig be skinned and the hide tanned, to be hung on a wall somewhere. "Oh, no, no!" she moaned. "I'd just as soon have Jack's hide nailed to the wall as the hide of my favorite horse."

Weather in this high country was always interesting. It either hindered or helped crops, livestock, and work. And it was interesting just in itself. Gram would say, "Well, I'll go out and see what the sky has to say." She would brace her sturdy legs, facing the southwest where our storms came from.

If it looked like snow, she would come into the house saying, "We're going to get more of The Beautiful, damn it." And we always got more of The Beautiful. Damn it.

But May always came, even though Gram was sure it would not. May! The soft air moved one's hair, and the sun brought up good odors from the earth. The bare, lacy aspen branches held an expectant glow. Cattle found a few green things; the hay had lasted or it had not, and that was that.

All winter Gramp kept a pile of manure in the barn so that it would heat. In the spring he would put about four feet of the manure into a very deep pit, top it with four to six inches of rich soil, and cover the whole thing with a glass frame made of photographer's plates which had been carefully saved from the early years when Gram took her first fling at photography. The manure would heat the soil and within three days some of the plants would be up.

All through the long winters we had nothing fresh to eat in the way of vegetables, except cabbage. As soon as the first dandelion greens peeped above the ground in May, Gram would call us and we'd be down on all fours unearthing them. Digging around in the dark, clean soil and smelling the fresh open earth was part of satisfying our hunger. Gram would say, "I know just how a cow feels when she tastes her first spring grass." But soon the dandelions were too big and strong to be palatable, and we hungered afresh for other greens.

But food on the ranch was good. Mother cooked with imagination and beauty and she did most of the cooking, but Gram had a way of putting things together, all her own, that made plain food wonderful. Since she had little respect for reading, she didn't bother much with a cookbook; she made things out of her head. She and Gramp both had a taste for unusual dishes. Every year or two a bear would be killed. The grease—pale yellow and soft like honey—would be used, among other things for deep frying. Gramp was sure that no fat could equal bear grease for doughnuts. And he always carefully skinned and prepared the feet for pickling. What a rare treat—pickled bear's feet!

Other specialties were pickled tongue of elk or pig; the marrow from a fresh boiled bone on delicate bread; hot boiled egg-bag, eaten with fresh bread; wild field mushrooms fried in butter (sometimes a dishpanful could be picked from the west field after a gentle rain, but they always had to be gathered young before the worms found them).

The majority of ranchers in Jackson Hole cooked the life out of any kind of meat, so the way Gram and Gramp prepared their elk steaks became known up and down the valley. In our kitchen galvanized pie plates would be heated piping hot in the warming oven while the fire was antagonized with pitch until the top of the stove turned red with heat. T-bone elk steaks were seared quickly on both sides, turned into the pie plates, spread with butter, and eaten immediately. Often, they were served with rings of onion sliced into thick sweet cream.

We were very proud of Gramp's cooking. It never failed to be good. And the nearest he ever came to bragging was on his food. He said, "If I have a frying pan with a little flour I can live a long time in the mountains. But with you kids it's different. You've got to know something. You've got to git an education."

By June the frogs were singing like mad in every pond and there was the voice of killdeer and crane, goose and duck. Cow elk could be heard barking to their calves near the rushing Buffalo River. From the river itself came the grinding sound of uprooted trees that were carried along the swollen current. Snowslides roared like early spring thunder high in the Tetons; we could hear them on warm, dripping days.

The loveliest sign of full spring was the wild clematis trailing from the cow's horn that hung against one wall of the dining room. Busy as Mother was, she would take time to walk to a pine-darkened hill beyond the ranch buildings and bring back the delicate purple flower and its vine. Gram would tramp into the house, drink her coffee with the spoon standing in it, admire the clematis briefly because she loved any and all flowers, and be gone—back to barnyard, hill, or field.

The beastliest sign of June was the mosquitoes. Gram would say, "Oh, my God, the mosquitoes." They whined over and around and through us. They were breathed in. They hung in a cloud over our heads when we stepped outside; they blackened the screen doors. There was no section of Jackson Hole where they were worse. The horses and cattle stamped in anger. We children had bloodstained arms and legs from the bites we scratched. Gram fought the abominable things with her two fists. Some-times she wore netting over her hat, pulled down, double, to her shoulders. "It won't keep out the damned little things," she once said, "but by doubling it, I befuddle them." Surely, her cursing helped too.

But in spite of mosquitoes and heavy work outdoors, Gram was seldom in trousers. She generally wore a house dress or a shirtwaist with divided skirts—know in Jackson Hole as double-barreled skirts—made of khaki, buttoned or hooked over well-laced corsets. A drive to Jackson, forty miles down country, called for dressing up in fancy shirtwaist and wool skirt with an added piece of jewelry, such as her handmade gold ring set with garnets, or the enormous sterling belt pin covered with her curlicued initials—LPS.

The only jewelry Gram wore at home was a pair of small, rough nugget earrings and a heavy gold band on the third finger of her left hand. Until her death, when she was eighty, I took for granted that this wide ring had been placed there by Gramp when they were married. But when the ring came to me, I found engraved inside it: *Carrie to Mama, 1902*. Why should Mother give this ring to Gram? Perhaps she was embarrassed because Gram wore no wedding ring. I shall never know the truth.

For Gram and the rest of the grownups summer was a short, warm breath filled with work: haying, seeing to the cattle on the range, repairing fence, washing, ironing, baking—and laughing. The days were longer now, so more work and more laughter could be crammed into the hours be-tween daylight and dark. When haying ended, fall was a swift, bright breath.

And in the fall, hunting for the winter's meat was a natural part of ranch life in the valley. However, any season of the year meant big game hunting for the people of Jackson Hole if they wanted fresh meat, in spite of an established season by the state.

There were guns all through our house; sometimes they stood three deep in a corner. Gramp was the best shot on the ranch, but he took no special pride in it. He hunted methodically, without lust, to get meat we needed. We were sure he couldn't miss an elk if he tried, because one moon-lit night in the dead of winter, when a herd of fifty or sixty elk came, in single file, into the north field to pilfer the haystacks that had been fenced away from them, Gramp got up from his bed, took up his gun, and from the bedroom window shot and killed the lead bull. Much to his annoyance he had to get into his clothes, go down into the field, and bleed and dress out the animal so that no meat would be wasted.

Mother was a very good target shot with a six-shooter, but she despised the killing. Gram loved the hunt. Apparently, it helped to satisfy the animal in her. Gram's theory was this: If it's fit to eat it ought to be killed; if it ain't fit to eat, it certainly ought to be killed.

When she first came to Jackson Hole, she always went big game hunting with Gramp if meat was needed on the ranch. (A rancher, in those days, seldom killed his beef. Cattle were raised to be sold, not to be killed and eaten at home. To bring them successfully to maturity was too expensive and too worrisome for ranch butchering.) Gram would help dress out an elk and drag it home by the saddle horn, or quarter it and bring it in on a pack horse if it were shot any distance from the ranch. Finally, she ventured out alone, when meat was needed and Gramp was too busy to go. Within a few hours she returned.

"I got an elk, Jack. A dandy cow."

"Where is it?"

"Why...back where I shot it?"

"Did you bleed it? Did you gut it?"

Gram looked sheepish. "I bled it; that's all."

He shook his head. "You've hunted enough with me to know better than that."

"It ain't easy to dress out alone. I thought you'd—"

He cut off her words. "Anybody that shoots an elk around here cleans it and drags it in or they don't go hunting. Go bring in your game."

Gram did as she was told, and though she laughingly cursed Gramp for being no gentleman, she was proud that he made her complete the job. After that she often went alone for meat and brought home the kill.

After the quick brilliant beauty of fall, grass, trees, river, and clouds all moved with the wind, carrying everything into winter. Heavy clouds would shroud the Teton Mountains and, when they lifted, the peaks would be covered with fresh snow. Gram would say, "The mountains are putting on their winter underwear," and shake her head and talk about the gosh-damned wind, and insist that the weather had turned to the devil, and complain about winter coming wrong-end-to. She didn't like winter and she fought it.

But, in truth, she was never held in or down by weather or anything else. She had too many interests and too much work. In winter she carried out her hobbies. Once she decided to study taxidermy. She tried to mount a hawk, but she failed to apply the knowledge she had learned to the whole bird; flies got to the wings—maggots dropped out. The hawk had to be burned. After a little more study, but not enough, she tried to mount a skunk, but the tail wouldn't stan up, it dragged on the floor, so she lost interest in "the art of preparing, stuffing, and mounting the kinds of animals in lifelike form."

Photography was of more lasting interest—and far more expensive. Gramp said, in his quiet way, that it took the price of one steer a year to keep her in film and other necessary supplies. She snapped pictures of everyone, coming and going. Usually the clothesline, the woodpile, or the toilet was in the background. Gram had no eye for setting. Or had she? Maybe her goal was to get all three in one picture—clothesline, woodpile, and toilet!

She spent the evenings one winter braiding a fancy horsehair bridle for Mother—sixteen strands. It was professionally done, with tassles hanging all over it and along the braided reins. She always had some other kind of handwork in progress too: paste beads, a melon-seed bag, delicate embroidery. Gram had no eye for color where her clothes were concerned—she might combine green, purple, and red—but the embroidery that lay waiting to be picked up would be white, intricate and expertly done on linen. Now and again, of a winter evening, Gramp would pick up the embroidery and work ten or fifteen minutes, his huge hands dwarfing the piece; yet one could not tell where Gram left off and Gramp began—his work was that well done. How proud we were to think he could brand a calf and embroider with the same two hands! But, of course, Gram could also do both.

We never knew from month to month what her next interest would be. Neither did she.

Gram never wanted Mother to have children, but after we sneaked by her into the world, she was proud of us, though we would never have guessed it by her words. Once when we all got in her way, she said to Mother, "Carrie, it's a good thing you didn't have triplets or quadrupeds too or I'd a wrung their damn little necks. If there's anything I hate it's a snarl of kids around." She would fuss about the stringiness of my hair, about Ruff's mouth forever hanging open, and would tell Bill, my twin, that his sharp shoulder blades reminded her of the running gears of a katydid. And she would say to Mother, "My God, Carrie, you don't make these kids eat right and you don't make them comb or wash." Mother, with a week's work piled ahead of her to be done in one day, would only laugh in her light, musical way and tell us what a joy we were to her, what a satisfaction, no matter what we ate or didn't eat, or how we looked. "You are my life," she would say, "I couldn't live without you."

But through Gram's harsh words of ridicule we could feel her pride in us, and read it in her eyes—when we didn't neglect our duties. And we could feel her love for Mother anchored on bedrock, even though she continuously yelled, "Hurry, Carrie, hurry!" as Mother moved slowly through her work. She leaned on the broom or mop and read a magazine until Gram yelled, "My God, hurry!" The handle of the churn slowed down with her reading until Gram screamed, "Hurry, hurry!" She washed and ironed and scrubbed and sang, and though Gram tried to drop a rock into her thoughts, Mother was always mentally free. She could never be chained to scrub pail, broom, churn—or to Gram: she lived an inner life of her own, unrestrained.

And so lived the rest of us.

But Gram was the freest of all. She never tried to be anything but her own unbounded, funny self. Her life was complete. She needed no one from beyond these mountains so long as we all were here. And seldom knowing the need of anyone beyond the ranch, she never ceased wishing her neighbors were in hell—a cheery sort of hell.

For twenty-two years she and Gramp ranched in Jackson Hole. In this valley Gram found her happiness and in this valley she held it.

Work was her life—laced with laughter. And the laughter came easy because the work was good.

18

THE BET I MADE WITH UNCLE SAM (1989)

JOE JONES (1873–1936)

Joe Jones had spent time as a gambler and a prospector before he landed in Jackson Hole. Among his winnings was a rundown homestead on the south end of Blacktail Butte, land that would eventually become part of Grand Teton National Park. He and his unprepared family decided to give it a try.

This is the ironic, sarcastic story, told by Jones, of his struggle to prove up on his land before "starving to death." The stunning view of the mountains did not help his family to survive on what Jones described as "second-choice land." This is a tragic but entertaining story of settling a land that was not meant for farming. It is a story of what took place on much of the high and arid lands of the American West.

There is, however, a bright side to Jones's story, taken from a collection of stories published in 1989 called Preserving the Game. *He did prove up, but he then sold and moved his family to the town of Jackson, where Jones became a successful businessman. More important, his land and those of many others in the same dilemma were sold to John D. Rockefeller Jr. or the National Park Service, making possible the park we have today.*

The local land commissioner dropped the money into the drawer of his desk and handed me my receipt. As I stood a moment folding the precious paper the commissioner turned toward me and whimsically asked, "Who wins?"

"What do you mean?" I inquired, puzzled.

"Why, haven't you just bet Uncle Sam sixteen dollars against 160 acres of land that you can stick there for five years and not starve to death?"

Naturally, I laughed, for it appealed to me as quite a joke. I was in the mood for merriment, for hadn't I just acquired the right to fence, plow, plant, harvest, put up buildings, dig ditches, and in fact do just as my fancy dictated with a lovely tract of land, and for only ten cents an acre? Yet grim reality eventually dulled the point of that joke for me.

I had been raised in the West and for many years had been eligible for Uncle Sam's land patrimony. I had viewed board shacks on the parched plains of California; the structures of stone and adobe that clustered the water holes of Nevada and Arizona; the shake buildings of Oregon and Washington and the log houses that turned the cold in Idaho and Montana. The homes of the open country had always seemed so hopeless; not a tree to relieve the monotony or cast a welcome shadow. There was the fierce heat of summer and cold winds of winter; the mire of mud when the rains fell and the caked earth when the sun shone.

The Homesteader's Pride

In a manner, there was a bond among all my neighbors, for they, too, were struggling against odds. Perhaps problems that fretted me did not annoy some of them, and then again others were confronted with difficulties that I did not have. There was a spirit of generosity among them, for those who suffer know how to help others. We all wrote brave letters to our friends and relatives, and sometimes women confessed that they reviewed their former dreams of homesteading life and found them a reality. Yet occasionally these letters acted as boomerangs, for relatives or friends came to visit and much cheerful explanation was necessary to harmonize their colored epistles.

Yet who could criticize the dreams that widened those dreary walls and changed crude furnishing to artistic setting?

A homesteader who has sufficient money to keep a hired man is a rare individual and has no place in this article. Again, one who is financially able to put up buildings, purchase machinery, tools, food, horses, wagons, milch cows, and remain steadily at work on his land until it returns a living, is just as rare an individual as the former. Therefore it is necessary for a

Joe Jones and his wife Fidelia Humphrey at their wedding in 1899. They acquired a homestead at the south end of Blacktail Butte but found it so difficult to survive that they eventually moved to town. Collection of the Jackson Hole Historical Society and Museum, 1958.2442.001.

homesteader to work away from his land, often long distances, for in a sparsely settled country the opportunities for earning money are few. The wife must then do the milking, chop wood, care for the horses and do all the man's work during his absence. These brave women are always so willing to help. They care for the garden and search out a market for eggs and butter. Often, they work in the field and assist their husbands at tasks needing the labor of two persons.

Those who are unequal to the struggle quit the game, and sometimes those of strong character and clear vision do the same; but pride holds the majority to complete a task so hopefully started. Few ever dare to count the costs, the grind, the calloused hands, the faded beauty and vanished dreams;

the cloud of debt, uncertainty and endless toil that envelops them. Yet worst of all are the meager opportunities of the children for education and social life, for 160 acres is a large area of land, and of necessity schools must be long distances from many of the homes. This feature was particularly bad at the period when homesteaders like myself were settling second-choice land in the West.

The early settlers located on the bottom lands and cut wild hay or sowed crops and irrigated them with the easily diverted water. Returns from the land were quickly acquired, and with unrestricted range for stock they soon became prosperous ranchers. The next wave of homesteaders located the high mesas or made filings far back on mountain streams and springs. Here the struggle was keener and often friction developed with those who grazed stock on these areas. Those who located in the open country were often compelled to haul water long distances, and the wood problem was ever acute. Irrigation ditches were usually constructed by a few together, or in some instances a large number combining on the work.

These waterways were the cause of much dissatisfaction among the builders. Invariably there were those who sloughed their share of the work, and when some were ready to build ditches others were not. I never knew one of these neighborhood canals to snap through quickly. Usually the homesteaders did their own surveying, and the amount of dirt to be removed was just a rough guess. Generally, their grades were quite accurate, but the work required to build these ditches usually far exceeded their calculations. Many of them dragged along for years and frequently bitter quarrels developed. I have in mind one project that took twenty years of bickering to complete. Without friction, the same men could easily have constructed it in two working seasons.

It is easy to picture the misery of these people, anxiously awaiting the water that means so much to their land. Each year they hang on, hoping that work will progress faster, and they grow old and bitter in the waiting. Worst of all is the discovery, after the water does eventually reach them, that there is still friction and lack of quick results.

Assuming that their land is properly prepared for irrigated crops, they always find the legal amount of water far below their requirements, for raw land sucks up water like desert heat. In addition to this, frequent breaks occur in the new ditches and the evaporation of water moving slowly for a long distance is great.

For instance, if you turn the legal amount of water into a new six-mile ditch, and ten men hold ownership, and each one diverts his proper allowance, those at the end of the ditch will receive little or no water. This feature is often overcome by turning more than the law allows into the ditch, and then the homesteaders who divert water on the stream below retaliate by sicking the water commissioner on you. So, it is hell if you abide by the law, and hell if you don't.

Too Stringent Water Laws

The amount of water allowed by the Wyoming law for the irrigation of seventy acres is so small that it needs careful attention properly to irrigate twenty acres of raw land with it. After the land has been well flooded for several years it is possible that this allowance will meet the irrigator's requirements.

Your crops are burning, and you work all the daylight hours and much of the night in guiding the tiny stream to points of vantage. Suddenly the volume of water decreases or fails entirely, and you hasten up to the ditch to find the cause. Sometimes it is a break that needs much labor to repair, or perhaps a despairing neighbor has taken the water in a desperate chance to save his crops. So, you are constantly at high tension and in a mood for quarrels. The returns from your land are of vital importance to your existence and you see red when the other fellow sneaks a drop of water that is legally yours. No wonder that some of the homesteaders get water on the brain and shoot their neighbors full of holes! Indeed, the ditch that usually starts with a joyous assemblage of neighbors and picnic dinners eventually becomes a flowing line of friction.

I was granted a permit by the state to place water on all my homestead land. At the end of a certain period I would be entitled to a water deed, provided I had completed my ditch and made useful disposition of the water on each legal subdivision of my land. I made careful compliance with these requirements according to my interpretation of the water laws, but when I submitted proofs before the commissioner, he refused to grant a deed to other than the twenty acres I had plowed.

This decision canceled my old permit and my only recourse was a re-opening of the case or else a new filing. If I made a new application, I would have to accept a flood-water right, for during the period between my application and proving up, a Carey-Act project had filed on all the unappropriated water in the river that my ditch led from. As I constructed laterals and diverted the stream so as to improve the growth of the native grass, I decided to contend for a deed under the terms of the old permit. After several years of grief my point of contention was sustained and a deed granted. What heartaches are sometimes caused by an ignorant public official! Yet Wyoming irrigation laws have for years served as a model to other Western states in solving much of their water problems.

Much of the high lands in the West are planted to grain, and crops are entirely dependent on the uncertain rainfall. Large production means low prices, and a good market in an off year does not equalize with a short crop. Each morning the dry farmer sniffs the air and hopefully scans the heavens for signs of rain. Each day he despairingly watches the sun suck the scanty moisture from around the roots of his struggling grain. Crop failure usually means curtailment of credit, and a man must seek work away from home to provide food for his family. Water is so vital to these localities that it is an ever-present thought and serves as a basis for conversation among neighbors. Many of these homesteaders are without springs or wells, and water must be hauled long distances in barrels after the day's work in the field is done. Also, lack of moisture precludes the chance of successful diversified farming. The irrigator thinks this own skunk highly obnoxious, but the dry farmer claims one that outranks it!

Building a Barn Single Handed

When spring came, I again planted the twenty acres to oats. Having exterminated most of the rodents, I was successful in raising a good garden that year. Ditch work, care of the crop and necessary chores took up the summer months, and I spent most of the fall in the hills with a hunting party. I was paid $160 for my services, and we made this sum do for our winter clothes and groceries.

The grain crop was a failure and brought little return. The store of hardy vegetables helped out greatly on our food problem.

Late that fall I erected a good-size barn. The logs were dragged into position on the ground, properly notched, and then rolled up skids with the aid of ropes. As the building grew in height the work became increasingly slow. I would fasten two ropes to the top of the building and encircle them on the log that next went into place. I would then toss the ropes to the inside and pull one end of the log a couple of feet up the skids, make it fast and repeat the performance with the other rope.

Then came the delicate task of placing it in position, and sometimes it slipped to the ground. With the exception of a little assistance from my wife in rolling up the largest logs, I did the work entirely alone. The roof was of green poles, covered with straw and dirt. The finished building was warm and serviceable.

That winter's trials were but a repetition of the previous year's, only had to guard the straw carefully from the elk, for I now had more stock and less feed.

In the spring I planted several acres to potatoes, but an unprecedented frost left nothing but blackened rows. I had invested heavily, according to my finances, in seed for this crop, and I strove by intense cultivation to overcome a measure of the setback. The green tops sprouted slowly again; but not so the weeds, for the latter grew with marvelous rapidity; so each day became an intensive round of rustling water and fighting weeds. What a snap farming would be if crops of value thrived as pigweeds do!

I was unable to procure machinery to aid me in accomplishing my tasks to best advantage. My oats and potatoes proved such a failure that the gross receipts for the two crops were less than $200. Also, I had given them so much attention that I was able to work out but little for wages that year. However, we tried to live within our income, and the old expense book that my wife has just dug up shows that our clothing bill was $42.10. As there were now seven of us, and this amount was largely for shoes and overshoes, it plainly reveals a story of needle and thread, and of cloth that descended from father to son or from mother to daughter.

This winter was long and severe. I had fifteen head of cattle and horses, and I ran out of hay. My neighbors were short of feed and I was able to purchase but a small amount. Finally, I saved my stock by feeding the straw that covered the barn and chicken house.

In the spring, after planting the twenty acres, I started fencing the balance of my land. It was late fall before this task was completed, for ditch work, care of crop, and chores, consumed much of my time.

In August, 1912, I made my five years' homestead proof, and a few months later received a patent from Washington, D.C., signed by the President of the United States. I had won my bet, and yet, somehow, my victory failed to thrill me. In fact, my feelings were like the fellow's who cleaned up a poker game and found that there was no money to cash the checks he had won.

I took stock of my circumstances. I had started with $3,000 and had given five years of toil to that piece of land. My family had suffered many inconveniences and, in some instances, actual hardship. Too much realism had dulled the romance of successful achievement for my wife and me. I was several hundred dollars in debt, and if I farmed successfully, I must have more machinery and horses. All that I had accomplished had been my uphill work. To receive an income from the land that would return just a living, I must plant a good acreage to grain, alfalfa and potatoes. To do this I must have equipment and hired help. Possibly I could borrow $1,000 on my homestead; the rate of interest was 12 percent.

The cold facts revealed nothing in the years to come but self-denial to earn a scanty living. There appeared no hope that I could expand and pay out. It took five years to get land in condition to mortgage, with the prospect of twenty-five to pay it off in. My children were growing up with but a few opportunities for education. If a stranger appeared, they were like a flock of chickens when a hawk swooped on them. I had, besides, the evidence of my neighbors, some of them experienced in farming methods, floundering just as hopelessly as myself in the mesh of homestead trials. I had conceived the idea that when I had a deed to my land things would be different. I found out that they were—in the shape of increased responsibilities and taxes.

Sold Out and Glad of It

That fall, as I made preparations for winter, my mind was constantly analyzing our circumstances, and slowly a decision was reached. I sold my cattle, and on a November day, with a cold wind sweeping snowflakes out of the north, I piled our household goods into the rig, the children climbed to position on top, and with my wife beside me I gathered the reins and we turned our backs on the only home we possessed. I had no work in sight, no real objective, just a desire to place distance between me and that homestead.

It is now nearly twelve years since I quit, and not once have I had occasion to regret my decision.

19

A WOMAN'S LIFE IN THE TETON COUNTRY

Geraldine L. Lucas (1994)

SHERRY L. SMITH (1951–)

Contrary to its northern neighbor, Yellowstone National Park, much of Grand Teton National Park was settled by homesteaders well before 1950. Homesteading in northern Jackson Hole was tough. As Joe Jones wrote, it was a bet that the government usually won, with the homesteaders abandoning or selling out their claims. One notable exception was Geraldine Lucas, who filed for a homestead on an unsurpassed site on Cottonwood Creek. She built her cabin in the summer of 1913, proved up her land, and enjoyed her single life until her death in 1938.

In the 1980s, when the National Park Service considered removing Lucas' cabins, historian Sherry L. Smith decided to research Lucas's life. What she found was that Lucas came from a prominent Ohio family, married and eventually divorced a New York City jeweler, enrolled at Oberlin College, then returned to teach art and music for fourteen years in New York City. She did all this before she had considered Jackson Hole. When Lucas retired from teaching, she headed west to join briefly her two brothers, Lee and Woods, who had entered into the cattle business.

Lucas lived a quiet life at the base of the Tetons. She worked on her homestead land and read books from her library. Her most acclaimed accomplishment was to climb the Grand Teton, which she did at age 58, the first local woman to do so. However, Lucas's ability to live as a homesteader in a beautiful yet difficult environment may be her greatest achievement.

What follows are a few excerpts from Smith's article, published in Montana: The Magazine of Western History *in 1994, which gives us a flavor of what Lucas believed and how she lived.*

At the summit of Grand Teton Mountain, a climber can find etched into the granite: "G.L. Lucas—1924." There is a story behind this simply inscription. "G.L. Lucas" was fifty-eight-year-old Geraldine Lucas, the second woman to reach the crest of the Grand and the first local woman to achieve such heights. In scaling this peak Geraldine Lucas undoubtedly attained a personal goal.

Since a number of these excursions were launched from the Lucas ranch, Geraldine undoubtedly knew about them. At some point, she decided to make the trip with Petzoldt. And several other young men. In August 1924 at the age of fifty-eight, Lucas scaled the Grand. The Jackson Hole newspaper carried only a brief notice of this event, although in the same story they indicated W.O. Owens climbed the peak again that summer and was the "oldest man ever to make the climb." Lucas held a similar distinction, of course. She was the oldest woman ever to make that climb—but perhaps she preferred to avoid any notoriety linked to the touchy issue of age.

Although little publicity about the climb came Lucas's way, it was nevertheless a remarkable feat. It was not only an "enterprising" thing to do in 1924, according to historian Leigh Ortenburger, "it was a fearsome thing." Moreover, it was highly unusual for a local person, man or woman, to climb any of the Tetons in those days. After listening to Lucas's own account of the trip, family members remembered later that "it sounded pretty scary"—particularly the point where she had to crawl on her stomach over a very narrow crevice. It was also physically exhausting. In an image reminiscent of that other dauntless woman mountain climber, Isabella Bird, who climbed Pikes Peak in 1873, some of the men in her party ended up "hauling" Lucas to the top. Whatever the measure of grace involved, no one could deny Lucas's achievement. The photograph of Geraldine at the summit reveals her unbridled delight and pride over the accomplishment. It was a moment of triumph.

Geraldine Lucas's homestead rested at the base of the Grand Teton. She loved the mountain, and at age fifty-eight she convinced Paul Petzoldt to take her up. She was the first local woman to make it to the summit, a great triumph. Paul Petzoldt provided the flag. Collection of the Jackson Hole Historical Society and Museum, 1958.0351.001.

Besides her climbing feat, Geraldine became a single-woman homesteader. But as Smith explains, Lucas wasn't interested in farming but settled on Cottonwood Creek for another purpose.

Joining the move, Lucas took up her homestead not in the nineteenth century but rather in the twentieth. Although many Americans still associate homesteading with the earlier period, Lucas was one of those who acquired their share of the public domain after the turn of the century. Not

surprisingly this generation found itself forced to migrate into the less attractive lands of Montana and Wyoming's high plains—less attractive, that
is, if the landscape's potential for agricultural development determined
one's sense of aesthetics. By Lucas's era, however, Americans were reassess-
ing their attitudes toward the land. Mountains, once viewed as obstacles or
at best receptables of mineral wealth, took on value for their beauty and
for the recreational opportunities they offered. Certainly, Geraldine Lucas
planted herself at the foot of the Tetons as much for the grandeur outside
her window as for its agricultural potential.

Winters stretched for many months there, sometimes beginning in October and lasting through May. Fortunately for her sanity, Geraldine Lucas
was "a loner." Although family entertained her for several weeks at a time
in the summer months, once fall set in, she returned to her homestead
where she remained until the spring thaw. She gathered in sufficient gro-
ceries plus a wood supply, then settled in with her books and her sewing
machine. Lucas was, in fact, a fancy seamstress and "would sew until hell
wouldn't have it," according to her nephew. He never knew what she did
with the clothes she made, however, for she wore only knickers. Lucas was
also a prodigious reader. At the time of her death, she owned a library of
more than 1,350 books—all carefully catalogued, listed, and numbered in a
sectional bookcase. One neighbor remembered her as a "deep thinker." She
also had a piano but no radio or phonograph.

*Lucas was known to her friends as "Aunt Ger." She lived on her Cottonwood
Creek homestead until her death in 1938. Her last years were enlivened by the
park controversy and the desire of the Snake River Land Company to purchase
her land for the park. She was never tempted. When one agent approached her, she
purportedly replied, "You stack up those silver dollars as high as the Grand Teton
and I might talk to you."*
    Sherry Smith reflects on Lucas's life and legacy.

After her death Geraldine did not exactly disappear. Russell Lucas, surely
following his mother's orders, had her remains cremated and placed in a
huge granite boulder that rests at the western edge of Lucas's property—facing the Grand Teton. Her ashes remain there to this day. So do her cabins....

She might enjoy the notion that her life choices—pushing against the boundaries of acceptable behavior for women in education, marriage, livelihood, and recreation—those aspects which made her susceptible to charges of eccentricity and worse; are now choices western women can make with far fewer psychic costs. Yet Lucas did not set out to challenge convention for its own sake or, apparently, to open doors for other women. Rather, she settled in the Tetons as a nonconformist who co-existed with the government and the community on her own terms. Those terms centered on family loyalties, limited friendships, a love for the country, and above all, independence in thought and action.

PART IV

PRESERVING THE BEAUTY

20

THE STARVING ELK OF WYOMING (1911)

STEPHEN LEEK (1857–1941)

An attraction of Jackson Hole is the abundant wildlife. For local hunters the game provides food and challenging hunt, but for most visitors they offer a unique viewing opportunity. In the summer the elk escape to southern Yellowstone and the green-carpeted thoroughfare country, but as the aspen tree leaves turn and the days grow short, they migrate by the thousands to the National Elk Refuge just north of the town of Jackson.

At the turn of the twentieth century, however, there was no refuge. Cut off from their normal migration patterns by fences and roads, elk either died of starvation or pilfered ranchers' haystacks. It was a pitiful predicament, particularly the winter of 1908–1909 when elk carcasses littered the whole valley. The survivors wandered about desperately seeking nourishment. One pioneer captured the drama through his camera. His name was Stephen N. Leek, and if asked to identify the person most responsible for a winter home for the elk, one would be hard pressed to name a more important individual than Leek. Rancher, guide, and wilderness lodge owner, Leek also loved photography, and he used his skills to arouse the conscience of the nation. The following article appeared in the May 1911 edition of Outdoor Life.

Probably never before in the history of the universe (and I hope never again to be witnessed in the same enormity) has such a sad plight been evidenced among the wild animal kingdom as that which has been witnessed in Jackson's Hole, Wyo. during the past few years. Never until late years have the

149

elk ranges been fenced off like they are now by settlers, and never again, I hope, will the government allow these animals to suffer and die as they have in the past. The last appropriation by Congress and by the state of Wyoming show that the people have at last awakened to the necessity for immediate action—but oh! how long the aid has been a-coming, no one but we who are settlers of the "Hole" and see it with our own eyes every winter can fully realize.

The summer of 1910 was unusually cold and dry, which resulted in a scant growth of grass on the winter range of the elk in Jackson's Hole. An early heavy snowfall in the mountains, with rain in the valley, caused the herds to come down unusually early. This condition prevailed with light snowfall in the valley till about February 15, 1911, when it began storming, and kept it up until the snow was about three feet deep in the valley. Then, turning warmer, it rained for 48 hours, after which it turned colder, snowed some more and finally froze up, effectively shutting the elk from the little remaining grass. For feed they were confined to the willows (two-thirds of which had been killed by the close browsing and peeling to which they were subjected the two years previous), and to what hay they could steal from the settlers' haystacks.

Before the storm ceased, on February 26th messages were sent to Cheyenne, where the Legislature was in session, calling attention to the need and asking for aid. Four days later we received a reply saying that a bill had passed the House appropriating $5,000 for the relief of the elk. We were further informed that this bill was sure to pass the Senate, and that the Governor would send a man in immediately.

A week later, with no further word from Cheyenne, the calf elk getting very weak and many of them dying, and it being plain to be seen that if any of the calves were to be saved feeding must commence immediately, I sent the following message to several addresses:

JACKSON, Wyo., Feb 7, 1911.—Unless fed, five thousand elk will perish within two weeks. S. N. LEEK.

This might have been putting it pretty strong, but I thought the end justified the means, and in just four days after sending out the message Sheriff Ward of Evanston, Wyo., arrived at Jackson with authority to act, and three

Pioneer photographer Stephen Leek's images of starving elk inspired the state and federal government to establish the National Elk Reserve in 1912. Collection of the Jackson Hole Historical Society and Museum, 1993.4937.001.

days later, February 13, the first load of hay was fed to the elk about one mile north of Jackson. Two days later feeding was commenced on my place, three miles south of Jackson, and on Mr. Kelly's place, one mile farther south.

It was now found that very little hay could be procured in the valley, and Mr. Ward was not authorized to offer a sufficient price for hay to induce or justify any stock to be driven to Idaho. So it was impossible to feed all the elk. Feeding was commenced to about 3,000 head of those in the worst condition, and this has since been extended to about 5,000 head, though the very limited hay supply (255 tons) makes it necessary to feed barely enough to keep them alive. Feeding was commenced too late to save but very few of the calves, and at this time the hay supply is nearly exhausted. Therefore, if winter does not break soon there will be a very heavy loss yet.

Such, in brief, is the history and situation to date for this year—a repetition of former years. Should I tell you some of the terrible sights we are forced to see—to what extremities the elk are driven for feed or the settlers to save their hay—you would not believe the half of it. But I submit herewith photographs taken on the ground, that will tell more than words.

Nearly the entire calf crop of three years in succession, with many old elk, has perished for want of feed, and including those killed this loss has reduced the magnificent herds of three years ago to less than half their number at that time. As a result, we have, in place of young elk coming on, practically all old cows with very few bulls.

The annual report of the ex-State Game Warden for 1910 says: "About the usual number of elk died in Jackson's Hole last winter." I asked Mr. Crawford, an old resident in the valley, and at present feeding the largest bunch of elk being fed, about what percentage of the elk calves died last winter. He said, "80 percent." I next asked Mr. George Wilson, another old resident, the same question. He said, "85 per cent." Mr. Kelly said 75 per cent. The calf crop each year is about 30 per cent of the whole, while there are very few young elk growing up.

It is therefore a fact that we, by permitting this annual normal loss among the elk for want of feed, by allowing one-third or one-half of the calves to perish year after year, are destroying the males only, and making it necessary that the breeding must be done by immature and inferior males, thereby raising degenerate, weak calves that succumb easily to hard winters.

It is necessary in breeding farm stock to select the best sires. In breeding among wild animals, nature's intention is to eliminate the weaker, inferior animal, for in their fights during the rutting season the stronger, more mature male drives the others away. In the case of the elk there is not enough mature bulls to go around, and this is causing inter-breeding to some extent, all of which has a tendency to create weak offspring.

Now, the state of Wyoming and the National Government are going to try another experiment—drive the elk like cattle to a better (?) feeding ground. We hope they may succeed, on this proposed new elk range.

21

VALLEY IN DISCORD (1965)

MARGARET MURIE (1902–2003)
OLAUS MURIE (1889–1963)

Margaret and Olaus Murie came to Jackson Hole in 1927 when Olaus became head of the National Elk Refuge. For some thirty-seven years they participated in the life of the valley.

Conservation has always been a dominant issue. Since the turn of the twentieth century, homesteaders, residents, politicians, developers, and federal officials have asked a basic question: "What should we do with this beautiful place?" Like all thoughtful questions, there are no easy answers. After a long struggle, the National Park Service laid claim to the mountains when Grand Teton National Park was established in 1929. However, that was just the beginning of land acquisitions. With John D. Rockefeller Jr.'s money and National Park Service cooperation, much of the private land in the northern part of Jackson Hole was purchased with the intent that his land would become part of an enlarged national park. However, as the Muries explain, this deprivatization of land did not happen easily. Valley residents were divided, creating what the authors term a "valley in discord." Tempers were short, families were often split, and "there was no such thing as getting together and talking it over."

In this essay, published in the Muries' book Wapiti Wilderness *(1965), the Muries capture the flavor of a local feud that had national consequences. When the dust settled, what emerged was the pristine park enjoyed by so many today.*

Our car begins to take the zigzag turns and we put it into low gear just to be sure. Glancing up the slope, we soon see a piece of the road directly above us, and we know we are approaching the top of Teton Pass. Yes, there is the dip in the ridge just ahead. We leave the hairpin turns, and glide out onto the little flat at the summit.

On every trip over "the Pass" we stop for a bit, and look. Out through the gap fringed with spruce and fir and pine we look into the misty valley far below and see the blue white-flecked mountains beyond. Beside us there is a rustic sign: "Howdy, Stranger. Yonder is Jackson Hole, the last of the Old West."

Those of us who are not strangers, those of us who live down there in the misty blue, will, if we are honest, confess to a little tightening of the throat each time this view bursts upon us. Is that slight mistiness in the scenery, or in our eyes? We don't think so much about "the last of the Old West," but those forest-clad slopes, the very air we breathe, spell HOME.

The valley of Jackson Hole lies here snugly among the mountains that rise on every side. The scenery, the game herds, the wild flowers, the entire ensemble of natural attributes has combined to produce a recreational environment that gives satisfaction and inspiration to hundreds of thousands of people each year. Yet it would seem that the sheer beauty of the place, as it might be with a beautiful woman, has actually been the cause of discord and petty quarreling to a degree almost unique. Neighbor against neighbor, group against group, the feelings have smoldered, leaping out in open conflict from time to time, the bone of contention being: What to do with this beautiful place?

We all praise the memory of that group of frontiersmen of 1870 who in the face of temptation to exploit the Yellowstone region decided to boost for a great national park, the first in the world. But their problem was simpler. They were a small group, and with just a little altruistic feeling among them they could come to a decision. In the 1940's in our valley we were dealing with a situation that had settled into a stubborn groove of tradition.

Yet altruistic impulses were felt in the Jackson Hole country, too, in earlier years. They began with explorers who saw the valley in the previous century. In 1892 Owen Wister wrote: "Of all places in the Rocky Mountains that I know, it is the most beautiful, and, as it lies too high for man to build and prosper, its trees and waters should be kept from man's irresponsible destruction...."

In 1923 there was a notable occurrence, which is commemorated by a bronze plaque at the doorway of a simple log cabin on the banks of Snake River at Moose. The plaque reads:

THE MAUDE NOBLE CABIN

This cabin, erected on its present site in 1917 by Miss Maude Noble, has been preserved and renovated to commemorate a meeting held here on the evening of July 26, 1923, at which Mr. Struthers Burt, Dr. Horace Carncross, Mr. John L. Eynon, Mr. J.R. Jones and Mr. Richard Winger, all residents of Jackson Hole, presented to Mr. Horace Albright, then Superintendent of Yellowstone National Park, a plan for setting aside a portion of Jackson Hole as a National Recreation Area for the use and enjoyment of the people of the United States. The purpose of that plan has been accomplished by the established and enlargement of the Grand Teton National Park. The broad vision and patriotic foresight of those who met here that July evening in 1923 will be increasingly appreciated by our country with the passing years.

Jackson Hole Preserve, Incorporated

The words on this plaque indicate only the beginning, and the end, of a stormy period in the history of Jackson Hole, a period running from 1918 into the 1950's. The purpose of the meeting at Miss Noble's cabin in 1923 was to devise a means of saving the beauty of the valley from commercial exploitation, from the ruin of its natural beauty; an appeal to have it placed under the supervision of "some public agency." Here is a memorable example of the recognition by a very few people, for the benefit of the future, of the need for safeguarding a meaningful segment of our country from the uses of commerce.

Why the need for such concern, for such an appeal? A simple chronology of events will show, I think, what threatened the valley and what human motives were at work in its history.

Environmental activists Olaus and Margaret "Mardy" Murie in many ways represent the heroes of the park and Jackson Hole. They were tremendous advocates of the park and the community, reminding people of the value of wild places in both Jackson Hole and Alaska. Collection of the Jackson Hole Historical Society and Museum, 2011.0034.001.

The years 1918 to 1923 were trying years in Jackson Hole. In 1918 Congressman Mondell introduced a bill for the extension of Yellowstone National Park to include the northern part of Jackson Hole only. Everyone in the valley was opposed to this seemingly thoughtless dumping of a part of the valley into another already large national park. Nevertheless, it was twice introduced, and twice failed. During these war years the cattlemen of the valley were able to get good prices; they had visions of expanding their herds and later securing much more of the summer range in the previously created Teton National Forest in the northern and eastern parts of the valley, which at that time had been set apart for the elk herds as the Teton State Game Preserve, under control of the Wyoming State Game Commission. In 1919 the Forest Service began curtailing some use of the ranges by cattle, for the protection of the elk, and this caused angry reactions from cattlemen. Even so, the Park Service, not the Forest Service, was the most hated government bureau. The administration of Yellowstone was suspected of wanting to "swallow up" all of Jackson Hole and do away with cattle ranching and every form of private enterprise. Thus, this early in the play, the Park Service was cast as the villain of the piece.

The tragic flu epidemic of 1918-19 was followed by a severe drought and a short hay crop, but when cattle prices began to tumble after the end of the war, the Jackson Hole ranchers held on, hoping the market would rise, hoping to use more of the valley for cattle ranching; and having had to pay high prices for hay to supplement their own short crops, they found themselves in 1920 bankrupt or heavily in debt or heavily mortgaged by the local bank.

In an attempt to remedy the situation, a few cattlemen made an effort to bring sheep into the valley. Other ranchers and most of the citizens rose in hot protest, and won out, but worry and strife now permeated the clear mountain air.

These were the local events. Added to them were more ominous threats. An engineer in Cheyenne had formed a corporation known as the Teton Irrigation Company and had filed in 1909 and 1912 on the waters of the Gros Ventre River, the Buffalo River, and Spread Creek, the most important Snake River tributaries in the valley. They claimed the purpose of this was to "water" the beautiful sagebrush floor of the valley in the front of the Tetons, Antelope Flat, which had been set aside by them under the provisions of a federal law, the Carey Act. But of course, the real intention was to sell the water to Idaho farmers, and although the law required the completion of their work in five years, their privilege was extended, by succeeding State Engineers of Wyoming, for a total of twenty-seven years.

In this same unsettled period, through connivance with some local homesteaders, an Idaho corporation known as the Osgood Land and Livestock Company secured an interest in the water-storage rights on two of the valley's lakes, Emma Matilda and Two Ocean. Two years later a citizen of Jackson Hole, in going through some records at the state capitol at Cheyenne, discovered a secret filing by the Carlisle group on the waters of Jenny and Leigh lakes, the two gems at the base of the Tetons themselves.

Here were threats to the natural condition of all the main lakes and streams of the valley, and a threat to the floor of the valley itself. By 1923 the danger seemed very real and ominous to Struthers Burt and his friends who met in Maude Noble's cabin that July evening. They knew that, inexorably, the danger would grow. The water resources of Jackson Hole would be a constant temptation to the acquisitive and the greedy. Owen Wister had been wrong. Jackson Hole did *not* lie "too high for man to build and prosper in." And it now needed to "be kept from man's irresponsible destruction." There were immediate threats to the lakes and streams.

These are reasons for the meeting in Maude Noble's cabin, for the beginning of what was later known as "the Jackson Hole Plan." I have seen the original of a petition requesting preservation of the upper end of Jackson Hole, and on it are the signatures of men who a few years later fought bitterly against establishment of either a national park or a national monument. In 1931, as in 1923, many cattlemen and businessmen were in favor of some kind of preservation plan which would not jeopardize their lives and their business, and the essential purposes of the Jackson Hole Plan were endorsed by the Jackson Hole Cattle and Horse Association. When in 1926 John D. Rockefeller, Jr., became interested and began purchasing ranches and other private lands in upper Jackson Hole with the avowed purpose of later turning them over to the federal government, he was acting on the same motive, but in a practical way. The chronology, however, does not yet become peaceful.

The banker at Jackson was Rockefeller's agent. I talked with him many times, but he was very secretive; in those first days, neither the purchaser nor his plans were disclosed, and this is understandable. I asked the banker if he thought the people of Jackson Hole would be behind the project, whatever it was. He assured me that they would be, and that it "would be a great thing for the valley."

What happened next I shall not attempt to explain. For some reason Rockefeller selected a new purchasing agent. And that changed the whole climate of the valley. From that moment on, the banker and all his associates, many of them cattlemen, were bitterly opposed to the Jackson Hole Plan. They now seemed to see in it the ruin of the cattle business and all freedom of enterprise in Jackson Hole. The plan did not take in the whole valley, but they felt they could not trust the forces behind it; they felt there were Park Service people who wanted everything "rim to rim."

Grand Teton National Park was established in 1929 by mere transfer of National Forest lands covering the mountains and the lakes at the western edge of the valley, which had always been federal lands. The first superintendent of the new national park met the banker on the street in Jackson and was introduced. The banker said: "Well, we fought you as long as we could. You won. Now we will cooperate."

A handsome speech, under the circumstances. One can hardly imagine any substantial number of people, in or out of Wyoming, who would now consider the creation of this park ill-advised. But Rockefeller's program of purchasing private lands in the upper and eastern parts of the valley went on, and opposition to it went on too. As the years passed, it settled into a tradition. The cattlemen became somehow convinced that all their grazing rights would be taken away; the federal government was going to gobble up everything; they had forgotten that quite recently they had petitioned that a great portion of the valley be preserved for recreation and inspiration for all people for all time. As with most feuds, this thing went beyond the state of reasoning for or against a plan; it had become a personal battle, a case of loyalty to one side or to the other. As Dick Winger, the new purchasing agent for Rockefeller, and a resident of the valley since 1913, testified at one of the several Congressional hearings held in Jackson to try to straighten out this controversy: "We don't have clean killings in Jackson Hole; we just worry each other to death!"

Soon after this I got into Dick's car one day to ride home with him. He glanced over at me with a quizzical smile: "Aren't you afraid you'll be condemned now, after being seen riding with me?"

Thus it went on. Jackson Hole might be isolated from the rest of the world in winter, but it always had two burning topics for winter conversation: the elk herd and the park. Card parties, dinner parties had their embarrassments if certain ones prominent on "the other side" were present. In some inexplicable way an atmosphere was created in which one felt inhibited from even mentioning the subject. There was no such thing as getting together and talking it over. Congress and our state officials, the federal bureaus, and all the cattle and chamber-of-commerce organizations were concerned, yet through these years it was largely a local feud, a family quarrel. At intervals new rumors drifted up and down the valley. How many more ranches had Rockefeller bought? Was it all going to be added to Yellowstone, or Grand Teton, or what were they going to do with it? Then came a day in March 1943.

I had been up the valley, tramping along the banks of the Gros Ventre River counting dead elk, for March is the month when the weak and sick succumb. As I drove back into town, I stopped my car near the post office, and I noticed "Buck," the successor to the former banker, and a real leader in the community, standing in a group of people on the sidewalk. Buck and I were working together in the Boy Scout troop in which his son and our Donald were both members, and I suddenly remembered that I must ask him about the next Court of Honor. I stepped over and began to speak, but didn't get many words said. "Boy Scouts!" he exploded. "Boy Scouts! How can we talk about Boy Scouts now? Haven't you heard what they have done? The President has put our whole valley in a park!"

Thus I received the news that Franklin Roosevelt had, by Executive Order, made a National Monument of all the Rockefeller lands and some remaining federal lands in the east and north parts of the valley. At first, I too was stunned. When I came through the back door, Mardy looked up from her mixing bowl: "What's the matter?"

And when I told her, her first reaction was: "But we're in the middle of a *war!* Why do it *now?*"

So we lived through a few more years of battle over the beautiful valley. Bills were introduced in Congress to abolish the Jackson Hole National Monument; more hearings were held in Washington and in the field; the State of Wyoming even brought suit against a superintendent of the Park and Monument, since it would not sue the federal government. Signs appeared in the windows of many business houses: "We are opposed to the Jackson Hole National Monument." A large sign on the outside of one store was partly blown away by a March blizzard, leaving only the word "opposed"—which pretty well expressed the current attitude. If we of the valley, all of us, were to stop now and take a calm look back, I think we might wonder what it was all about. The ranchers of the middle and north parts of the valley had all sold because they wanted to; and yet the other ranchers clung to the idea that their lands and livelihoods were going to be snatched away.

One has to live a dreadfully long time in Jackson Hole to be considered an "Old-timer." I don't think we were considered old-timers even after thirty years of living there. But in spite of this I do think that Mardy and I sensed a bit of how the "real" old-timers, the cattlemen, the long-established towns-people, felt about this "invasion" of their own chosen valley by government, by tourists, by more and more dudes, by proposals to do this or do that with the valley. It is not easy to give up a natural proprietary feeling of ownership and let all the world in. How did the Indians feel at the unheralded arrival of white settlers in land that had always been theirs?

One old-timer, a woman, expressed this feeling rather well when, fourteen years after the establishment of Grand Teton National Park, the bombshell of the Jackson Hole National Monument proclamation dropped into the valley: "We GAVE them the Tetons! What *more* do they want?"

Here is the ubiquitous problem: who is "They"? Grand Teton National Park now includes the Monument lands and nearly all of the lands purchased by Rockefeller, and the noise of battle has died away. Gradually we all have learned to live with it, to recognize the good it holds, to be firm in opposing practice we think bad. We growl about some of the Park Service architecture at the headquarters at Moose, but it at least is limited to one spot. As one drives into and out of the town of Jackson, 14 miles to the south, passing through an unsightly parade of billboards that scar the charming scenery, one cannot help but breathe a sigh of gratitude after crossing the park boundary to find a quiet and serene landscape, marred only by a too-modern highway. It is our park; it is our government; we are they, and they are we. The American public decidedly will not leave this region alone, nor can we ask them to. They will be coming in increasing numbers; it is their country, too.

Now the cattlemen have their grazing rights on the national forest lands, and the right to drift their cattle across national park lands to reach these permits; people still have their homes; dudes still have their summer homes. No one, Old-timer or Newcomer, would now deny that the National Park has vitalized the economy of the valley a thousandfold. These material results are obvious. Our problem now is not the number of acres that are under state or private or federal jurisdiction, but whether or not we can keep most of these acres unspoiled by man; whether or not we can keep our souls receptive to the message of peace these unspoiled acres offer us.

Jackson Hole is not merely a sky-piercing range of mountains for tourists to aim their cameras at. It is a country with a spirit. Grand mountains, to be sure, but also lesser hills harboring on their wooded slopes the bulk of the game herds; a fringe of aspens in the foothills; the sage flats of the valley floor where in primitive times buffalo and antelope grazed; the Snake River bottoms, where white-tailed deer found congenial habitat within the memory of men still living. There is, as one of our neighbors said, "something about it." Those of us who have our homes here and are raising families can help interpret to the visitor the spirit of Jackson Hole, forged out of long controversy, tempered with our love for the valley, for "the something about it."

In our St. John's Hospital in Jackson there is plaque honoring the parents who donated an operating room to the hospital in memory of their daughter who lost her life in the Tetons, and whose last entry in her diary that long-ago summer had been: "God Bless Wyoming and Keep it Wild."

22

SAVING THE TETONS (1978)

MARGARET SANBORN (1915–2005)

Journalist Margaret Sanborn came to the Tetons to write a popular work on the mountain range. Much of her work is a colorfully written story on the fur trade and early cattle industry, or as she states, "taming the Western wilderness." However, in her afterword she narrates the story of "saving the Tetons." In this entry, taken from Sanborn's book The Grand Tetons *(1978), Sanborn tells of the fight to create the 1929 park. Her straightforward story is a companion to the Muries' more personal account of the fight for an enlarged park, finally created in 1950.*

A procession of fur trappers and traders, prospectors, big game and trophy hunters, cattle and sheep ranchers, horse raisers, lumbermen, and farmers went into Teton country over the years following its discovery by John Colter. Concerning themselves only with what could be turned to immediate profit or use, they killed the wildlife, converted the stands of pine, fir, and spruce into logs and lumber piles, and dammed and drained the lakes for irrigation projects. They displaced the native herds by ploughing up the herbage and feeding their stock on wild grasses. Overgrazing by sheep stripped the Teton high country of much of its original beauty. By robbing the native bighorns of their food, men drove them ever higher among the peaks. There herbage was scare and many starved. Domestic sheep transmitted to them their diseases and parasites which, in conjunction with the lack of forage, caused the bighorns to virtually disappear from these mountains.

The very presence of settlers in the Teton valleys disrupted the migration routes of moose, elk, buffalo, antelope, and deer. Fencing land, draining marshes, and felling trees further altered the habitat for these animals, and affected bears, beavers, muskrats, trumpeter swans, geese, songbirds, and nearly every other wild creature. Ranchers, resenting the indigenous grazers feeding on the natural hay, killed them ruthlessly. Swans, hunted for food or simply for sport were virtually exterminated. Poachers, living at the north end of Jackson Hole, preyed on the migrating elk who, in moving south each winter, left the protection of Yellowstone Park. Thousands of them were slaughtered.

Men searched the Teton canyons, slopes, and streams not for the beauty they might find there, but in the hope of striking a bonanza. They found enough gold along Trail and Moose creeks, in North Leigh and Whetstone canyons, and at the head of Bitch Creek to encourage them. In hunting for the mother lode, believed to be the source of the fine flakes they saw in nearly every stream, they discovered deposits of silver, copper, coal, asbestos, gilsonite, and lime, and near the mouth of Horseshoe Canyon, oil. So they blasted tunnels, dug prospect pits, built sluices, diverted streams, set up lime kilns, and formed companies to mine, drill for oil, irrigate, and lumber. On the west side, nearly every canyon had a sawmill.

In 1906, Jackson Lake was dammed so that its waters could be taken west to develop Idaho's semiarid Snake River Basin. Few were concerned that the contained and increased waters covered the historic Indian and trapper trail leading to Conant Pass, drowned ancient Indian artifacts and campsites along the shore—invaluable in the study of those people who first came into Jackson Hole—or that hundreds of conifers which ringed the natural lake were killed, leaving unsightly stands of bleached snags. Several years later, water storage rights were filed on Two Ocean and Emma Matilda lakes, and then on Jenny and Leigh, with plans to dam them and pipe their water west of the Tetons.

As early as 1897, Colonel S.D.M. Young, superintendent of Yellowstone Park, proposed to the secretary of the interior that the reserve's limits be extended south to include part of Jackson Hole, as a means of protecting the migrating elk from poachers. The next year, Charles D. Walcott, director of the United States Geological Survey, made a tour of Jackson Hole. He was so favorably impressed by everything he saw there, he suggested that a separate national park be created rather than an extension of Yellowstone. Both proposals were submitted to Congress, but no legislative interest or support was around.

Throughout the West there were countless mountain ranges still not fully explored, their highest peaks unclimbed, and many yet unnamed. It was therefore difficult for senators, congressmen, and other government officials who had never seen the Tetons to understand why this one small group of peaks should be preserved. Although they were unlike others in this country—there were already being called the Alps of America—it was impossible for them to compete in popular appeal with the novelty of Yellowstone's geysers, boiling lakes, bubbling mudpots, and roaring caves. Even John Muir found these thermal curiosities exciting and wrote enthusiastically about the wonders of Yellowstone, while giving the Tetons only passing mention. He saw these peaks only from a distance, and apparently made no effort to get any closer views, or explore them.

If the Hayden Surveys had been continued, the doctor's energies would have been doubtless direct next toward the creation of a Teton national preserve, for these were his favorite Western mountains. With William Henry Jackson and Thomas Moran to supply visual proof of their unique beauty, the reports of his specialists, the enthusiasm of Nathaniel Langford on the speaker's platform, and his own persuasiveness, the Tetons and possibly both east and west valleys would have been made into a park half a century earlier.

Wilderness areas were at this time still so plentiful in America they seemed inexhaustible to the average person. To most residents of the Teton valleys, so recently settled, and to their representatives in national government, wilderness was considered an obstruction to progress. Repeated efforts by conservationists to protect the Tetons and Jackson Hole from exploitation and commercialization failed. Years of education on the part of such men as Muir and John Burroughs were required to awaken in the public an appreciation of nature an awareness of the necessity for preserving wilderness as a refuge from the stresses and demands of daily living.

By 1923 nearly all of the lakes and streams on the east side were threatened by irrigation projects. Rows of tourist cabins and a dance hall were spoiling the beauty of Jenny Lake's setting. Advertising billboards were dis-figuring the sagebrush plains that form the Tetons' foreground and enhance their rugged sheerness.

Gasoline stations and refreshment stands were lining the roadsides in Jackson Hole. The Forest Service, which by then had jurisdiction over the valley's timber stands, was proposing to license commercial lumbering at Jackson Lake, to allow a number of mines to operate at the north end of the Hole, and to open tracts for summer homes. Recently a proposal had been made to build a highway up through the wilderness along Pacific Creek and across historic Two Ocean Pass as an alternate route into Yellowstone Park.

That July a meeting of concerned residents (five in number), headed by author-due rancher Struthers Burt, met in Maude Noble's cabin at the site of Menor's Ferry, to discuss the valley's future with conservationist Horace Albright. Albright was then superintendent of Yellowstone Park, and long an active advocate for extension of the park's boundaries south to include the Tetons and Jackson Hole.

The committee did not agree that the Tetons should be made a part of Yellowstone Park; they were in favor of some form of national recreation area that would allow cattle and horse raising, grazing, hunting, and dude ranching on a limited scale. They made an appeal for money among those wealthy eastern sportsmen who came regularly to Jackson Hole, but were unable to raise enough to buy the amount of land they had planned to in-clude in the preserve. Congress was also approached, but prove unreceptive to that form of federal protection.

Horace Albright continued his campaign to save the Tetons. Whenever important or influential visitors came to Yellowstone, he talked to them about park extension and usually managed to take them to see the Tetons from Jackson Hole.

In the summer of 1926, John D. Rockefeller, Jr. brought his wife and three of their sons to Yellowstone Park. He had already seen a part of Jack-son Hole but was anxious to see it all, and he readily accepted Albright's offer to drive him and his family there.

He and his wife were troubled by the sight of so many tourist cabins, re-freshment stands, gas stations, dilapidated ranch buildings, and billboards—one stood directly in the foreground of the Grand Teton—which detracted from the overall beauty of the valley and mountains. After they had passed through this exploited area Rockefeller asked Albright to send him a map that would show the locations of these structures, and also an estimate of the value of the land on which they stood. Albright agreed.

While stopped at Hendrick's Point to look at the view, Albright told them about the meeting at Maude Noble's cabin, and the other plans and efforts to preserve the valley and protect the Tetons. The Rockefellers made no comment, he recalled, nor did he ask for their support or mention the subject again.

That winter Albright took the map, and the estimates to Rockefeller's New York Office. After examining the map, Rockefeller told Albright that he had a much larger area in mind—in fact, all of that part of the valley which could be seen from Hendrick's Point. He wanted to acquire the entire northern section of Jackson Hole and eventually add it to Yellowstone Park. His two reasons for considering the project where "the marvelous scenic beauty of the Teton Mountains and the Lakes at their feet," which were seen at their best from Jackson Hole, and the fact that this valley was a natural feeding ground and necessary refuge for elk, deer, moose, and buffalo. It was an ideal project, he said, and he was only interested in ideal projects.

By February 1927 he was ready to act. To avoid unwanted publicity and inflated land prices, his name was kept out of the project. The Snake River Land Company, a Utah corporation, was organized, with New York lawyer Vanderbilt Webb as president, and Jackson banker Robert Miller as the resident purchasing agent.

Rockefeller made it clear that in buying the land his representatives were to pay fair value for it, and that in every case the owner's financial circumstances were to be appraised sympathetically. The company was to hold the acreage until it could be turned over to the federal government for inclusion in the park system or some other form of preserve that would benefit the general public. However, the ultimate disposition of the land was also to be kept secret.

On February 26, 1929, after thirty-two years of agitation, the conservationists scored a victory when President Calvin Coolidge signed a bill creating Teton National Park. The east face of the range from Webb Canyon south to Granite Canyon, and a narrow strip along the base that contained Leigh, Jenny, Bradley, Taggart, and Phelps lakes, were included in the park. The rest of Jackson Hole, except for that land held by Rockefeller, remained unprotected. The west side of the Tetons and Pierre's Hold had never been considered in this struggle for preservation.

There was little opposition to a park that consisted principally of high peaks. Only a few cattlemen objected, chiefly on principle, since their association had taken a stand against park extension.

In April 1930 the Snake River Land Company made its plans public, at the request of Wyoming's governor. When the people of Jackson Hole learned that the company's holdings were to be included in Teton National Park, the valley became embattled. Feelings ran high as everyone took sides, and many an old friendship was broken. One men's service club in Jackson passed resolutions against adding the Rockefeller lands to the park, while another took a vigorous stand in favor of it. The *Jackson Hole Courier* was strong pro-park, but it soon had a rival, the *Grand Teton*, established purposely to fight park enlargement. The bitterest opponents were the cattlemen who were convinced, in spite of assurances to the contrary, that their grazing rights would be abolished, and foresaw the end of all free enterprise in Jackson Hole.

Throughout this decade, frequent attempts were made to get congressional approval for inclusion of the Rockefeller lands, but every effort was frustrated by powerful lobbyist pressures. For nearly ten years, while he waited for the government to accept his gift, Rockefeller held around thirty thousand acres of taxable land. In November 1942, his patience wearing thin, he wrote to Harold Ickes, Secretary of the Interior, to say that if the government did not take advantage of his offer within a year, he intended to sell it on the open market.

In his reply Ickes assured him that the "great conservation project" which he had made possible would have been accepted long before, had it not been for "selfish local interests." He assured Rockefeller that he would do all he could to effect the inclusion of his lands within the park.

Certain that Congress would still resist park enlargement, Ickes drew up a proclamation that set aside 221,610 acres in Jackson Hole as a national preserve. On March 15, 1943, President Franklin Roosevelt, by executive order (allowed under the 1906 Antiquities Act), created Jackson Hole National Monument.

The entire state of Wyoming was outraged at what was regarded as an arbitrary act on Roosevelt's part. The proclamation seemed to indicate total indifference to popular opinion and disrespect toward their elected representation in national government. Within four days Wyoming Congressman Frank Barrett had introduced a bill abolishing the monument. It passed both houses of Congress but was promptly vetoed by the president. In May, the state of Wyoming filed suit in the federal district court to prevent the government from taking control over the monument.

Throughout the 1940s, the battle continued to wage locally and nationally, with most of the country's newspapers taking sides in the controversy. But by the beginning of the new decade much of the bitterness was tempered. On September 15, 1950, President Harry Truman signed a bill that included the monument in the Grand Teton National Park. Two of the most militant and vocal opponents of park enlargement, Senators Hunt and O'Mahoney of Wyoming, had introduced the measure.

It was the ambition of the early conservationists like Muir, Burroughs, Hayden, Langford, and Albright, to encourage as many people as possible to go to the national parks and forest reserves. "Wander here a whole summer, if you can," urged Muir, "roaming... in rosiny pinewoods or in gentian meadows, brushing through chapparal...parting sweet, flowery sprays... jumping from rock to rock...panting in whole-souled exercise and rejoicing in deep, long-drawn breaths of pure wilderness."

Naturally, none of these men could foresee the American public's present mobility, nor anticipate that the parks and reserves would ever be faced with the problems of overuse by tourists.

Three million people visit the Grand Teton National Park each year, a number that will continue to increase as long as the people's mobility remains uncurbed. During the summer, the most popular season, picnic and campgrounds, lodges, dude ranches, scenic turnouts, lakeshores, and trails are crowded to excess. The noise of automobiles, motorcycles, and powerboats obtrudes on natural sounds—birdsongs, aspen leaves rippling in the wind, the plop of feeding trout, the footfalls of small creatures in the woods, the drum of grouse, the drone of bees. Exhaust fumes from these vehicles overwhelm the delicate smells of dewy grass, lichen, pine needles warmed by sun, bracken, and alder groves. The indigenous sounds and smells are as vital a part of the enjoyment of Teton country as are the peaks themselves. It is doubtful whether Muri, at least, would approve of the summer throngs. He once wrote: "Only by going alone in silence…can one truly get into the heart of the wilderness,"—comprehend its essence.

Those who agree with Muir must avoid the summer season. In doing so they will miss the finest displays of wildflowers and songbird choruses, and the sight of waterfalls and streams at their fullest. But they will discover other wonders, for there is no season in the Tetons without them.

The struggle to protect Jackson Hole from exploitation and commercialization still goes on. Business interests are continually agitating for enlargement of the airport to accommodate big jets, for the construction of more ski lodges and winter sports areas on the park's environs, the building of high-rise hotels in the town of Jackson to attract all-season tourists, and tract housing. The valley's future lies in the hands of planners who seek permanently effective ways to protect the Tetons' setting from encroachment by inappropriate and unwise land use.

John Muri was well aware that "the battle for preservation will go on endlessly. It is part of the universal battle between right and wrong." Fortunately, the most important victories in this battle for right have been won. The east side of the Teton Range, its forests, lakes, and wildlife, and the greater part of Jackson Hole are being held inviolable for present and future generations to enjoy.

"The clearest way into the Universe is through a forest wilderness," Muir observed. Because of the foresight of a few, and their unflagging labors in the realm of conservation, those who also wish to comprehend the macrocosm by way of a Teton wilderness may do so. They may also heed the injunction of that great naturalist—"climb the mountains and get their good tidings."

23

POSTSCRIPT FOR A PARK (1982)

ROBERT W. RIGHTER

A major theme of Grand Teton National Park *was the difficulty of its creation. As Margaret and Olaus Murie noted, it was a bitter fight pitting friend against friend, and occasionally family against family. For over twenty years the two factions fought with no resolution.*

Finally, in 1950 the two sides produced a compromise that created the park we know today. Of course, neither side were fully pleased with it. But the agreement did resolve their dispute, and its sagacity was eventually accepted. When I was writing Crucible for Conservation *(1982), from which this selection is taken, I often thought about what might have happened if the efforts of the two sides had failed. I decided to write a brief scenario if the 1950 efforts at compromise had come to nothing. It is reassuring to note that in over thirty-five years, no one has really questioned this literary fabrication. Fortunately, it is only a fairy tale: a fantasy that never happened.*

Park or no park, throngs of people would have descended on Jackson Hole, for it does not take the National Park Service to inform visitors that this is a place of exceptional natural beauty. They would have come, but had not Rockefeller, Albright, Struthers Burt, Olaus Murie and so many others fought with infinite patience and determination, they would have found a different valley. Perhaps it is not proper in a work of this nature to indulge in futuristic scenarios, but one can not help but speculate on what might have been. The southern end of Jackson Lake would have been festooned with some four hundred summer homes, possibly attractive, yet preventing access for the general public. We can also assume that Jackson Lake would have faced pollution problems from seeping sewage, not unlike Lake Tahoe, California. Inevitably the land would have been scarred by construction and the valley bisected with power lines. Jackson Lake might have been desecrated further by a small logging operation, utilizing logs on the west side of the lake, transporting them across the lake to a small lumber mill. The mill might have been located at Moran. As is so often the case with a logging operation, air quality would have been diminished. We might also expect the lake would have been drained, particularly during drought years, to the point of being an eyesore.

Inevitably, the road from Jackson to Jenny Lake would have become an extension of the town of Jackson. Motels would have been built further north, each claiming the best view of the Cathedral Group, and yet collectively diminishing the pleasure of that scene by their very existence. Along with the motels we could expect fast and cheap food service, facilities for automobiles, and crowded campgrounds featuring electricity and sewer hookups in lieu of trees.

The bypass road on the east side of the Snake River might have been spared such intense development. However, since this is the route of the tourist-in-a-hurry, we might expect the most audacious commercialism to slow him down. Perhaps a model might be Highway 16 from Rapid City to Mount Rushmore. "Gravity spots," reptile gardens, aquatic displays, a "wild" animal park, and the ubiquitous Indian souvenir shop, *ad infinitum*, could be expected, replete with billboards out of all proportion in size and number to the attractions advertised.

Perhaps this scenario is unduly pessimistic. Let us presume that this development would have been done tastefully, eliminating the worst excesses. The result would still have detracted from the pristine beauty of Jackson Hole. It would have focused the tourist's attention on man-made objects and on individual transient needs, rather than allowing his spirit to soar briefly to the heights of this awe-inspiring mountain range as he hurriedly traveled the highway east of the river.

Of course, none but the most crass, opportunistic resident would have sanctioned this scenario at any time during the long struggle over land use, but inevitably it would have happened. It would have happened because those who opposed the National Park Service favored individualism, property rights and local control. Given the conservatism of local residents and their attachment to "laissez-faire" economic principles, it is difficult to see any other outcome. Certainly the group that met at Maud Noble's cabin in 1923 recognized this scenario for the valley and were determined to remove somehow the land use decision-making power from local control. They knew that although there might be professions to the contrary, money would be the measure in Jackson Hole and unrestrained development would be the result. And why shouldn't that be the pattern? Why should Jackson Hole be spared? That is a question which perhaps will never be answered.

PART V

THE MOUNTAINS

24

THE MATTERHORN OF AMERICA (1892)

WILLIAM O. OWEN (1859–1947)

William O. Owen, a professional surveyor headquartered in Laramie, Wyoming, roamed the Rockies at the turn of the twentieth century. Mountaineering was his passion, and by the time he was thirty, he was familiar with the peaks of the Uinta Range, the Rabbit Ears Pass area of Colorado, the Big Horn Mountains, the Wind River Range, and most of the lesser ranges of the northern Rockies.

Owen's reputation, however, is linked to the Teton Range. Leigh Ortenberger, today's most knowledgeable historian of climbing in the Tetons, has stated that "there is perhaps no name better known in association with the Teton Range of northwestern Wyoming than William Octavius Owen, 'Billy Owen of the Tetons.'" Such a tribute is based upon the fact that Owen was a member of the three-man Franklin Spalding party, the first party to indisputably scale the Grand Teton in 1898. Until his death in 1945, Owen claimed the peak as his conquest, and he was so successful that the closely associated Mt. Owen was named in his honor.

Although the Spalding party was the first with an absolute claim, reason tells us that the first human being to summit the mountain was a Native American. On the south side of the Grand Teton and about eighty feet from the summit is The Enclosure. It is a small, horseshoe-shaped space built by Native Americans for protection from the elements or for rituals, such as vision quests.

While Owen did not discuss The Enclosure, he did write a great deal about the Tetons. But much of what he wrote was colored by his obsession to discount Nathaniel Langford's 1872 claim to the first ascent of the Grand Teton, which does not make for engaging or inspirational reading. However, Owen was a talented writer, and in 1891 he was free of crusades. In that year he, his wife, another couple, and a guide unsuccessfully attempted the climb. Later, he published this account of their adventure in Frank Leslie's Weekly.

In the northwest corner of Wyoming, about twenty-five miles south of the Yellowstone National Park, form a range of rugged and perpetually snow-clad mountains whose christening dates back some seventy-five years, rise three of the grandest peaks in North America. They are known as the Three Tetons, and are mentioned in Irving's "Captain Bonneville," and by the renowned pathfinder, John C. Fremont, in his official report to the government covering his exploration.

These three peaks, by name, are probably more familiar to the tourists who have visited this Western country than any others in the entire Rocky Mountain system and yet I believe it perfectly safe to assert that they are in reality as little *known* as the giant snow-clad summits of equatorial Africa. The reason for this latter fact is readily to be found in the great difficulties that must be encountered in reaching them—difficulties that can be overcome only by excess of nerve and first-class physical endurance.

From the west, these peaks are easily seen two hundred miles distant, and viewed from this point they are seemingly as sharp as needles. The summits lie in a northeast and southwest direction and are almost exactly a mile asunder. The farthest north of the three is known as the Grand Teton, and has an altitude of 14,150 feet; the other two rising respectively 13,400 and 13,100 feet above the sea. These figures were obtained from careful transit and barometrical measurements and are the means of twenty independent observations.

They are truly Alpine in character and in this respect, if in no other, lie entirely without the realm of comparison with other North American peaks. That the loftiest of the three has not yet attracted the attention of the mountaineering fraternity is little short of wonderful, for it possesses every feature that gives life and charm to mountain climbing.

The Grand Teton bears a marked resemblance to the famous Matterhorn of the Old World, as seen from the Riffel, and has many physical characteristics in common with its far-famed prototype. In one respect, at

William O. Owen is credited with the first recorded ascent of the Grand Teton in 1898. As evident in the photo, he had talents other than climbing mountains. Collection of the Jackson Hole Historical Society and Museum, 2004.0055.008.

least, it surpasses that celebrated mountain. The Matterhorn from its base rises about five thousand feet, while the Teton, on the east side, lifts its head 7,500 feet above the valley at its immediate base, in a smooth, unbroken slope of granite so steep as to be entirely inaccessible to man. Pike's, Gray's, Long's and the host of other Rocky Mountain summits are tame when compared with the Grand Teton, and, viewed in the light of difficult and dangerous climbing, are not to be spoken in the same breath with it. It is absolutely peerless.

To attempt an ascent of this mighty peak, Mr. Dawson and myself, accompanied by our wives, proceeded to Market Lake, Idaho from which point the journey was completed by wagon, packs, and foot, the last eight miles being impassable by either of the former two methods. Market Lake, the nearest railway point to the Three Tetons, lies a hundred miles west of the peaks, and from this point these giant landmarks seemed to pierce the sky in their awful reach heavenward. At Basin River Ranch, thirty miles from the Teton Range, we secured an excellent photograph of the three peaks bathed in brilliant sunlight and carved on a band of bluest heaven. They looked bare and inaccessible. Proceeding eastward we reached our last camp on the Teton River, eight miles from the peaks and at once began preparation to "foot it" the remaining distance, wagons or packs from this point forward being out of the question. Taking a limited supply of bacon, flour, coffee, and sugar and barometer, thermometer, and camera, we set out the following morning accompanied by Alonzo Daw, our guide. Bedding was, of course, entirely out of the question.

At four o'clock in the afternoon, after a day of frightful climbing, we found ourselves on the west brink of the Teton cañon, a wild gorge of appalling depth and awful grandeur. From our feet a slope of forty-five degrees over beds of bowlders and ancient glacial moraines fell swiftly sway to a snow-fed river at the bottom of the cañon three thousand feet distant.

We camped on the brink of the river, in a grassy plot amid a cluster of firs, at an altitude of 9,200 feet, and proceeded at once with the preparation of our evening meal. The women were in the best of spirits, and had borne up under the fatiguing tramp with heroic fortitude, and were now eager to begin the ascent.

Our camp at this point was extremely picturesque, pitched as it was amid solemn pines, the sombre cañon walls rising hundreds of feet on either side, and broidered at the brink with mammoth banks of snow, affording the birthplace for a hundred cascades that leaped noisily over cold vertical walls of naked granite a thousand feet high.

Supper over, a bed of pine boughs under shelter of a huge log was arranged, and a large pile of wood collected with which to replenish the fire during the night. Having no bedding, it was necessary to keep up a good fire throughout the night. We retire—if I may use the expression—at dark, with nothing save the star-studded firmament for a covering, and as I lay there in the awful depths of that cañon mentally weighing the chances of success or failure for the morrow, the full moon rose tranquilly over the granite battlements of the Three Tetons, completely filling the cañon with its mellow light, and touching with a hand of gold the snow-capped pinnacles that stood like sentinels on the brink of the gorge.

I have never seen a more glorious exhibition of nature's wild beauty than here lay before me. There may be steeper cañons than this, and perhaps more beautiful, but there are none wider nor more rugged; and save for the golden sheen of the world-renowned Yellowstone cañon were difficult indeed to choose between them. After a hasty breakfast, provided with coils of rope, barometer, and thermometer, we crossed the snowy river and began the ascent of the steep comb or ridge that lay to the east, completely shutting the peaks from view. Two hours of painful climbing over beds of loose rock that were ready to start at any moment brought us to the crest of the ridge, no wider than a horse's back, and which, sweeping in a semicircle to the south, joins the main range at the south side of the middle Teton. Looking eastward through a mile of superlatively clear atmosphere, we beheld the Grand Teton, unveiled from foot to crown—a giant monolith rising a clear 5,000 feet from the glacier valley at its base, and terminating in a point as sharp as the steeple of the church.

Words cannot convey the impression one gets while viewing that awful spire from this point. Its size and appalling height are simply overwhelming. In an experience of fifteen years of mountaineering I have seen absolutely nothing comparable with it. Five thousand feet of naked, cold granite, with not a spear of vegetation nor vestige of soil on the whole mountain. Sky, snow, and granite the only elements in this wild picture!

Descending gently, we encountered the west edge of a glacier lying peacefully in the amphitheater-like valley, resembling in contour the half of an oyster-shell with its small point broken off. It is nearly a mile wide, almost the same in length and has a maximum depth estimated at two hundred feet. The rope, to guard against accidents, was now put to use, but the glacier, having a gentle slope, and no crevasses to speak of, was crossed without difficulty. We were now at the actual foot of the peak and the ascent began, our path proceeding over a mass of loose rock, to scale which entailed the greatest danger to life and limb. At times large bowlders, becoming detached, would rush down the steep slope with irresistible velocity, filling the valley with echoes and threatening to carry the entire mass of loose rock to the bottom.

A thousand feet from the base, resort to the rope became necessary, and for the remainder of the distance scarcely a foot's progress could be made without it. Crevasses forty or fifty feet wide, filled with deep blue ice, were frequently encountered, constituting obstacles of a most dangerous character, and which, without the rope, would have been simply impassable.

Up, up, over nearly vertical walls of snow and ice-robed granite we toiled, reaching, after a desperate struggle, an altitude of 13,200 feet, at a point on the south side of the peak.

Here, toward the east, the face of the mountain sweeps down in a long, unbroken slope of glacier-polished rock for six thousand feet, meeting at the base a score of Alpine lakes fringed with lofty pines. And at this point defeat stared us in the face at every turn. A thousand feet above our heads towered bare, rocky pinnacles without crack or crevice to afford hold for foot or hand, and as vertical as a plumb-line. It might be possible to make the ascent from the north side, but we had no time to reconnoitre, for it was already three o'clock and camp was a good distance off. We were completely baffled, and none felt the disappointment so keenly as the women, whose skill and courage thus far had been little short of marvelous.

A hundred miles to the southeast, shimmering in the blue, stood Fremont's Peak, conspicuous among a host of others whose giant forms stood in faultless definition.

Being unable to continue the ascent, we chiseled our names on the rock, and erected a large cairn in which we deposited an airtight can containing the date and brief account of our trip and an excellent portrait of our Secretary of State, Mr. James G. Blaine. It had been our intention from the beginning, if we reached the summit, to christen this peerless peak in honor of our great statesman, as being the only mountain in our country worthy to bear his name.

Beginning the descent, we were soon enveloped in a blinding snow storm with ragged flashes of lightning and terrific peals of thunder, whose vibrations detached large blocks of stone that came thundering down the mountain side with the velocity of a bullet. I had often read in Whymper's "Scrambles Among the Alps," of cannonades on the Matterhorn, but never realized before now the terror that such an exhibition can inspire. The snow, completely wetting the rock, rendered the descent far more dangerous than the climb had been, and compelled the use of the rope continually. However, we reached the glacier in safety, which terminated the more difficult portion of the descent, and proceeded to cross the field of snow, which had become, during our absence, literally covered with blocks of stone, rolled hither by the jar consequent of the heavy thunder accompanying the storm. Without an accident we reached camp at seven o'clock thoroughly drenched and cold, and considerably cast down by our failure to reach the summit. A large fire, however, soon dispelled the gloom, and served in a great measure to restore our spirits.

Whether the Teton be inaccessible or not, I am not quite prepared to say. It is no mountain for novice, however, for failure certainly awaits any but the most skillful, and even such a one will require every appliance known to the fraternity to overcome the obstacles which beset him on this grandest peak of the Rocky Mountains. There are many peaks in the Rockies as lofty as the Tetons, but beyond this point all parallelism ceases.

The country surrounding the peaks is rugged and wild beyond the power of words to convey, and when this region becomes more accessible, by means of railroads already projected, it will doubtless rival, as a pleasuring ground, the famous National Park itself.

The scenery of the whole Teton country is intensely interesting. Its sombre forests, opening gradually upward and terminating in scattered groves of individual beauty; its deep and rugged cañons with massive, precipitous walls; its turbulent and varied cascades; its extensive snow fields with broad patches of virgin white gracefully trimming the lofty, needle-like summits, together form a combination of grandeur and beauty which may not be described.

And then, in addition to all this, stands that awful spire of granite whose storm-swept summit knows not the foot of man—a naked column of rock rising abruptly seven thousand feet from the valley and terminating in a point sharp as the spike of a warrior's helmet. However exalted may be the expectation, none can behold and be disappointed. It is a peak in every way worthy the attempt of that veteran mountaineer, Mr. Edward Whymper, and wears with distinguished honor the second title we gave it—the Matterhorn of America.

25

TETON CLOUDS AND SHADOWS (1938)

FRITIOF FRYXELL (1900–1986)

A great many writers have attempted to describe the Teton mountains. It is difficult to mold the English language to depict such visual grandeur. Perhaps the most successful was Fritiof Fryxell. His background partially explains his success. He earned a master's degree in English from the University of Illinois and then a PhD in geology at the University of Chicago. It was his education in both literature and science, combined with his love and knowledge of the mountains, that provided the tools for exceptional prose.

Fryxell first saw the Tetons in 1924. When the park was established in 1929, he became a ranger-naturalist, spending his summers in Wyoming and the school year teaching geology at Augustana College in Illinois. From June through August he climbed, crawled, scampered, and camped in almost every part of the range, taking scientific and literary notes on his mountain encounters. By 1935 he was ready to write—to distill his experiences. Later he said, "I hoped to convey as best I could the impression [the mountains] had made on me—both during the first three summers when they served as a 'backdrop' for the valley, and as I got to know them later from traversing the canyons and climbing the peaks."

This excerpt is taken from his book The Tetons: Interpretations of a Mountain Landscape *(1938).*

Into the Teton landscape enter many elements which are ceaselessly changing, producing combinations that are new and beautiful. Even the contour of the range undergoes change, as we have observed, but in the large view this is imperceptible, so that seeking permanence in a universe of change we turn to mountains such as these for a symbol of everlastingness.

Over these seemingly changeless mountains, in endless succession, move the ephemeral colors of dawn and sunset and of noon and night, the shadows and the sunlight, the garlands of clouds with which storms adorn the peaks, the misty rain-curtains of afternoon showers. On the range are often set the rainbows; more rarely appears the alpenglow. Along the lower slopes appear the varying shades which the seasons bring to the aspen groves, and in the open meadows unnumbered flowers spring to life and beauty, each for its period and soon replaced by others, perhaps of equal brilliance but of different hues. High above are the snow fields, likewise changing and assuming new patterns as from spring to fall they dwindle, until at last all lose their identity in the mantle of breathless white silence that winter casts upon the region. We see the range now shining with snow, now darkly fearsome in storm, now serene and clean-washed after rain. Always it is changing, yet always it is beautiful.

Early and late in the day the sunlight falls aslant upon the range, throwing its features into strong relief by high lights and shadows. Then it is that the tremendous depth of the chasms is most apparent, as are also the faceted character of the summits and the finer sculptural details everywhere graven in their faces. Then also the range is most awe-inspiring, and yet at the same time it has a mystical, entrancing beauty.

There is no jutting crag or promontory that does not at some hour catch the sun, and at others withdraw into the shadow. The shadows are never harsh blacks. They assume pastel shades of blue and purple that run through every conceivable tone, each of which deepens when seen through an opening in the green forest, an optical phenomenon that almost everyone discovers for himself sooner or later.

The hours of early morning or late afternoon provide the best conditions for viewing the Tetons, and there is no better way of seeking a first acquaintance with them than to visit, at these hours, some point far enough distant to afford an unbroken panorama embracing the full sweep of the range, from Buck Mountain on the south to Eagles Rest and beyond on the north. Deadman's Bar, six miles out on the flats, is one such place often visited, and there are others with much in their favor. If time is very limited, a short stroll out into the sagebrush will suffice to open up a part of the view.

In the middle hours, the illumination, being from above, is intense and searching, and falls with too nearly equal value on all the landscape to produce strong contrasts. The shadows on the mountain walls then pale or vanish, the lighting grows severe, and the range assumes an aspect of flatness all out of keeping with its actual rugged relief.

All this the artist knows full well. He also knows that the mirrorlike morning reflections on the lakes are not for the late riser, for as soon as air currents begin to move up the canyons ripples disturb the placid surface of the water. In some respects, it is the artist who acquires the clearest understanding of the mountains, for he cannot successfully paint them without first having studied them attentively to learn their varying moods. He who is astir with the mountaineer before sunrise, and who a few hours later returns with a canvas that his critic may yawningly dismiss as "overdone" because, having never seen a mountain dawn, he cannot believe that such color effects exist. But whatever the artist's objective or schedule, his paint-box is usually put away from ten in the morning until three in the afternoon, the interval during which colors, shadows, clouds, and reflections are likely to be least impressive.

Late in the afternoon as the sun sinks behind the Teton Range a great shadow moves eastward across the floor of Jackson Hole. Probably few of the thousands who pass through the valley, or even those who spend their lives there, give thought to this daily phenomenon other than to note, perhaps, how the rampart range to the west shortens the length of day in the valley; yet in the perspective that one may gain from the Teton heights the afternoon shadow is a marvelous thing to see, reproducing as it does in silhouette the profile of the range. Unseen, this spectacle has been reenacted daily through the ages; even now few witness it because it takes place at an hour when most hikers and climbers are well on their homeward trek, and already have descended too low. Also, in its swift and soundless course across the valley it may pass unnoticed, for we can be unbelievably oblivious to Nature's offerings, failing to observe unusual cloud displays, celestial phenomena, and the aurora largely because we have the world too much with us even when in the wilderness. Someday the Teton shadow range will become celebrated, and then many will gladly climb the heights to see it, as now they seek them for the sunrise.

I first saw this spectacle in 1929 from near Ramshead Lake, after a late descent from Symmetry Spire. Chancing to glance downward, my attention was riveted by the scene on the valley floor. The shadow peaks of Rockchuck, St. John, and Symmetry Spire were already formed; and from a point a little lower and less obstructed those of Teewinot, the Grand Teton, and Nez Perce came into view (the shadows of Mount Owen and the South Teton merging with those of their forepeaks). At first low and blunt, the shadow peaks lengthened until each had attained its proper relative height, and the full profile was recognizable as that of the familiar Teton skyline. Only for a moment was this so; to have held this picture one would, like Joshua, have had to bid the sun stand still. With increasing distortion and accelerated speed as they were cast more and more obliquely, the shadow peaks pushed onward, crossed the Snake, and, grown to narrow, needle-sharp points, grotesque exaggerations even of peaks as slender as these, raced across the final stretch of Antelope Flats to the far edge of the sagebrush. The Grand Teton shadow was the first to reach it. With all the valley in shade, the peak shadows could still be seen mounting the wooded slopes beyond, but at last these, too, were all obscured, and the phantom range was gone.

Travel to the Tetons is largely confined to the summer season, which at best is brief. In the spring, swift storms continue to whiten the peaks, along the base of which lie persistent snowdrifts that mark the avalanches of the past winter. But on by one the passes are opened, until, by June, from the four points of the compass visitors stream over the mountains into Jackson Hole. The busy weeks of summer which follow are few and fleeting and, while they last, filled with a beauty so enchanting that time passes unheeded and one is never prepared for the brooding gray days of late August. Then more frequent storms again bring fresh snow to the summits as a prelude to Indian summer, sunset of the year, when one hears in the distance the bugling of the elk, and on the mountainsides sees the aspens turn to gold.

A dweller of the city or lowlands, finding his way to the Tetons at any of these seasons, will discover that here earth and sky meet on terms of undreamed intimacy. Here summits rise aloft to form steps whereby he can literally no less than imaginatively ascend to the very clouds. And here

Geologist and writer Fritiof Fryxell made many first ascents in the
Teton mountain range. A professor at Augustana College in Illinois,
he worked as a climbing ranger every summer, giving campfire talks,
advising climbers, and sometimes leading rescue parties. Collection
of the Jackson Hole Historical Society and Museum, 1958.0138.001.

clouds in their turn ofttimes descend to earth, there to re-new association
with glaciers and with lakes.

Impressive beyond any telling are those mornings when one awakens
to find that in the night clouds have taken possession of the range. Daylight
reveals them, poised over the cirques, wreathed about the peaks, or draped
in festoons between them, settling into the canyons and trailing slowly
along the mountain front. There are days when clouds sink even to the
level of Jackson Hole, and with cool, moist fingers touch the tips of the firs,
or come to rest over the sill lakes. For all that may be seen now, the nearest
mountains might be a thousand miles away. Sooner or later the gray curtain
rises, and there come into view all up and down the range the gleaming

white cascades and waterfalls, each revived and refreshed from the rain that has fallen above.

Many of the summer storms come in the afternoon. As I have seen them year after year from camps on Jenny Lake, these are brief and dramatic.

Though perhaps foretold several hours by clouds gathering in the range, such a storm almost always breaks with startling suddenness. An arresting sound comes from the west shore, that of the wind bursting from the mouth of Cascade Canyon and encountering the heavy forest. Simultaneously a white line appears on the lake, which advances swiftly. By their agitation the on the shore also mark the progress of the storm front. The sound of a gale in the pines is always impressive, and at times alarming. It is sustained like the held notes of cellos in an orchestra, but as the storm approaches there is a crescendo such as no baton ever summoned. Now it sounds in the trees overhead, all about.

The lodgepole pines give proof of their marvelous elasticity. It is remarkable that all are not snapped or uprooted, considering the violence with which they sway and toss. An occasional report does tell of a breaking stem, accounting for broken snags and windfalls throughout the forest—the toll of past storms.

The lake is rising, its surface flecked with white. The first gusts tear the wave crests into sheets of spray. With good reason rowers are cautioned to stay near shore when a storm is imminent, for with wind coming from the canyon like this is a boat in the open might be caught in desperate plight.

Usually rain does not set in at once. One can stand by the shore for several minutes as onlooker of the pageant in which all Nature takes part. Gradually the agitation of trees and waves becomes more subdued, and when the first big drops strike the water the whitecaps may all have disappeared. From high in the range thunder speaks for the first time, quickly the mountains vanish behind a veil of rain, and the pines straighten, holding out their arms to the rain which now descends in generous measure.

We had come to believe that the wind brought destruction only to the trees that were poorly rooted or otherwise weakened. Then on the stormy night of September 22, 1933, came a blast from Cascade Canyon that swept across the lake and through the forests beyond, felling almost every tree within a quarter-mile strip across the moraine and devastating much of the

Jenny Lake campground. Thousands of trees were uprooted or broken, all thrown eastward away from the canyon. Fortunately, no one had remained in the camp so late in the season. One large pine fell across and demolished the tent which I, with my wife and little son, had vacated not many days before. The wreckage of the storm was eventually removed, but the forest clearings remain to record a weather caprice such as has occurred but rarely, if one may judge from the continuity of the forests elsewhere.

A summer of periodic rains is one of few forest fires and, therefore, of freedom from worry on the part of the rangers responsible for the protection of the forests. But occasionally come times of drouth that cause great anxiety, necessitating ceaseless watchfulness and special fire patrols. Each new cloudless day heightens the tension, and as week after week the mountain slopes grow drier and the trails more dusty the menace of fire becomes of grave concern to all.

At such times a thunderstorm may relieve the situation, at least locally, by bringing drenching showers; but if there is little rain the storm may paradoxically make the situation even more critical by leaving in its wake a scattering of fires set by lightning. These, however difficult to reach, must be extinguished at once. So effective is the protection afforded by the ranger staff that no fire within the park has yet gotten out of control, or even assumed serious proportions.

Snow is possible in any month. As a rule, the cloud formations that bring it are larger and more formless than others, and linger over the range in a curiously caressing manner.

The snow of summer or early fall comes with a delicate beauty of its own. Perhaps the peaks have long been nearly bare, when one night rain comes to the valley. Because they are mantled with clouds, one knows not the fate of the peaks until at sunrise the mists begin to disperse. Then here and there through cloud rifts are revealed the summits; and behold, they are covered with new snow. It lies on ledges and along the couloirs, emphasizing unsuspected lines in the faces of the most familiar peaks. So white is it that by comparison the shining clouds seem gray. The revelation is brief, for the sun of the new day drives away the clouds, and within them the snow also takes flight. But the scene is imperishably engraved in memory.

Clouds—creatures of sky, to be sure; yet they are thoroughly at home here among the mountains, enjoying close fellowship with peaks and canyons. Large is their contribution to the landscape, adding life and movement to scenes otherwise in eternal repose. When they are absent, the mountains seem austere and bare, and in periods of prolonged drouth one feels vague uneasiness and expectancy. On their return, how unfailing is one's response to their beauty, how eagerly all their movements and changes of form are again followed.

So, for the Teton visitor, clouds and their ways become subjects of absorbing interest.

In the lowlands clouds seem more remote than in reality they are, there being no means of estimating their height. But in the Tetons the range serves as a scale, conveniently graduated as it is with lakes, glaciers, and summits of known elevation.

It is a July day and, high above, a thousand silvery cumuli are silently afloat, casting blue shadows on the slopes and valleys below. As they drift slowly along, they clear the highest of the peaks, evidence enough that they must be well over 7,500 feet above our station on the valley floor. But on another day such clouds, possibly larger and darker, less regular of form, are sufficiently low to graze the Grand Teton. They are, then, about 7,000 feet above us and nearly 14,000 feet above the level of the sea. Eventually, as they mass more heavily, they obscure the Three Tetons and Mount Owen, just touching the summit pinnacle of Teewinot. Now they are about 1,500 feet lower than when first observed.

The range not only intercepts the passing clouds; it actually gives birth to many. These are the most fascinating of all. Their forms are legion, and many of their ways devious past finding out, yet one can, with observation, learn much concerning their place and manner of formation.

One type seems fairly obvious. The glaciers and snow fields chill the overlying air so that at times its moisture condenses. On frosty mornings little cloud caps so formed may often be seen, for instance, over Falling Ice Glacier and the east-face snow fields of Teewinot, this despite the general absence of clouds elsewhere. Such clouds are ordinarily short-lived, but if the air is still, they may persist for hours.

Other clouds are probably produced by the air currents that encounter the range. Forced sharply upward, these expand and cool. Condensation may occur at various altitudes, depending upon the prevailing conditions of temperature and humidity. When it takes place at low elevations, great cloud banks roll up along the range, and at times bot it from view; when higher, more scattered clouds from here and there among the peaks. As the currents flow along lines predetermined by the contours of the range, they tend to produce clouds at points where they must rise over divides and peaks. Some clouds are best explained in terms of convection, or by the mixing of air from currents of difference humidity and temperature.

It is not uncommon to find clouds forming at the very mountaintops. These may linger where formed, may drift some distance away before vanishing, or may be launched in a train miles long, reaching clear across and beyond Jackson Hole.

Teewinot, it has seemed to me, produces the most varied and unusual of clouds. Of many memorable displays, I recall one with special vividness. Late one August afternoon it alone of all the peaks in sight started to form a summit cloud, a solitary formation that grew with extraordinary rapidity, both outward and upward, until in less than half an hour it had become a towering edifice with rounded, glistening white contours, wonderfully smooth and substantial looking. A structure so grandiose could not stand long, and, as I watched, it sank about the summit into shapeless ruins. There was still no other cloud in the range.

Very different was the situation on another August day, suggested in the following note made at the time: "A scene today such as I have not previously observed. At noon when I passed Timbered Island a little cloud cap was hanging over each of the major peaks all the way from Buck Mountain to Eagles Rest. East of the valley were two more, over Jackson Peak and Sheep Mountain. But they were all increasing in size, and an hour or two later, when I again passed this way, nearly all had merged."

Such scenes cannot lose their interest though watched year after year, and references to them crowd my summer journals. To quote a few from one month:

"July 4. Awoke to an overcast sky. Air cool and misty. For several hours this morning the thunder rumbled solemnly over the range (without, however, any distinct peals) as though the peaks were conversing. If peaks could speak, such, I fancy, would be their voices."

"July 11. Storms and sunshine have alternated about the high peaks both yesterday and today with a swiftness almost bewildering."

"July 21. All day clouds have been streaming about among the crags of the near-by peaks, especially St. John, and our handful of visitors have been watching them from the ranger cabin. They have said little, and spoken only in hushed tones of the changing scenes up above, feeling well repaid, I am sure, for the rain and muddy roads they braved to get here. At evening the clouds miraculously dissolved and the summits emerged, fresh and radiant in the sunset."

As was true on that particular July evening, during the hour of sunset the range almost always joins with the heavens in declaring the glory of God, and frequently it happens that of the two the mountains show forth the greater splendor.

For at this time the lofty, richly sculptured north walls of the ridges and peaks one by one emerge from their shadows, even as the other slopes sink into obscurity. Receiving full on their faces the light from the northwest, they take fire, till every crag and pinnacle shines with the brilliance of burnished gold. When the sun passes beneath the horizon this direct illumination is cut off, and now the great precipices assume various colors, crimson, lavender, or rose, whose tones and intensities vary with those in the evening sky from which they are reflected. Slowly, reluctantly, these colors fade from the mountains as they fade from the heavens, but they linger long into the dusk on the very summits on Nez Perce, Teewinot, and others of the high peaks.

Late in the evening, should one stroll down to the lake for a final view of the range, the peak faces might be found still touched with a pale light, as if giving back the last of a few hours earlier, is silvery and unfading, for it is a light that is shed from the stars. Through the long hours of night, it continues, unless extinguished by clouds or, at moonrise, merged in a sudden greater brightness.

Moonlight in its fullest flood brings a spectacle of beauty causing one to abandon every thought of rest, and, heedless of the hour, to set forth anew, as though it were the dawn of day and not its close. For again the features of the range are lighted, but gone now is every trace of austerity, the severeness that by day may frighten or appall. This nocturnal outpouring of light, as revealing almost as day, is infinitely soft and tender, and is deeply fraught with mystery.

No denying fancy now its sway. Are not the peaks grown taller, of nobler stature even than before? Motionless, yet they are alive, these spectral figures, this night met in voiceless conclave for deliberations man may neither share nor comprehend. No matter; enough to be abroad at such a time. And as one starts forth in the night it is with bated breath and cautious step, least any sound escape and break the reverent silence.

26

THE SONG OF THE WHITE PELICAN (1996)

JACK TURNER (1942–)

Jack Turner grew up on the coast of southern California and attended the University of Colorado, Stanford University, and Cornell University, where he earned a PhD in philosophy. For a time, he taught at the University of Illinois at Urbana-Champaign. But classroom teaching did not suit him, and the Illinois countryside was far too flat for his taste. He left for the mountains and wilderness, leading treks to Pakistan, Nepal, Peru, and even Bhutan, relishing in the landscapes but also the people. In time, he always returned to "the mountains I love most,"—the Tetons.

Jack lives at the base of the Tetons, where he thinks, reads, and writes. From his pen have come such outstanding works as Teewinot: A Year in the Teton Range *and* Travels in the Greater Yellowstone. *What follows, however, is a selection from* The Abstract Wild, *entitled "The Song of the White Pelican." Soaring birds (eagle, hawk, osprey) are always a fascination in the park, but here Turner tells the intriguing story of the white pelican, their soaring ability, and his captivation and speculation about them.*

I am lounging on the summit of the Grand Teton surrounded by blocks of quartz and a cobalt sky. It is mid-morning in July—warm, still, and so clear the distant ranges seem etched into the horizon. To the east, the Absaroka, Gros Ventre, and Wind River; to the south, the Salt, Snake, and Caribou; to the west the Big Hole and the Lost River; and to the north, the Centennial, Madison, Gallatin, and Beartooth. Directly north, and closer, is the still-snowy summit of the Pitchstone Plateau, and beyond it the fuzzy blur of a geyser somewhere near Old Faithful. To the northeast are slices of Yellowstone Lake.

Despite the breadth of view I always feel this summit is a place of great simplicity. I have just climbed the Exum, or south, ridge of the Grand Teton with clients. They are taking photographs. Since I have climbed the Grand for thirty years, I have my pictures, and since I am fifteen years older than my oldest client, I am tired. So I rest and enjoy the clarity and count shades of blue as the sky pales into the mountains. Then I hear a faint noise above me, and my heart says, "Pelicans."

The sounds are faint, so faint they are sometimes lost—a trace of clacking in the sky. It is even harder to see them. Tiny glints, like slivers of ice, are occasionally visible, then invisible, then visible again as the sheen of their feathers strikes just the right angle to the sun. With binoculars we see them clearly: seventeen white pelicans soaring in a tight circle. I have seen them here before, as well as from the summit of Symmetry Spire and from the long ridge of Rendezvous Peak. But it is rare—in part, I think, because the conditions for hearing and seeing them are so rare. Perhaps they are often above us, but with the wind and clouds and the ever-present anxiety of climbing, we fail to notice them.

The white pelican (*Pelecanus erythrorhynchos*), one of seven species in the world, is a large bird often weighing twenty pounds, with some individuals reaching thirty pounds. The only other pelican in North America, the brown pelican (*Pelecanus occidentalis*), is smaller and restricted to the coasts. The white pelican's wingspan is smaller and restricted to the coasts. The white pelican's wingspan reaches nine and a half feet, equal to the California condor's. Of North American birds, only the trumpeter swan is consistently larger.

Though huge, a pelican, like all birds, consists mostly of feathers, flesh, and air. The beak, skull, feet, and bones of a twenty-five-pound pelican weight but twenty-three ounces. Its plumage is brilliant white except for the black primaries and outer secondaries, and pale yellow plumes on the crown of the head during breeding season. Occasionally there is pale yellow on the chest. Their eyes are the color of fine slate.

The summit of the Grand Teton is 13,770 feet high, and the pelicans above us are at the limit of unaided human vision. Since in good light a flock of white pelicans is easily visible at a mile, these pelicans are at least a mile above us, or higher than 19,000 feet. This seems high for any bird, but geese have been photographed at 29,000 feet, and I have watched flocks of Brahminy ducks from Siberia cross the ridge between Everest and Cho Oyu, which is 19,500 feet at its low point. So although 19,000 feet is impressive, and no one knows how high pelicans can or do fly, the more interesting question is this: What are they *doing* up there? Soaring. Clacking. Yes, but why? I don't think anybody knows, and this mystery, along with the inevitable speculations, are a large part of why I find them so appealing.

For years I asked biologists and birders about pelican sounds, and they are unanimous: they have never heard a pelican make a sound. The popular bird books do not mention pelican sounds, and most of the technical literature reports that pelicans are mute except when breeding. Then the authors go on to admit they have spent little time around breeding pelicans. There are, of course, good reasons for this. The white pelican so dislikes human presence during breeding seasons that if approached, they will abandon their nests and raft on nearby water. The eggs, or chicks, are then exposed to the sun, to cold, and to the depredations of the ever-present gulls. An hour, or less, is sufficient to wipe out the breeding colony. If repeatedly harassed, white pelicans will abandon a rookery forever. For these reasons, monitoring the white pelican population is usually done from airplanes, increasingly with aerial photography. In one sense this is commendable, but in another it is sad, for fewer and fewer people know less and less about pelicans. The hard data are known—the average length of the bill, the average time of arrival and departure during migration, the average number of eggs—and no doubt will increase, but our understanding of pelicans, a way of knowing that requires intimacy, is nil.

We could, of course, let pelicans comes to us. This is the difference between seeking and stalking and just sitting and waiting. It is an old difference, as old as hunting, but a difference that is hard for us to choose because we are, as a nation and as a civilization, a people of seeking and stalking, though exactly why this is so remains fugitive.

I used to visit an old Sherpa in Khumbu who had served on perhaps fifty Himalayan expeditions. His name was Dawa Tensing and he lived in a village just north of Thyanboche Monastery on the trail to Everest. He was famous for saying, "So many people coming, coming, always looking, never finding, always coming back again. Why?" Once, in all sincerity, he asked me: "Is America beautiful? Why you always come back here?"

It took a long time for Dawa's "Why?" to sink into my thick skull, and it took even longer to prefer his question to the closure of an answer. I suspect now that if we wish to know pelicans intimately, we must begin with a preference for questions and a preference for sitting and waiting. Perhaps it would be better if ornithologists were to become glider pilots, mountaineers, and fishermen, flying in the thermals, lounging atop great peaks, fishing great rivers, and waiting for pelicans to come to them....

Dōgen's famous lines in the *Genjo Koan* are always suggestive, even when removed from their spiritual context:

> That the self advances and confirms the ten thousand things is
> called delusion;
> That the ten thousand things advance and confirm the self is
> enlightenment.

The Japanese word here translated as "enlightenment" can also be translated as "intimacy." Perhaps it is time to realize that the knowledge won from hard data is limited; perhaps it is time to allow wild animals to establish the degree of intimacy between us. No radio collars, no netting, no banding, no intrusion into their lives. We wait; they decide.

A few people have spent time sitting with pelicans. In 1962 George Schaller spent 367 hours sitting in a canoe watching pelicans breed. He heard lots of sounds. Other researchers have noted that pelicans hiss when angry, snap their mandibles together as a warning, and while mating make sounds that have been variously described as piglike or low-toned grunts, subdued croaking, a deep-voiced, murmuring groan, and grunting quacks. Audubon said they made a sound like blowing through the bunghole of a cask.

Although pelicans do make sounds, they are, relative to other birds, quite silent. There may be phylogenetic reasons for this. The newer species of birds are the most vocal and produce the greatest variety of sounds, while pelicans are very old—they've been around thirty-five to forty million years. We have one fossil record from the Pliocene, and we know they have been in the American West since the Pleistocene. Ornithologists have discovered prehistoric nesting sites on mountains that were once islands rising from the Pleistocene lakes that covered much of the Great Basin.

The silence of pelicans, along with their great age, contributes to their dignity. And this is no doubt augmented by the fact that the pelican is not a popular bird. The Hamilton stores in Yellowstone offer no pelican postcards or posters or stuffed pelicans or pelican candles or pelican-shaped coffee mugs—the kind of merchandise that nibbles at the dignity of other animals....

Of all places available to pelicans, mountains provide the most opportunities for soaring. Where the prevailing wind meets a mountain, it flows over it like water over a boulder in a rapid. Just as beyond the boulder is a hole followed by smaller standing waves, so there are standing "wave trains" of air currents beyond the mountain, and pelicans can soar up each one. Since our prevailing summer wind is from the southwest, the wave trains behind the Grand Teton point straight toward the Molly Islands.

Pelicans can also soar in thermals. As the ground warms, patches of warmer air rise, puff out at the top, peel off, and are suck back into the vortex that keeps rising again and again through the center of the thermal. The stronger the rise, the stronger the thermal, and the tighter the circle a soaring bird can cut. The Teton range has strong thermals, and the pelicans above the Grand Teton always soar in tight circles, carving into the wind for lift, then dropping around for the tailwind, then farther around and into the wind again for more lift. Thermals tend to stack up in a long "thermal street" and drift downwind, allowing a pelican to climb in one thermal, cut out and glide to the next, climb again, cut out again—all with virtually no expenditure of energy. In the summer, the Grand Teton's thermals stack up in a line heading toward the Molly Islands.

Pelicans also soar in thunderheads, which suck cold air down from the upper atmosphere. When it hits the ground, it spreads out, displacing warmer air which, in turn, goes upward, creating more good soaring places. The Grand Teton has some of the most dazzling thunderstorms of any place on the planet, with lightning to match. During the most intense period of one recent storm, lightning struck every two minutes, and the storm lasted sixteen hours. Pelicans often wander the edges of great storms and I envy them this freedom, even with its risks. In one account, thirty-three pelicans were knocked out of the air by lightning in Nebraska. In a storm in Utah, twenty-seven were killed. The same thing must happen over the Tetons.

Ten years ago my guided party was hit four times by ground currents while descending the Grand Teton. We watched green bolts of lightning ricochet through glaciers like bullets. Yet I still climb mountains, and pelicans still soar in thunderheads. After thirty-five million years, they must know about lightning and its risks, just as mountaineers do, but it no more changes their behavior than it changes ours.

So there are many good reasons for the pelicans to above the Grand Teton, but exactly why remains a mystery. The pelicans we see there in July are not migrating. Yellowstone pelicans winter in Mexico and the Sea of Cortéz. Then in late March or early April they fly to the Great Salt Lake. In late April or early May they fly to the Molly Islands. Perhaps the pelicans over the Grand Teton in July are returning from a foraging mission. Perhaps they are nonbreeding adults on a lark. Perhaps someone will put a radio collar on one and find out, though I hope not. Whatever science would discover is not worth the intrusion into their wild lives. What interests me is not that pelicans can soar, that soaring is useful, or that they soar here. What interests me is the question of whether pelicans love to soar.

The pelican's love of soaring is only hinted at in ornithological literature, but it is there. In his *Handbook of North American Birds*, volume one, Ralf Palmer uses the word "indulge" in the cryptic grammar of scientific description. He says the pelicans "often indulge in high-soaring flights" and that "while soaring in stormy weather [they] may indulge in aerial acrobatics with much swooping and diving" (270). This is not exactly the language of mechanistic science. Does this mean that pelicans are, sometimes at least, soaring for pleasure? Do they play in thunderheads for fun? Do they fly in thunderheads knowing full well the danger? Do they experience ecstasy while soaring so indulgently? What could it mean to attribute these emotions to a bird?

Consider Doug Peacock's film footage of the grizzly he named Happy Bear. In the spring, when the streams are still frozen, Happy Bear likes to sit on his butt in small meadow streams and break off chunks of ice, bite them, push them underwater with his huge paws, then bite them again when they pop up. He does this a lot. I don't think we can say why Happy Bear is doing this without using analogies and metaphors from human emotional life.

Or consider the gulls in Guy Murchie's *Song of the Sky*:

Many a time I have seen sea gulls at the big Travis Air Base near San Francisco flapping nonchalantly among the huge ten-engined B-36 bombers while their motors were being run up. The smoke whipping from the jets in four straight lines past the tail accompanied by that soul-shaking roar would have been enough to stampede a herd of elephants but the sea gulls often flew right into the tornado just for fun. When the full blast struck them they would simply disappear, only to turn up a few seconds later a quarter mile downwind, apparently having enjoyed the experience as much as a boy running through a hose—even coming around eager-eyed for more.

Simply disappear. Like paddling a kayak into Lava Falls.

It is not popular now to attribute human characteristics and processes to wild animals, since it projects onto the Other our biases and perceptions and limits our view of their difference. But all description is merely analogy and metaphor, and as such is forever imperfect and respectful of mystery. We are more ignorant and limited than we can conceive. Even scientific descriptions and theories are contingent and subject to revision. We do not understand even our dog cat, not to mention a vole. Even our knowledge of those we know best—our lovers and friends—is fragile and often mistaken. Our knowledge of strangers in our own culture is even more fragile, and it seems that despite our volumes of social science, we have no understanding of native peoples. Language may probe the mystery of the Other, but the Other remains a mystery.

We also fail to appreciate that many of our descriptions and explanations of human behavior are appropriations from wild animals: the lion-hearted hero, the wolfish cad, the foxy lady. And this suggests that life is a spectrum where unity is more pervasive than difference—a rudimentary truth for the Apache and the Bushman, but a truth ignored by our epistemologies.

It is no more odd to say that pelicans love to soar and do so in *ecstasy* than it is to say what we so commonly say of human love and ecstasy:

that our heart soars. Or, to take another example, to describe meditation as Dōgen does in the *Mountains and Rivers Sutra*: "Because mountains are high and broad, the way of riding the clouds is always reached in the mountains; the inconceivable power of soaring in the wind comes freely from the mountains."

Some people fear that extending a human vocabulary to wild animals erodes their Otherness. But with is *not Other*? Are we not all, from one perspective, Other to each and every being in the universe? And at the same time, and from another perspective, do we not all share an elemental wildness that burns forth in each life?

When I see white pelicans riding mountain thermals, I feel their exaltation, their love of open sky and big clouds.... I believe the reasons they are soaring over the Grand Teton are not so different from the reasons we climb mountains, sail gliders into great storms, and stand in rivers with tiny pieces of feathers from a French duck's butt attached to a barbless hook at the end of sixty feet of a sixty-dollar string thrown by a thousand-dollar wand. Indeed, in love and ecstasy we are closest to the Other, for passion is at the root of all life and shared by all life. In passion, all beings are at their wildest; in passion, we—like pelicans—make strange noises that defy scientific explanation.

If pelicans are soaring above the Grand Teton in ecstasy, how should we describe their clacking? I can find only one reference in our immense literature on birds to the clacking that pelicans make at high altitude. In his *Life Histories of North American Petrels and Pelicans and Their Allies*, Arthur Cleveland Bent quotes Dr. P. L. Hatch as saying, "This immense bird usually signals his arrival in the early part of April by his characteristic notes from an elevation beyond the range of vision except under the most favorable circumstances. The sound of those notes is difficult to describe, but unforgettable when once certainly heard from their aerial heights" (291). Why do they utter that unforgettable sound only when they are so far up in the sky—at the limit of our vision? Olaus Murie once said of the coyote's howl that "if the coyote could reflect and speak he would say this is his song, simply that." Simply that: the song of coyote. All things have their song, and few questions about songs have answers.

I believe the clacking in the sky over the Grand Teton is the song of the white pelican. I believe they sing their song in ecstasy, from joy in an experience unique to their perfections. I know climbers who whistle, sing, and yodel when they are up in the sky. William Blake died singing to the angels he knew were leading him to heaven. Some sing, some whistle, some yip, some clack in the sky, some make love to a violin. Why saw at strings of gut stretched over holes in burnished wood? Why sing cantatas and masses and chorales?

All life contains its anguish, even a trout-eating pelican's life—the Buddha's first noble truth. But all life must occasionally experience a release. In passion and ecstasy, all life lets go—of what?

27

AT THE HEIGHT (1993)

PETE SINCLAIR (1935–2015)

No one need be told of the centrality of the Teton Mountains to the park. Without the mountains there would be no Grand Teton National Park and many residents would live elsewhere. Of course, the valley—featuring the free-flowing crystalline water of the Snake River—would be an attraction, but only a secondary one. The Tetons, with their verticality and absence of foothills, transform one's thinking. One reaction among vigorous visitors is to want to climb the Grand Teton. Many have.

We Aspired (1993), from which this passage is taken, is the account of Pete Sinclair's experience as ranger-in-charge of mountain rescue in Grand Teton National Park from 1959 to 1970. His was not a boring job! In the summer numerous park visitors decide to take on the mountains when they shouldn't. These ill-prepared climbers become the responsibility of skilled mountaineers called the Jenny Lake Rangers. In his book, Sinclair writes of his many climbing adventures and rescues. The most harrowing was the 1967 rescue of an injured climber on the North Face. "At The Height" tells the dramatic story, for which the six NPS climbing rangers received the U.S. Department of Interior Valor Award.

Rocks started booming down. The litterman tried to secure, or knock off, as many rocks as he could before he got below them. Inevitably he missed some, and the "running cable" sent them after him. We were lowering the Stokes litter in a horizontal position, both because of the nature of Gay's injury, and because that way he could only look up. When you're helpless, there's something to the warning not to look down. That meant that he lay face up to the rocks. The litterman tried to shelter him with his body, which more reassuring than effective. It's amazing that he did not take a serious hit. Still, the lowering to the First Ledge wasn't too bad.

Leigh, knowing well why I had asked him to stay on, had proceeded directly to the First Ledge to search out a way off the mountain. Every climber knows that Leigh Ortenburger was the author of *A Climber's Guide to the Teton Range* and assumes correctly that he was a very experienced climber. Many climbers know also that his guide established a new standard of accuracy and thoroughness. What perhaps only I knew was how reassuring such a historical perspective can be in a situation like the one we were in. There were possibly a hundred climbers in the country who were technically better than Leigh but not one I would have rather had there. We didn't know yet what we had to do on that mountain, but we had with us the one man in the world who knew exactly everything that had been done on that mountain.

I regarded Rick as my persona reservoir of strength. From him came the energy to overcome inertia. His mind, his muscles, and his wit were constantly at work.

Ralph was the spirit of sacrifice, quietly doing the unwanted work as if feeling privilege to be there.

I puttered about, muttering to myself or to anyone who would listen to me.

Once on the First Ledge, forward motion mired down in indecision. Even the morphine couldn't keep Gay happy as we talked first this way and then that. Leigh had scouted out the possibility of reaching the Grandstand with 600 feet of cable. That is, we could drop straight off the Ledge to the north. I could estimate a 120-foot rappel within a margin of 10 percent. I had no confidence in judging twice that distance, and I could not contemplate looking down five times that and having any notion at all about what I was looking at. Usually I knew how far up I was because I knew how many leads had been made. I had a lot of practice judging distance looking up. Even on a tall building where the surface is uniform, looking up feels very different from looking down. On a mountain, the two perspectives are totally foreign to each other. A 10 percent error in 600 feet is a five-story building. I was prepared to believe that Leigh's estimate was very close, but we couldn't see any ledges below us on the alleged 600-foot wall. The litter would be down there, and we wouldn't be able to rappel down to it. Even if Leigh was right, the advantages of a single 600-foot lowering appeared to be outweighed by the disadvantages.

The advantages were three. One, we'd only have to set up one really solid anchor. With the time that would save, we could set up an anchor that could hold the entire rescue team and gear if need be. Two, the wall was vertical to overhanging, meaning there would be little bumping, dragging, grunting, and sweating and fewer rocks pulled down. Three, it was an elegant solution. Just cast off and drift down the mountain in the invisible gravitational current, like a spider descending from the ceiling.

The principle disadvantages were that after lowering the litter, the six remaining at the top would have to descend the North Face route, following the First Ledge down to its lower end and then descending fairly straightforward but rotten rock a thousand feet or so to the glacier. Then they would have to climb back up the Grandstand a thousand feet to the litter and take it back down. Second, the litter would have to be lowered unbelayed. The rockfall would be less, but the ones that came would be coming from a long way up. However strong the cable, stretched taut over the lip of an overhang and taking a direct hit? Or if it didn't reach and they had to dangle there for six or eight hours? I remarked to Leigh, "The man who went down that six hundred feet wondering if it would reach, listening to rocks sail by him, might never get entirely back to us." He agreed that this was a possibility. We dropped rocks off and counted the seconds. Some said six seconds, some said eight, an uncertainty of two hundred feet. We were also uncertain about what would happen when we came to the end of the first reel and had to join the second three hundred feet of cable to it. Most of all, I, at least, did not want to split the party. The regular route it was to be.

We stuck to that plan for one hundred feet down the First Ledge. Then Leigh made the first move in what has become one of the legendary feats of American mountaineering. He had gone down the ledge, looked over the edge, and announced in a tone of undeniable authority that, one, we could get to the Grandstand in two 300-foot lowerings and, two, the rest of us could follow the litter because there was, in addition to the ledge

300 feet below us, a smaller intermediate ledge exactly halfway down the first 300-foot pitch. It was inadequate for the litter, but adequate for the rest of us. This meant that we could tie our 150-foot ropes together, hang them double down to the intermediate ledge, rappel 150 feet to that ledge, retrieve our rope by pulling on one strand, and repeat the process to join the litter at the 300-foot level. If there was no comparable ledge in the lower 300-foot segment, we could use the two 150-foot lengths as one fixed and irretrievable 300-foot strand. We would have to abandon them and somehow get off the Grandstand with two 120-foot ropes (we'd had to cut the third one for slings), but the problems on the Grandstand were more manageable. Suddenly, Leigh's view seemed reasonable.

The debate this time was shorter. These discussions, I now realize, were as much acclimatization time as they were times of rational deliberation. We needed to accustom ourselves to the scope of the thing. A kind of pressure had been building in me since dawn. It took a long time to get across the traverse, and the traverse had to be counted as not even part of the problem but blessedly easy access to the accident site. I began the day with a feeling akin to being late for an appointment. The constant reviewing of the options had made me uncertain about decisions already made. No decision had been self-evident. Furthermore, the whole world seemed to be tuned in. Radio communication in the park had been shut down so that the channels were for our use. We knew that everyone we knew who could get near a radio, including our families, was keeping track of us. We were asked many times for estimates of our progress, information needed in order to coordinate our support below, should we ever reach lower slopes, and my estimates had been consistently too optimistic. I even found time to worry about my upcoming doctoral examinations. I hadn't covered half the material I had planned to that summer. The Climber's Camp had been closed, and an era was ending for climbers in America and for me in the Tetons. Relations with my superiors were not good. Things weren't so good in the country in 1967 either. My big tests were coming all at once; the values and efforts of a lifetime were being tested, and I felt unprepared.

Certain worries I could, and did, enumerate to anyone who would listen. It seemed to help them to have me complain. Emerson discovered on the Everest expedition that if A expresses doubt, B expresses confidence.

I didn't want to face the fact that we were going to have another bivouac. I didn't like being out of food or worrying about the other party, which had climbed up to us and had started the descent back down the regular route. I found their shouts of joy, when they arrived safely on the glacier, obnoxious. Irvine and I had enjoyed grumbling to each other for years. Now he was being excessively chipper. Sleeping bags had been flown up to the base of the glacier on the strength of one of my optimistic predictions. A team had assembled there ready to bring them up to us, but we weren't going to get anywhere within reach. Most of all, I didn't like the sound rocks made as they came by with a slicing whir or hit with a crack. I didn't like where I was, what I had done, or what I had yet to do. But Leigh's solution was a thing of beauty, and we'd do it.

Now we truly were racing against the descending sun, trying to get down before it did. Leigh tested his claim, that the unknown distances were known to him, by rappelling into the unknown in search of the two ledges. He went on and on. We were fishing for a ledge with him as bait. He radioed back, "I've got one!" The first three-hundred-foot lowering would work. As we got the litter down to the three-hundred-foot ledge, it appeared that we were holding our own against time, if the rest of us were fast enough in getting down as well.

I was one of the last down to the intermediate ledge. I was shocked to find that the ledge was a large detached flake with a flat top. The last man off a rappel has to go without a belay. I assigned myself that duty as a sort of punishment for having made so many bad guesses that day. I studied the flake I was on, and my curiosity was rewarded with the discovery that the flake was not part of the mountain! My hands became moist. The flake was delicately balanced, a piton driven behind it would pry it away from, and possibly off, the wall. I was not at all delicately balanced. Every time I moved, the cable reel in my pack tried to pitch me off the wall. I was sure that soon my legs would begin trembling uncontrollably, sewing machine legs, as we called it. It happens sometimes when you overload on oxygen and adrenalin. I had to stand balanced on that flake because when I leaned against the wall, I thought I could feel the flake move outward. I had to lean against the wall because soon my legs wouldn't support me and I would fall off the mountain.

My eyes wouldn't focus on one thing. The knot at my waist. It's untied! The carabineer. It's open! The piton. It's pulling! The gap behind the flake. It's wider! I wanted to check everything at once. I jerked my eyes from one to the other so fast I didn't check any of them. I started the rounds again, knot, carabineer, piton, piton crack, rope. I felt as if I was standing on grease. I couldn't see anything wrong, which made it worse. Where is it? What's going to do it?

I felt as if I were floating in my boots. My boots. They're untied! They weren't. Boots untied! Jesus Christ, what am I going to do, cut the rope and jump off? I won't have to. I'll be shaking so hard I'll shake myself off. But I'm not shaking, idiot. I wasn't. While all this was happening, nothing was happening: I'd glanced around twice and shifted my weight once. I laughed and that was it. For years, I had awaited the moment when I would not be able to will myself to do what I was afraid to do. All that while, something had happened. Over the years I had learned the right habits. Rock was rock, mass and gravity were mass and gravity, balance was balance, a knot was a knot, routine was routine. I didn't have to understand anything. All I had to do was what I'd done hundreds of times before. I had no extraordinary mental resources, just discipline born of experience and mindless habit. Aristotle said virtue is habit. It had taken me twenty-three years to learn how to rescue my brother properly.

Not that everything became suddenly peachy. I got down to the big ledge and found that the anchor that had been laboriously placed wouldn't do. It was thirty feet too far to the east. Thirty feet horizontally along the ledge here meant a vertical difference of sixty feet down on the Grandstand. The cable might reach, but the rope wouldn't, because some rope had to be used in knots and in belaying. Someone suggested that the litterman rappel off the end of his belay rope and hang from the litter for the last few feet. It was too late and we were too tired for anything as fancy as that, but I found the idea attractive. Bob quietly and firmly objected. He was right. That did not change the fact that I had never wanted anything in the world more than I wanted to get down to that Grandstand before dark. The drill bits were dull; we would lose an hour drilling new holes. I got two solid whacks on my hard hat from falling rocks just for aggravation. The new holes would have to be drilled thirty feet to the west, on what we hoped was the other side of an intervening rockfall area. I decided to be the hero. I should have been thinking, and I knew it, but I wanted to pound on the mountain for a while. I didn't pound long enough and ruined the first hole by driving in the bolt before the drill hole was deep enough. My friends were standing over on the ledge, with the valley becoming dark behind them, waiting for me to do my job, and I was just flailing away at it. Finally, I called on the reserves and asked Rick to drill the holes properly. The mountain may have gotten me on the run, but I knew it couldn't get him off balance.

Then things started to work. Rick got the anchor in. Leigh tested his theory that it was three hundred feet and not more to the Grandstand, as he had tested the upper half. He went over the edge. If he was wrong, he would have to climb back up three hundred feet. The friction of a single rope with the weight of three hundred feet creates a tremendous amount of heat. Because two ropes had to be tied together, no mechanical device, like a rappel bar, which would absorb and dissipate the heat, could be used. Leigh had permanent burn scars from that rappel. But when he stood finally on the Grandstand, the end of the rope dangled chest high. The distance was within three feet of being exactly three hundred feet, a margin of error of one percent, half that for the whole six hundred feet. As they say, not bad for government work.

Mike joined Leigh; he too was burned. The sun was well down. I offered to let someone else take the litter, but they declined. Since I'd been babbling about little else for the past two hours, they'd guessed that I badly wanted off. With that rappel to think about all night and falling rocks to keep them awake, they couldn't have expected to get much rest, but my need was greater.

I caught a glimpse of the last red as Gay in the litter and I, attached to a sling outside, went over the edge of an overhang and rotated freely four feet from the wall. The head lamp I had borrowed from Gay was almost out. Leigh's penlight, two hundred feet below, looked like a single ray of light pointed at the heavens. My sling seat cut into my legs, and I thought about circulation and retaining consciousness. I had eaten only four bites of cheese, two bites of candy, and half a C-ration can of beans that day. I was, nevertheless, happy. I was on a grand piece rock, massive, uncluttered, and overhanging for the last 260 feet.

I was proud of my skills with the litter and would like to have shown Gay how smoothly I could get him down. There was more important work to do. The litter could not be allowed to swing too far to the east, or it wouldn't reach. I had to concentrate on that. For the first time, I began to warm to Gay. Up to this point, he had contributed far too much to the discussions about the tactics of the rescue for my taste. His interest in the matter was understandable, but I'd rather that victims be spectators. There's something to be said for my position, too. The victim's judgment is not unbiased.

Dangling from the end of that tiny cable, smaller in diameter than a pencil, we were similarly in a largely passive situation. We chatted about what was happening to us and got so we could anticipate the jolts in the cable. Gay felt that he could distinguish between a jolt caused by a strand rolling off another strand on the reel and a jolt caused by the friction of the cable over the terrain, which created varying tensions in different segments of the length of the cable. He'd had a lot of time to ponder about what caused the jolts. We sounded like two sidewalk superintendents at a construction site.

We approached a bulge not far above Leigh. By hanging from my slings underneath the litter, I could reach the rock with both hands and feet. Scratching and crawling, I pulled the litter a few precious feet westward along the wall. Gay, though he was being badly bumped, reported my gains and spoke words of encouragement. Suddenly there was nothing for me to grasp, and we pendulumed sickeningly eastward, but then stopped and swung back. "It caught! Right there!" cried Gay. I struggled back into a vertical position and saw that the last three inches of a projecting rock held the cable in exactly the right position. Now we could talk to Leigh in normal voices, and I was almost ebullient. Leigh said, "M'God, Sinclair, is that dim glow your head lamp? I thought you were smoking your pipe." I had actually started to smoke my pipe during the lowering, but the stem was too long. By neglecting to bring a short-stemmed pipe, I had missed my chance to become a legend. Leigh had cleared out a place for the litter under an overhang. With the radios to carry our instructions, we swung Gay into position a few inches at a time as neatly as would a dragline operator. We propped a couple of rocks under the foot end, and with the cable for a belay, he was safe for the night, with his head and torso protected, though his legs were exposed. Thoughts of the full length of cable exposed all night to unknown and unseen quantities of rockfall gave me a second's pause. I had an image of the cable being severed near the top, its full length whipping down the face to jerk the litter out of its bed, but fretting about things like that was no longer as entertaining as it had been on the detached flake. I jammed another rock in beside the litter and let it go at that. There couldn't be any such thing as absolute safety.

Objectively speaking, we weren't in all that terrific a position. Four men were perched on a sloping, wet ledge, at the wrong end of a three-hundred-foot, overhanging, flesh-burning rappel, with the singing of falling rocks to lull them to sleep. I derived a small amount of comfort from the thought that all four, Rick, Ralph, Bob, and Ted, were Salt Lake City climbers, if not the fathers, at least the uncles of the new generation of hard men coming out of that area. They weren't all Mormons, but they were all clean-cut and uncynical. Their virtues would protect them. Mike was alone, one hundred feet below us, where he had gone to explore the route. We had been slow, but not because we didn't keep pressing. Mike had gone down alone while we were fiddling with the litter. We'd made use of every second of daylight.

I too had lowered my weary bones into better bowers. Leigh and I were on a little platform scratched into the debris in the moat between the face and a snow patch. I was at the edge of the platform. (I'm certain Leigh planned that while I was busy with the litter.) When I dozed off, my hand slipped from my lap and hung in space. I didn't like that sensation. My legs were cramped, and when I dozed, my feet slid into the snow. When they tingled with cold, I woke up and wiggled my toes to restore circulation. Rocks dropped in occasionally. One hit the snow between Leigh's foot and mine and filled the neck of my down jacket with snow.

"What's that?" I said, as if I didn't know.

"I dunno," muttered Leigh, as if he didn't either, and went immediately back to sleep. If the rocks wanted us to pay attention that night, they'd have to hit us. My dreams were of YMCA showers with steam rising from the floor, a way of accounting for the tingling in my feet.

The next day we found that the mountain hadn't done with us yet. The rappels were sloppy. Without the two long ropes, we'd lost flexibility in setting up belay positions. The fussing to set up a solid position seemed interminable, like the rappels of beginners. We were a long way down the mountain now, so there were plenty of places for the rocks to come from and plenty of time for them to achieve terminal velocity. At one point, out of sheer perversity, I calculated the amount of rock falling around us. During one lowering, two hundred pounds of rock landed within thirty feet of me. I didn't see how we could escape taking a hit. This continuous assault from above, combined with fatigue and hunger, developed in us a condition which can be called rock shock. The most dramatic instance of what we'd become like occurred after Rick made the last, difficult overhanging lowering from the Grandstand to the snow at the top of the glacier. As the helicopter, carrying Gay to the hospital, started its engine, the roar crashed down on us from off the mountain walls. Those of us who were still on the mountain instantly cowered as if overtaken by the largest and last rockfall, believing that the mountain had waited until this last moment to get us.

The last two rappels, with the taste of beer practically in our mouths, turned out to be three.

It was here that we regained a small measure of dignity. Someone suggested that we just leave the ropes on the last two rappels in order to save time.

"No need to leave ropes behind," said Leigh. He wasn't thinking of their value. They were so chewed up they'd have to be discarded anyway. It was a question of style. The mountain had thrashed us to the bones, but in our retreat we would walk, not run.

The helicopter returned and carried, in relays, to the meadow outside our cabins, knowledge in Leigh, strength in Rick, reason in Bob, foresight in Mike, selflessness in Ralph, and compassion in Ted, courage in all, my comrades, who had made this the noblest adventure of my life, and given me, finally, self-possession.

28

"THE EXUM RIDGE" AND "TWO DOGS CLIMB THE GRAND" (1998)

Glenn Exum (1911–2000)

Glenn Exum is legendary in Jackson Hole. He came to the Tetons as a young professional dance band musician but stayed a lifetime. When Charlie Craighead compiled his biography of Exum, he called it Never a Bad Word or a Twisted Rope *(1998), from which the entries here are taken. It was a perfect title, for Exum was a true gentleman and a great climber and guide. Paul Petzoldt introduced him to mountain climbing. They became fast friends, two young men committed to a sport that was rather exotic in 1930. They formed a guiding service that eventually became the Exum Mountain Guides, which still exists today.*

Glenn had many talents and one of them was storytelling.

His passion for fly-fishing and his climbing adventures in the Swiss Alps provided material, but his life and profession centered on climbing in the Teton Range.

I have selected two stories. The first is Glenn's rather serendipitous discovery of the Exum Route up the Grand. The second is a playful account of guiding seventeen boys and two Labrador retriever dogs up the Grand Teton.

The Exum Ridge

Paul had taken me up the Grand Teton the summer of 1930. I had finished high school and was going to Moscow to the University. Paul was going there too, so we continued our friendship in the winter. The next summer, in '31, we came out and I was playing in the band at Jenny Lake and working on the trail. One day Paul said, "Ex, I'm going to make a guide out of you."

214

I said, "This is rather sudden. I've never climbed except last summer with you, and I don't know anything about it."

He said, "That's all right. You have the aptitude."

"Why," I said, "I don't have any shoes."

Paul used to play center on the University of Idaho's football team, and when he invited me to go on this climb he said, "I have a pair of football cleats you can use."

The shoes were about two sizes too big, so I put on some extra socks. I didn't know any better at that time because I was young and quite agile. They were kinda like a pair of roller skates, but they must have gripped something.

Anyway, as we were going up the couloir on the way to the Upper Saddle, Paul said, "Ex, why don't you go over there, take a look at that ledge, and if you think it'll go, why go, and we'll meet you on top. If you don't think it will go, call me and we'll wait for you." Paul had seen the ledge from the top of the South Teton back in 1924, and once in a while from up there in the couloir.

That day the wind was blowing from the southwest and I got up there to the end of that ledge and it scared me, but when I called out to Paul, he couldn't hear me and didn't answer. I walked away from the ledge seven times, until I finally got up there and saw those little handholds and the boulder on the ridge. When you get to the eastern extremity of Wall Street, why, there isn't any place to jump from. So I climbed as high as I could until I was sorta secure, and I jumped from a standing start.

Once I got across there, I was mortified. Almost paralyzed. But I just decided that from then on I was going to change my whole attitude about it, because there was only one way to go, and that was up.

And you know, the other party was over on the ridge next to us, the Underhill Ridge, on that same day. And I was screaming at them just to get their attention, and they never did yell back at me. Phil Smith, he said later, "I thought you were over there just watching us."

And I said, "Hell no, I was over there trying to climb the mountain, and I just wanted to talk to somebody but you never answered." I think I was probably yelling because I wanted to communicate with somebody. I was really alone, but I thought if I could at least get in a word with them, it

Exum, musician and mountain guide, stands before the mountain range he loved. He and Paul Petzoldt created the Exum Mountain Guides in 1926, the oldest mountain guide service in the United States. It still thrives today. Collection of the Jackson Hole Historical Society and Museum, 1991.4055.001.

might be some comfort, you know. It was kinda crazy and I didn't know anything. My equipment wasn't very good. I was wearing that pair of football shoes. Finally I said to myself, "Well, I'm just going to climb and quit talking." The fear left me and I just started floating along. Just going.

I never saw Paul and the Austrians until he got clear to the top. I had been sitting up at the top of the mountain there about an hour and a half. I was looking off to the south and Paul, he comes up from the west, and the first thing I saw of him were those bushy eyebrows, you know, and he saw me and he couldn't believe it. He said, "My God, Ex," and started to run, and he forgot the Austrians were attached to him. They were just little guys, hitting the rocks. And he came over there and gave me a big bear hug and said, "This is somethin' else. Do you know what you've done?" I had no idea about the significance of my climb at all. I didn't really know the history of the mountain. Nor did I have any idea that I was doing what I did. It was not mapped out, it was just something that happened, you know. I just happened to do it.

We all made it down to the Lower Saddle and I took off because I had to play in the band that night. Paul had gone to take a look at the route. I thought when he got out to the end of Wall Street I heard him holler down, "Any old lady could do this," you know, and that kinda made me mad, so I ran all the way down to Jenny Lake. Later I found out that he said, "Exum, you're crazy to do this."

Two Dogs Climb the Grand

In the summer of 1952, 17 boys from the Teton Valley Ranch qualified to climb the Grand Teton through my guide service. Dick Pownall, one of my senior guides, and I were to take them up. The morning we left on the climb, Dick came to me and said, "Glenn, I have a number of things to take care of in Jackson. Would you mind if I met you at base camp on the Lower Saddle of the Grand later this afternoon?"

There was no problem with that, so I took the boys and arrived at the Saddle by 4 p.m. In those days we had no hut to stay in, and had tried most every type of tent, including pup tents and even an umbrella tent which blew away shortly after we put it up. The wind on the Saddle seemed to blow in all four directions at the same time, and it was difficult to keep any kind of structure in an upright position for long.

We found, after much frustration and experimentation, that a large tarpaulin served us best. We would take a climbing rope and stretch it between two boulders about fifty feet apart, take the tarp and lay it on the ground between the boulders, then pull it under and back over the rope. After we had placed the sleeping bags in a neat row, we would put our clients in the bags, pull the tarp over the rope and stretch it tight over the clients, and then place rocks on the edges of the tarp. The guides would then slip in the sides of the tarp, resecuring the tarp with additional rocks. We were "snug as a bug in a rug," warm and out of the wind.

The boys and I had done all of this preparation and decided to go down to the big snowfield on the east side of the Saddle to fill our canteens with water and prepare the evening meal. We had just filled the last canteen when I glanced down at the Middle Teton glacial moraine. Dick was walking at a fast gait with two large black Labrador retrievers following him. In about 45 minutes he arrived at the tarp, the dogs closely behind him. I inquired, "Dick, where did you get the dogs?"

He responded, "They started following me on the lower stretches of the trail. I told them to go back. I even swore at them and finally threw rocks at them. They seemed to have an affection for me and kept right on coming, so here they are."

I asked Dick how the dogs got up over the headwall. It is an eighty foot pitch and a dog could not possible climb it.

Dick responded, "Oh, I helped them a little bit."

In turn, I replied, "Oh."

We ate our evening meal and shortly after the sun set, decided to retire. We lined the boys from west to east in their sleeping bags, and then thought about the dogs. I said, "Dick, I understand that the body temperature of a dog is much higher than that of humans. How about sleeping with them? You pick one of the dogs and I will take the other one." Dick was in accord, so he took his dog to the west side of the tarp, threw back the flap, coaxed the dog under the flap and closed it. After sliding the rocks into place, we too were snug.

At 3:30 a.m., when our alarm went off, Dick and I took our dogs from under the tarp and fired up the Primus stoves. I was elated. "You know, Dick, that's the warmest, most comfortable night I have ever spent on the Saddle," I said.

"You're right, Glenn," Dick answered. "We shall call this the Two Dog Night."

We roused the boys, ate our breakfast, prepared our packs, and were about to leave when Dick asked, "What shall we do with the dogs?"

I said, "Dick, there's no way we can take them with us. There are some short sections of rope over there in the cache. Tie the dogs to a couple of those boulders. Keep them separated."

After Dick tied the dogs up, they immediately started to howl, bark, and jump like they had lost their marbles, so I said, "Turn them loose." Dick and I have never seen such tail-wagging and tongue-licking affection. The dogs were in ecstasy, running among the boys, who were murmuring with affection. The stars and moon were out as seventeen boys, two guides, and now two dogs started the trek up the mountain.

One hour later, we reached the point just above the Needle's Eye and the Belly Roll, almost to where the Owen and Exum Routes meet. I said, "Dick, you have graded all of these boys. Pick the eight best climbers and one of the dogs and head for Wall Street and the Exum Ridge. I'll take the other dog and the rest of the boys with me and climb the Owen Route."

Dick selected his eight boys and chose one of the dogs. But something wasn't right. After some thought, Dick and I decided that if we were going to climb with the canines, we needed to know their names. I said, "Let's call your dog Lord Mallory, after the English climber who said he climbed the mountain because it was there." Then I thought about my dog and added, "And since we are climbing the Owen Route, I shall call my dog Billy Owen after the man who first climbed the Grand Teton in 1898."

Dick took his boys and His Lordship and traversed over to Wall Street. My boys and Billy headed for the Upper Saddle. We saw Dick and his group silhouetted against the sky as they continued north on the Exum Ridge. Soon we were at the Upper Saddle and ready to rope up and get on to the route that was discovered by Bill Owen's party. The dog Billy hadn't had any problems to this point. I took him over the Bellyroll unaided. The boys all were carefully belayed across the Crawl. (These two leads were the crux points that opened the way to the summit in 1889.)

The Crawl is a horizontal crack that extends about 35 feet across the west face of the mountain. It is truly amazing; it almost looks artificial. Climbers are required to get into the crack and "coon." Billy Owen called it the Cooning Place, because one has to crawl like a raccoon to negotiate it. It is extremely exposed. A rock dropped from that point wouldn't hit anything for about 3,500 feet.

The Bellyroll is actually a flake attached to the west face, and to climb it one has to roll around the outside of the flake. We then came to a vertical chimney, which I knew Billy the dog couldn't climb. I made a little harness out of nylon streamers, put it on him, got a good hold of the harness, and actually threw him to a boulder protruding above my head. I chinned my-self up to him, then belayed the boys one by one up to the double chimney immediately above us. Billy was composed and patient. I felt that he could climb the next few pitches, so took the harness off him.

We quickly ascended the double chimneys and traversed the Catwalk, which took us almost due south. From there we climbed up a number of short chimneys, and were soon on the summit. It was about 10 a.m., the start of a beautiful day; the sky was a robin egg blue and studded with cumulus clouds.

As we enjoyed the beautiful view, Dick and his party came up the ridge to join us. There was something peculiar extending above Dick's left shoul-der. Closer inspection proved it to be Lord Mallory's nose. Dick had stuffed the dog into his knapsack. In a matter of a few minutes, he had his eight boys on the summit. I inquired, "What happened to your dog?"

Dick replied, "His Lordship just doesn't like to climb, so I have carried him most of the way."

We had the boys sign the summit register. Then I said, "Dick, what can we do about the dogs? We will have to leave some kind of a record of this unusual ascent."

Dick said, "I have some iodine in my pack." He quickly took a paper nap-kin out of his pack and doused it with iodine. We then took the right paw of each dog, pressed them into the napkin, and left two vivid pawprints on the summit register. Soon after we packed up our gear and started down the mountain, we found ourselves at the Pownall-Gilkey Rappel point. Dick and Art Gilkey had set up the rappel on the first direct ascent of the North Face of the Grand in August, 1949. Art lost his life on K2 in 1959.

The rappel station was the most direct route to the Upper Saddle, and cut out a series of traverses on the west face of the Owen route. The rappel is a spectacular one. It is 120 feet, the last 80 feet of it free—that is, the climber is suspended without touching the rock. We had the boys all lined up and ready to go down. After two rappelled, the dogs became very restless. I said, "Dick, we had better take the dogs down."

He and I emptied our two army packs, and put a dog in each. Dick tied the inside shoulder straps together, so the dogs were side-by-side, placed his arms through the outer straps of each pack, then got into a crouched position and lifted both dogs onto his back. He fastened the waist belts together in front of his belt buckle. He got on a double rope and tiptoed out to the edge of the overhang. As he disappeared over the brink, the dogs closed their eyes, noses pointed up, as if they were in ecstasy.

We soon had all of the boys and the dogs on the Upper Saddle and were ready for the descent. I said to the gang, "Let's see what kind of a route finder we have here." I turned Billy loose and he guided us all the way to the Lower Saddle without missing a turn. What a nose and memory for direction! We were all elated with our canine's super performance, and we continued back over the moraine, glaciers, and trails to our climbing school's headquarters at Jenny Lake.

When we arrived, my wife Beth couldn't believe her eyes as we walked into camp with seventeen boys and two dogs. During our climb, Beth had found out that the dogs belonged to John and Georgie Morgan, who were working on the Elbo Ranch on Cottonwood Creek. I told Beth, "I think these dogs should have a certificate of ascent."

She made one out for Lord Mallory and the other for Billy Owen. I delivered the dogs and the certificates to John and Georgie that evening. When I arrived at the Elbo I said, "John, we just completed an ascent of the Grand Teton with your dogs. Here are their certificates. You owe me $40." What fun!

29

THE TETONS (1984)

ELIZABETH D. WOOLSEY (1908–1997)

Elizabeth D. Woolsey has been described as an Olympic skier, a mountaineer, a horsewoman and fishing guide, and as a remarkable host at her Trail Creek Dude Ranch. She was all that and more. She set down her many adventures in Off the Beaten Path *(1984), an exciting read for anyone interested in high country and wilderness adventure and from which this section is taken.*

Woolsey first viewed the Tetons from the northern shore of Jackson Lake, where she was stunned, describing the range as "a great mountain barrier rising abruptly into the sky with no intervening foothills to hide the upward thrust." She compared it favorably to scenes of the Swiss Alps that she knew well.

Woolsey soon fell in love with Jackson Hole, bought an exquisite piece of land, and transformed it into the Trail Creek Ranch, a successful dude ranch where she lived and worked for the rest of her life.

In the following excerpt, Woolsey describes a couple of failures on the Grand and the North Face, finding falling rocks particularly daunting. But she returned "to the Tetons many times." Her favorite climb was Mt. Moran, even though it was the only time she had to bivouac overnight on a mountain ledge with her "legs dangled in space." Woolsey admits to climbing in the "old uncrowded days" when reservations were unheard of and a campfire was an enjoyable necessity. Like so many veterans of Teton Park, she advises to plan trips out of season, avoiding June, July, and August

The Waddington trip over, we said goodbye to Alan who flew back to Washington from Vancouver. Bill suggested, as we drove east through Washington and the Idaho Panhandle, that we detour south into Wyoming and have a look at the Tetons. This idea appealed to Fritz and myself as we were well rested after the cruise on the *Tranquilla* and full of energy; the summer was young and we had no pressing engagements in the East. Also, Bill had friends, the Dillworths, who owned a ranch at the foot of the mountains who had invited us to pay them a visit. We had heard that the North Face of the Grand Teton had not yet been climbed and that would be our main objective.

We drove through the lodgepole pine forests of Yellowstone Park, stopping often to feed the friendly bears who looked very small in contrast to the giants we had seen on the shores of Knight Inlet. I found the park interesting, but a bit oppressive, with miles of road bordered by thick stands of timber shutting out the view.

Our first sight of the Teton Range was from the northern shore of Jackson Lake; a great mountain barrier rising abruptly into the sky with no intervening foothills to hide its upward thrust. It was a scene to make the heart beat faster, comparing favorably with such classic mountain views as those of the Matterhorn above Zermatt, Mt. Blanc above the vale of Chamonix, or the Jungfrau group seen from Murren, across the Lauterbrunnen valley....

I was to return to the Tetons many times. A climb on Mt. Owen is memorable as it was the only time I was to bivouac on a mountain. Fritz Wiessner and I were joined by Jim and Gini Huidekoper, skiing pals who had been recently married, and we set up camp by the shores of Amphitheater Lake.

Gini developed a severe case of mountain sickness on the climb itself and, as I had already climbed Owen with Paul Petzoldt, I offered to stay with her. Gini became anxious about her bridegroom as soon as he got out of sight. As he didn't return till almost dark, there were long hours spent reassuring Gini rather than napping comfortably as planned. It was a long day.

The climbers returned at dusk, explaining they had missed the route and had forced a difficult chimney rather than retrace their steps. We started down in the half light, I particularly unhappy as I had only dark prescription glasses along and couldn't see with them or without them.

World-class climber and skier Elizabeth D. Woolsey on a vertical pitch in the Tetons. As a downhill skier, she led the American team at the 1936 Winter Olympics. Perhaps the finest athlete in Jackson Hole history, she established a dude ranch in the valley and managed it for the rest of her life. Collection of the Jackson Hole Historical Society and Museum, 2011.0005.087.

I persuaded the other to bivouac on a ledge wide enough for the four of us to sit on, though our legs dangled in space. We tied ourselves in and, as the ledge was wet, I sat on my felt cowboy hat and managed to doze off. It was a troubled sleep and I had a vivid dream, in color, when we reached the Amphitheater Lake there were gaily striped cabanas set up around the shore, crowds of people and radios going full blast. It wasn't a dream, it was a nightmare. I woke up, still perched on our ledge, from which we made our way down to a deserted Amphitheater. My dream was a foretaste of crowds to come.

I was to climb the Grand many times in the following years, but Moran, the northernmost and most massive of the major Teton peaks, is my favorite. I first climbed it with Dr. Becket Howorth, an orthopedic surgeon from New York.

The usual procedure is to bivouac one night as the climb is a long one, some 6,000 feet above the valley floor. I hoped, that by camping on Leigh Lake and using my boat, we could make the climb in one day. We would then eliminate the backpacking up to a high camp.

The mountain cast a spell over me that night, many years ago. My sleeping bag was laid out at the edge of the timber on the east shore of the lake. I walked down to a sandy beach as I couldn't sleep and looked up at the great mountain that rises right out of the dark waters of Leigh Lake. A bright August moon bathed its cliffs, glaciers and rock slides in a pale yellow light, accentuating its enormous bulk and towering height. I felt it to be a friendly mountain, one that would welcome me to its highest reaches and see me safely down to the valley again.

Some hours later, Becket and I were paddling across the lake to the foot of the climb. Our boat floated right into the reflected image of the mountain, now rosy in the first light of the sun. I had the illusion that we were already descending the peak, gliding smoothly down the precipices and steep slopes to the shore where we beached our boat.

The only sound was the drip of water, falling in drops from the blades of our paddles. We whispered as though we were unwilling to break the silence of the magical windstill morning. We landed to the sound of a small stream that had its source in the Falling Ice Glacier and the splash of a monstrous trout feeding by a big rock that jutted out from shore.

There were then hours of bushwhacking up steep slopes in timberline, hard going even without heavy packs. We ate a second breakfast and drank great gulps of ice-cold water, the last we were to find on the mountain, in a high meadow surrounded by rocks and stunted pine.

Thence our way led over easy rocks to the top of the isolated pinnacle. From this vantage point our route looked very difficult: a wall of steep, smooth slabs that must be climbed, just to the south of the black dike that splits the upper section of Mt. Moran. We descended the steep west face of the pinnacle, rappelling down over an overhang into the notch leading to the face of Moran proper, and the real start of our climb.

We worked our way up the slabs, taking the rope that was still in rappel position, with us. We tied it to a knob of rock for our use on the descent. The ensuing climbing was nowhere really difficult, but was airy and exposed. The rock was sound, unlike the conditions I had found on the Middle Teton. As we gained elevation, we had constantly changing views of the main group of the Tetons to the south of us and of the great granite wall of the Wind Rivers, far to the east.

Moran has a very comfortable summit, a surprisingly large meadow with patches of grass and wildflowers. That particular day it was swarming with butterflies that flew around us as we ate our lunch. It seemed an oasis, on top of the world, its approaches guarded by steep rock and ice. I lay on my back on the short Alpine turf and dreamed away a golden hour.

On a perfect day in the mountains, I have always a reluctance to come down from high places. This was such a day but we had a long descent ahead of us. We climbed down to our fixed rope, untied it and swung across the gap between the main face and the pinnacle above the overhang. This saved us much time. I was very proud of this maneuver as I had though it out all by myself.

The sun had now swung around to the west. The lower half of the descent was made beautiful by shafts of light reaching the v-shaped notches of Paintbrush and Leigh Canyons, forming bright bands on the dark waters of the lake.

We paddled across the lake to our camp site in the dark until the moon rose, low and blood red from behind the Gros Ventre Mountains. My last memory of that long day was of sprawling on the sand by our campfire, drinking mug after mug of steaming tea laced with rum and watching Moran turn to silver with the rising moon shining full on its east face.

PART VI

INSPIRATION FROM THE PARK

30

FOR EVERYTHING THERE IS A SEASON (1994)

FRANK C. CRAIGHEAD JR. (1916–2001)

Frank C. Craighead Jr. and his twin brother John were raised near the Potomac River. With the enthusiasm of their father, they were introduced to natural history, an interest that lasted for a lifetime. In 1937 the boys drove west to discover the Tetons and Jackson Hole. They vowed to return. After earning their bachelor's degrees at Penn State, the brothers did indeed return, buying land and building homes. They both became well-known naturalists for their writing on falcons and other birds of prey. In 1949 the two earned PhDs at the University of Michigan. In the 1950s John accepted an academic position at the University of Montana, but Frank and his family opted to remain in Jackson Hole.

The two brothers, however, soon teamed up to study grizzly bears in Yellowstone. In their twelve-year study, they made great progress in understanding the bears but also as pioneers in radio tracking of wildlife. Frank undertook many other studies for the U.S. Fish and Wildlife Service, NASA, and the NPS, and he also served as a senior research associate at the State University of New York at Albany between 1967 to 1977. Instrumental in advocacy of wild and scenic rivers, Frank's accomplishments are legendary.

Late in life, Frank embarked on another project with the assistance of his second wife, Shirley Cocker Craighead. The result was For Everything There is a Season *(1994), a compilation of a lifetime of observation. A gift to the park and the people of Jackson Hole, it is an ecological field guide based on timing for the fifty-two-week year. Here we reproduce the week of June 26 to July 2.*

When the white tufted seeds of hawksbeard and the flowers of western polemonium appear, young red-tailed hawks and nestling prairie falcons are in the feathering out stage of development, during which they continue to gain in weight and size. The towering stalks of green gentian are in full bloom as are the white wyethia and mules-ears. Great gray owl and kestrel eggs are hatching, and butterflies, moths, and dragonflies are active and numerous. Watch for the appearance of salmon flies.

Elk, deer, moose, bison, and pronghorn antelope are now less secretive and can be more readily observed with their young. The elk and bison are seeking grasses, sedges, and herbs; the moose, deer, and pronghorns favor the browse plants. The old, shaggy winter coats have been shed and replaced by slick, shiny pelage—the elk a deep brown, the moose almost black, the mule deer a reddish brown.

Nestling great blue herons are about half grown. A parent is usually standing watch nearby ready to protect them from maurading ravens. The nestlings are rapidly approaching the stage where they can defend themselves with their dagger-like bills. Spotted sandpipers and yellow warblers are incubating eggs. Juvenile mountain bluebirds and house wrens are leaving their nest hollows, and pine siskins are fledging. Young blue grouse a week old are keeping close to their mother while the pompous male diverts attention from the scampering brood. Fast growing, young Barrow's goldeneyes are trailing their mothers single file on beaver ponds, having left their hollow tree nests several weeks earlier for wetter and more open spaces.

With the yellow flowers of balsamroot no longer dominant, the now more conspicuous little sunflower (*Helianthella uniflora*) takes its place in the color scheme, being enhanced by the yellow shrubby cinquefoil (*Potentilla fruticosa*), sulphur cinquefoil (*Potentilla recta*), and another yellow cinquefoil, silverweed. Western Polemonium (*Polemonium occidentale*) appear as the white wyethia (*Wyethia helianthoides*) are in full bloom.

Young tree swallows congregate in groups on wires and limbs waiting to be fed by their insect-foraging parents. Hatches of stone flies, caddis flies, crane flies, and mayflies now more frequently inform the fly fisher of the dry fly to use.

The green berries of wild currant, holly-grape, buffaloberry, service-berry, black twinberry, elderberry, red-osier dogwood, and river hawthorn are all rapidly developing. The white flowers of thimbleberry (*Rubus parvi-florus*) and wild red raspberry (*Rubus idaeus*) are just appearing. A few wild strawberries are ripe, but they're usually scarce compared to the number of flowers observed earlier.

With the advent of summer, the orderly progression of blooming from year to year becomes more in sync with the flowering times of previous years. There is now less influence from weather variables such as snow depth, snow persistence, storms, chilly or freezing nights, extended periods of rain, overcast skies, or drought. Summer has arrived, and it is evident in the profusion and diversity of flowers and the varied nesting activities of a large number of bird species ranging from Calliope hummingbirds to golden eagles.

Young ground squirrels, meadow mice, chipmunks, pocket gophers, and yellow-bellied marmots are being picked off by coyotes, badgers, and red foxes—all with young to feed. They are taking their toll of the annual in-crease in the rodent populations. The mammalian predators are competing with the raptors for the same prey species, yet at the same time automati-cally collaborating in the reduction and control of rodents, species whose productivity is geared to compensate for such losses.

When the yellow clouds of lodgepole pollen are being whisked across the tree tops and are building up in yellow masses along the lakeshores, look for other but quite different clouds. These clouds are composed of hundreds of thousands of large-bodied salmon flies, largest of all the stoneflies, with wingspreads of three to four inches. They are called salmon flies because they are a beautiful salmon pink color. Emergence occurs at different times and throughout a number of days. It is largely influenced by warming water and by elevation, the flies appearing when water temperatures reach fifty degrees or more. Hatches occur in canyons or along vegetated stream banks and rocky shorelines. Here the nymphal form lives under rocks and debris in fast, well-aerated water. First emergence occurs down-stream and moves up as the water temperature rises. In late spring or early summer when the flowers of yellow sweet clover (*Melilotus officinalis*) first appear along highway shoulders, when little sunflower and blue flax are blooming, the salmon fly nymphs leave the water and crawl about on shore, where they cling to rocks, trees, and other vegetation. Here they shed their nymphal husks (shucks) and unfold and dry their wings prior to flying. Soon after they are airborne, the females fly low, dipping their abdomens in the water while depositing eggs in the stream.

In some areas, such as the Canyon of the Yellowstone River, I have observed late morning hatches that looked like locust hordes, the sky seething with the moving insects. Circling birds first indicated the presence of a hatch. Ravens and California gulls cut swaths through the moving mass as they fed voraciously on the insects. Trout gorged themselves on the limitless food supply and put on layers of fat that serve them well in leaner days ahead. I looked on, too entranced to feel disappointment at the trout's lack of interest in my artificial flies. This is an amazing spectacle, one that can provide a fly fisher enjoyment and satisfaction even if nary a trout is hooked.

31

THE RANGE OF MEMORY (2005)

TERRY TEMPEST WILLIAMS (1955–)

Terry Tempest Williams enjoys a national reputation. What is it about her? Her writing ability? Her capacity to express the best in nature? Her determination to protect the land and wilderness? Her love of the American West and its mountains? For our purposes, let us choose her love of mountains. Of all the mountains Williams has known, the Tetons come first. These iconic mountains are her "home range."

Williams is best known as a writer, but she is a fierce advocate of freedom of speech and issues of social justice. She is one who fights for the earth with both literary eloquence and pragmatism. Notably, she and her husband, Brooke, purchased a BLM oil lease with no intention of exploiting their right.

One might wonder at the origin of Williams's talent and passion. There are surely multiple explanations, but a dominant one is her intimate association with the Tetons. She and photographer Edward Riddell published The Range of Memory *in 2005, a collaboration of pen and image. In it, Williams shares personal anecdotes from her memory and diaries for some fifty years. I present a selection here.*

We are born in the minds of mountains. They hold our eyes on the horizon, shape our imaginations, and draw our gaze upward. We climb their peaks and touch clouds. We linger in the creases of their canyons and sit by streams and dream. Waterfalls. Wind rustling through leaves. Our legs and lungs propel us forward to the elevated seat of inspiration. Alpine meadows.

Rock faces. Cirques. The summit. The view before us is clear. We breathe in beauty.

This year, I turn fifty years old.

The Tetons are my range of Memory.

Rising from the valley floor, these granite peaks are sentinels, my guides and guardians of all that is true in the world. Grand Teton National Park is a storied landscape, a compass point, a place of pilgrimage where generations meet in a reunion of majesty.

Ten

"It all happens before the sun gets up," our father tells us as he wakes us before dawn to look for animals. Call it our family ritual. Once in the car, the headlights create a tunnel in the dark. My brothers and I are in the back seat, falling asleep, until the car pulls over, the engine turns off and our father's voice is quietly telling us to roll down the windows. Early autumn. Cold. We hear movement. Suddenly, with first light, we see the silhouettes of elk, dozens of elk, moving through the sage, females first, bull herding from the rear. Frost glistens on their backs and we witness their breath. We watch and wait. We wait to hear them bugle, one bull challenging another, and when the cry comes, we freeze. There it is: that blood-boiling scream rising out of the deepest muscular ache for power and possession. There it is again. Young bulls flee as one magnificent elk raises his head high trailed by his rack of perfectly sharpened tines. His harem gathers. He bugles again. It echoes through the valley. At the base of the Tetons, we hear wildness.

Eleven

Sunrise at Signal Mountain. Morning mist covers the valley below as the faces of the Tetons are painted in pastels. Blue grouse strut on the summit, backs arched, tails fanned, wings fluttering as red breast patches inflate like balloons. With my eyes closed, I can feel the drumming of grouse before I hear them. Gold over their amber eyes turns scarlet as they heat up their leks. Like Indian fancy-dancers at a powwow. I wonder who initiates whom.

My grandmother and I continue to walk around Signal Mountain until she stops and points to a snag draped in spider webs. I do not remember her words, only the way she paused to consider beauty created by creatures we fear.

Later, we stop at a pond where we breathe in a freshness known only to pines, drenched wood and mint. Sunlight meets the lilies and they open before our eyes. I do not trust what I see. An elk emerges on the edge of the pond to drink. Can one not believe in the common unfolding of a day?

Yellow-bellied sapsuckers tapping on aspen, violet-green swallows flying in and out of nest holes, kestrels hovering in a clearing hunting for prey, olive-sided flycatchers singing *"Cheep three beers…cheep three beers."* We fall in and out of shadows throughout the day. There is no end to my grandmother's curiosity, as well as her knowledge. "These aspens are all related," she says. "They call them clones. In the fall, each family group turns yellow or orange-yellow at the same time." I focus on the black marks on white bark. I see them as bird, the wing-prints left behind as they enter the trees….

Sixteen

The family who backpacks together stays together. This may or may not be true—but we commit to a Labor Day weekend hiking up Paintbrush Canyon where we spend the first night at Holly Lake. It's a rigorous climb up glacial stairsteps but the columbines are so beautiful along the way, I am distracted from the pull of calf muscles crying out for a rest. My brothers and I are strong. We've been raised for this and although I dread the initial ascent out of teenage obstinance, my love for adventure overrides any laziness that creeps in. Our family sets camp. Food is cooked. Stories told. And as night falls, we slip into our tents for that precarious sleep that comes and goes when outdoors. The next morning, we hike up to the Paintbrush Divide where the steep snowfield demands our attention. We feel both the cool air coming off the ice as well as the heat of the day. Joy replaces fear. We glissade our way down to Lake Solitude and make camp for the second night. In the glory of an early fall day, we dare each other to jump into the alpine water. Our father sleeps on a rock, his own ritual after a successful hike, and our mother finds her own place of serenity near the lake and a garden of mountain gentians. From my field guide, I identify a water pipit.

Seventeen

Deep snows. Temperatures below zero. We ski alongside the Snake River rimmed with ice. A red rose hip in winter catches my eye.

Eighteen

My father and I hike up Avalanche Canyon. There is no trail, hence its appeal. We want wild. We bushwhack our way toward Lake Taminah but it is much tougher terrain than we imagined. A map is a flat piece of paper, after all. Nothing but the ground itself can translate truth to the hiker's feet. The weather disrupts our plans. Temperatures drop and simultaneously, the sky turns dark with clouds. Thunder explodes and we seek shelter in the woods below the granite wall, pulling on our cagoules to stay dry. It rains violently. We huddle together watching pools of water surrounds us. Waterfalls are cascading off canyon walls. It rains harder and harder, no relief. For what seems like hours, we sit through the storm, often shivering. Rain drips off our heads and noses. More thunder. More lightning. A pause and then a clearing. The storm stops as abruptly as it arrived. Steam rises from decaying logs as the sun warms the land once again. We get up, take off our rain gear, shake it dry before stuffing it back in our packs. "Up or down," my father says. "You decide." We go down.

That night, we attend Gladys and Reginald Laubin's Indian Dance at the Jackson Lake Lodge. Admission is $1.50. This is my reward and choice of activity for surviving the storm. The performance is an homage to the Plains Indian People by a student and great respecter of their culture. My father is not impressed. After the fourth dance and repeated bows to the Four Directions, he walks out and waits for me in the lobby. I stay, mesmerized by the comfort of repetition.

Nineteen

Elk Creek Ranch is in Island Park, Idaho. I am working as a cabin maid but I dream of living in Jackson Hole, Wyoming. I read *Wapiti Wilderness* by Mardy and Olaus Murie.

> These are the adventures of the wilderness, the scenes and the music which make up Nature's great mosaic. Why do we so delight in the wild creatures of the forest, some of us so passionately that it colors our whole life? Why do we love Music, Art? Are not all akin, a part of beauty which we really do not understand?

Twenty

It is an ad in the local *Audubon* newsletter announcing a field trip in May titled, "The Natural History of Jackson Hole" taught by Dr. Florence Krall and Ted Major at the Teton Science School. I am a student at the University of Utah interested in both English and biology. This course is listed for three credit hours. I enroll. The place of my heart becomes a place of study. Suddenly, we are not just standing in a forest, but a community of lodgepole pine, Douglas-fir, and quaking aspen. It is a community of succession. Aspens appear first, becoming shade trees for evergreens. The evergreens eventually overtake the aspens. They mature until they fall prey to insects. Pine bark beetles drill into the cambium layer of lodgepoles. Pine needles turn orange, the tree dies becoming fuel for fire. Lightning strikes. The lodgepole burns. With the rising heat, "serotinous" cones explode, broadcasting seeds in the protected duff of the forest floor. The next year healthy saplings emerge. Underground, the roots of aspens sparked by shire shoot up like raised hands beginning the cycle of life all over again.

This is a familiar story to me. Ted calls it fire ecology. I call it resurrection.

I return. In June, I become the first intern at the Teton Science School and work through the summer as a volunteer-in-the-park taking bird walks. One morning at Blacktail Pond, we see an acorn woodpecker, the first sighting in Grand Teton National Park. It is disputed by authorities but later confirmed, luckily by a visitor's photograph. My eyes are open to possibilities.

There are mentors: Jack Major shows us how to use a plant key to identify wildflowers; David Love teaches us geology and lets us pan for gold; Frank Craighead speaks of grizzlies and their right to remain wild; Mardy Murie welcomes us into her home and tells us about a place called the Sheenjek. All I want to do is learn about the plants and animals I am living among and walk in wildness. I want to be a naturalist. Under the tutelage of the Tetons, Ditch Creek, and Joan and Ted Major, I learn to see ecology as the study of home. I am home.

We backpack in the Wind Rivers for a week. When we return to the school, a skinned coyote hangs like a crucifix from the cross beam of the old Elbo Ranch. "Some folks still don't want to see this dude ranch become a center for environmental education," Ted says as he unwraps the barbwire from the bloody carcass and carries the coyote down for a proper burial.

The artist Grant "Tiny" Hagen created a bronze sculpture inspired by an engraving by Ernest Thompson Seton. It is a man seated on the Earth with his legs outstretched. On his right foot sits a squirrel. The man lifts his large bowie knife to kill the squirrel. It is titled *The Thought*.

Twenty-One

The following year I return to the Teton Science School, this time with a husband. His name is Brooke Williams. Our engagement was all of three weeks. We met in a bookstore. He said his dream in life was to one day own all the *Petersen Field Guides*. I told him I already had them. I was nineteen. He was twenty-three. We moved from Salt Lake City to Kelly, Wyoming. We lived in a small cabin and taught students in the field. Our love for nature became our love for each other.

The image I have is this: A line of high school students traversing a snowfield in Open Canyon, each one walking carefully with the security of an ice ax. A bald eagle flies overhead. The students look up as its shadow passes over them. A new definition of freedom emerges as each one crosses the Mount Hunt Divide.

Twenty-Five

A child native to this valley alerts his mother that he has seen a white raven. Word spreads. He wears the cloak of revelation. He knows blue bison, silver coyotes, and fish in the Winds called golden trout. He knows how to call forth sun dogs and watch an eclipse without going blind. He is fearless because wild joy surrounds his heart whenever it grows dark.

Twenty-Six

If there is a common point of return it is at Oxbow Bend. Mount Moran presides over this holy meander like a mother. For years, I thought she was the Grand Teton until my grandmother told me otherwise. Here in generational waters, we see the passing of our own reflection. The heron rookeries of my childhood are gone. Where aspens once stood, there is now a forest of pine and fir. And the channel has widened. Change is the script of landscape—change and continuity. How many years, decades, have we counted on moose being here, right here at this particular turn in the Oxbow, the same solitary moose straining water on the edges of willows, here, now, always.

Yellow warblers. Yellow-throats. A pair of osprey tending a nest. Rafts of ducks are floating on rippled glass. With binoculars in hand, I isolate a pair of American wigeons, baldpates, and beyond them, otters play.

Twenty-Seven

Mother and I hike to Garnet Canyon with my father. He is ahead of us, moving fast, his lungs at risk of exploding from exertion or ecstasy. We saunter and talk, knowing we will eventually meet up with him. This is as close as we will ever get to the Grand. We reach the Saddle. Six weeks earlier, my mother was in surgery for ovarian cancer. Today, she raises her hands high above her head in triumph....

Fifty

White pelicans spiral above Teewinot. They turn—and appear—they turn again—and vanish. I watch in awe, aware of my own desire to soar. Like us, they cannot escape the lure of these mountains. Fifty years. Fifty millennia. Geologic time is sung slowly in the advancement and retreat of glaciers. For nine million years, the Tetons have patiently influenced the life that surrounds them: pelicans, human beings, the melting of waters from snowfields, the clarity of lakes, the animals who congregate. Life always returns to the beloved. Earth.

We are born in the minds of mountains. Life is dynamic. In process. Destruction begets creation. It is the fault of movement, what rises and falls, at once, that creates geographic relief. To learn to love a place.

I am of a place. Family is a place. The Grand Tetons—This Range of Memory becomes a silhouette of love that an erosion of time can never diminish. It is a rock-solid testament that life continues—splendidly—through the generations of all species in the shadow and light of animated granite.

32

"ANTELOPE DREAMING," "7 STARS FOR 7 BEARS," AND "CROSS FIRE" (C. 2010–2016)

LYN DALEBOUT (1955–)

Lyn Dalebout was raised in Salt Lake City. Her father was in the ski industry. Dalebout spent many delightful days on the ski slopes of Alta and elsewhere while pursuing her Bachelor of Science degrees in biology and geography. Her true loves, however, are literature, poetry, and astrology. She combines these interests with love of the outdoors and wilderness.

When Dalebout moved to Jackson Hole, she found both her physical and spiritual home. She often spends her days at Grand Teton National Park seeking spiritual contact with wildlife, particularly bears. She best describes her life in the park:

> *I have lived in Grand Teton National Park since 1980. I count this good fortune as one of the most valuable aspects of my life experience. I am continually inspired by outdoor adventures, the steady study of the Greater Yellowstone Ecosystem through four dramatic seasons, and the countless interactions with wild animals from grizzly bears to bison, and bird life from chickadees to eagles. I feel especially blessed to be part of a visionary and creative community.*

Dalebout is an environmental activist with a feathery touch. Her message often emerges from her poetry. For many people in Jackson Hole, she is the poet laureate. Clearly, Dalebout delights in the varied wildlife of Grand Teton. But beyond appreciation, she is a voice for wildlife that cannot speak for itself. She relishes the space and emptiness of Wyoming. As Dalebout expresses in her poems

"Antelope Dreams," "7 Stars for 7 Bears," and "Cross Fire," *Wyoming is a "state so empty of human diversion that we are a black hole at night on the satellite maps." She would not have it any other way.*

Antelope Dreaming

I run across these open plains
    as if I were an antelope
and needed no trail, only the wind.

I strike out across snow and these open places
    to return home at night. In spring
I never sink in and run like a coyote,
    homeward, with the wind.

It is my good fortune, and through many prayers,
    that I can walk all the way to Yellowstone,
if I had to, across open flats, like a river of wind.

I rise above the ground, like the marsh hawks,
    returning in spring, diving with their young,
as if the air had hollows, loopholes, hidden
    entrances and exits only they could see.

It is my good fortune to live in Wyoming,
    a state so empty of human diversion
that we are a black hole at night on the satellite maps.

We are broadcasting space, and we are broadcasting
    open space, and there is a silence to be heard
in Wyoming, and that's what we are here to do.

A place to counteract the noise and artificial light
    of those who have forgotten the night,
the place of dreaming. The antelope are dreaming now,
    I am sure, as I walk home across the space of

Dark Wyoming reflecting back the sky of nighttime.
    What if there were no stars, like in those mapped
cities of night? It would be like seeing with no sight,
    it would be unholy, maybe natural to another planet.

But not this one of antelope dreaming
    Wyoming into existence, breathing the notion of a state
large and empty and silent and observant.

Sit down before the last stars go out
    a billion years from now.
Sense how already, it has already ended.

7 Stars for 7 Bears

A Praise Poem for Grand Teton Grizzlies ~760 was one of these Bears

our Bears are numbered
610 and 399
a daughter and her mother
five cubs in tow
combined

we've watched them trade one cub
traveling between two moms
sometimes it seems all seven
are functioning as one

*

Ursa Major Ursa Minor
seven stars in each heavenly Bear

Ursa Major Ursa Minor
Great Bear and Little Bear

celestial Bears earthly Bears
mirror one another

emissaries visionaries
how do we live amongst each other

*

we are blessed by Bear ambassadors
fierce love and protection
inhabits their souls

Grizzly mothers
Bear mothers

in honoring them
we become more whole

*

are Bears' days numbered?
indeed if we ignore their needs

vast room to roam
    free
hundreds of miles to move
    unseen

our Bears are numbered
so in deeds
we must hold strong

guarding the wildness of territory
    more land
that's what keeps them from harm

*

These 7 Bears
are our 7 Stars

thankfully
they guide our hearts

Cross Fire

The elk pool at dusk
await the word of light
going down
await the dark.

They travel like
slow moving lightening
across Antelope Flats
awaiting dark coming down.
We see their instincts strong
as they've learned
to move at night.

We wait with them
and keep a silent vigil
for safe passage.
While we offer refuge,
first they must cross
fire, the shooting gallery
which lines their way
to safety.

We hope they are protected
from this hunt
which is not a hunt.
It's a betrayal
of an ancient pact
which is the hunt.
This is not a hunt.
It is betrayal.

33

SPRING (1995)

BERT RAYNES (1924–2021)

Raynes visited Grand Teton National Park in the 1950s. He and his wife Meg made the annual trek from Cleveland every year. A chemical engineer by profession, he was a committed naturalist by avocation. When Raynes retired in 1972, he and Meg quickly made their way to Jackson Hole. They never left. He soon founded the Jackson Hole Bird Club and was involved with park groups and civic organizations. He loved to observe nature but also to write about his experiences. Raynes authored a column in the Jackson Hole News & Guide *devoted to birds and his own reflections on humans and nature. He has continued to do so for over thirty years.*

Although never formally trained as a naturalist, Raynes has been bestowed with that mantle by both the park and the community. People call him regularly with their sightings or their questions. He is a font of information that freely gives. His dedication to conservation has resulted in awards by the National Museum of Wildlife Art, the Wildlife Heritage Foundation, and numerous other conservation organizations.

Raynes has published books and guides on birds in the Jackson Hole region. But he has also written books that reflect his razor-like wit and his subtle irony. Curmudgeon Chronicles *and* Valley So Sweet *represent a curl-up-by-the-fire reading experience. The following selection from* Valley So Sweet *represents the often-futile search for wildflowers and the irony of bison management. The second essay chronicles the strange antics of sage grouse at the "Lek" annual ritual.*

Death Recognition

We're poking around one of the places we go early in spring to hunt for wildflowers.

It's hardly a secret place: Kelly Warm Springs is adjacent to a plowed road. People drive here to see green when winter begins to drag. (Some people commence coming here by Thanksgiving, but they simply have a masochistic tendency, I fear.) It's April 1, and we could be on a fool's search. We don't think so. Sharper eyes have already seen orogenia in bloom.

Orogenia are tiny plants with dozens of inconspicuous whitish blossoms on a stalk less than an inch long. They're hardy and almost always the first to bloom; if not for those special characteristics, they'd be noticed only by botanists. If then.

We luck out, largely because we were told they're up. And then, even luckier, we come upon a few sage buttercup also in bloom.

Three bull buffalo saunter down to sample the green growth surrounding the warm spring. Bison, actually, but most call them buffalo. We watch with a mixture of admiration, curiosity and a certain uneasiness. Although we believe bison belong in Jackson Hole and their presence enriches and enlivens the scenery—that they simply belong—some people who control the fate of these creatures don't want them around.

There came a spring day in 1989 when wildlife managers from various state and federal agencies concluded some bison needed to be shot. By-and-large, "game management boils down to killing or not killing. This was a population reduction operation. Piece of cake. The bison were still on the National Elk Refuge, still in large groups, and conveniently near roads.

And so some uniforms were assigned (or volunteered?) to shoot 16 bison. Selected animals of every age and both sexes were killed. But there was a surprise: It turned out bison demonstrate an awareness of death in their kind.

When a female was shot, the remaining animals became agitated, excitedly moving about, tails up. First cows, then bulls, approached the dead cow to snuff, and sometimes nudge her carcass. One professional, experienced, management guy even went so far as to say their manner was "one of respect." (Gee. If I'd said that, he would have admonished me for being anthropomorphic. He'd be right.)

The much-beloved Bert Raynes: writer and naturalist. After a career as a chemical engineer in Cleveland, he and his wife Meg moved to Jackson Hole in 1973. Here he found his true calling as a naturalist, writer, and highly respected member of the community. Collection of the Jackson Hole Historical Society and Museum, 2011.0097.021.

When a bull was killed the entire herd went into a frenzy. Surviving bulls hopped about "like rodeo animals," bucking, bellowing, tails up, for up to 10 minutes. During this activity, many of the bulls deliberately gored and hooked the carcass. One bull which didn't die instantly was not only subjected to this savaging, but had another bull stand on him.

Cows were excited by the felling of bulls, too, but generally didn't participate in exaggerated activity. A few came up to sniff and to snort, but not to rake or gore.

We weren't witness to the killings or this death recognition business. Some 80 million buffalo were wiped out on this continent by—if not always literate, at least self-expressive—whites. We've read their exceptionally flowery and descriptive accounts of that near extermination. Examined paintings and seen movies. Read journals of travelers and hunters. But we have no recollection of hearing about this particular bison behavior. The stories portray professional hunters coolly killing first the lead cow and then the others as they stood there. Until the gun barrels got too hot to hold. One wonders if those old journals were edited, or if it just wasn't convenient for the killers to recognize feeling in their victims.

The killing on the refuge continued a second day. The remaining bison exhibited identical recognition-of-death behavior, but what appeared to the observers to be at a lesser level of excitement. Learning by the bison? By the killer? If by the bison, it was only learning of a sort, for after a century these animals still didn't grasp that firearmed man is their mortal enemy.

The game managers obliged (or delighted) to carry out this task appeared outwardly calm, detached. Professional. Yet, there were glimpses of behavior akin to a gang nine or 10-year-old boys nervously bolstering each others' guilty consciences after committing what is nowadays termed minor vandalism. A crime, that is. Ooof. Enough of such thoughts. It's spring. Flowers. Sagebrush above the snow pack. Bluebirds. Bison in sight and a chance to see moose. Recognition of life.

Time to Strut

In spring, it gets fancy.

Take sage grouse. Sage grouse aren't monogamous and don't pretend to be. They're into a modified harem arrangement in which a group of females yet particularly attracted to—or by—one. In the case of sage grouse it seems clear one male can't—or doesn't—satisfy all the demands placed upon him.

This seems to be the fate suffered by males of many animal species, up to and including the higher primates. Things are tough all over.

We went to watch the sage grouse strut this morning. Sage grouse gather just before dawn at historically selected places which look like nothing special...except to sage grouse. We call them "leks," areas where animals assemble to display and conduct courtship or mating rituals. Leks vary in size; some barely accommodate six males, whereas others extend several acres and are visited by 30 males and perhaps 120 females.

Our participation is simple. We show up at about 5:30 a.m. and position ourselves to have the anticipated dawn light at our backs. The grouse have already made their way to the lek, but sometimes a few more slide in on set wings from a half-mile or more away.

Pre-dawn on an April morning in Jackson Hole is cold. Sometimes it's windy and snowing. The grouse don't seem to care; we're talking raw sex here, so weather isn't a concern.

Soon we heard a peculiar plopping sound. This is an exhalation made by male sage grouse as they inflate then rapidly deflate air sacs prominent on their chests. Accompanying this display, they parade-strut with their spectacular tail feathers held erect and spread apart.

As the sky brightened, we perceived them clearly: a couple of big fellows in the middle of a loose circle of smaller, younger males and a gaggle of drab females pretending indifference. (Of course, it's feigned. They know it. Everyone knows it.)

Professional ornithologists—who too often are stolid and unimaginative—say that while the bigger, most aggressive male grouse are strutting around, showing off, and battling each other, a few females slip off into the sage with lesser-endowed, callow youth. Oh, well. I've noticed something similar in bars and on ski slopes. Nothing new.

I can't write about sage grouse mating rituals without recalling an old incident that still tickles us. The biggest lek in Jackson Hole, historically, is on sagebrush flat occupied now by a large airport. Old-timers would simply go to the airport to watch the grouse. The grouse and the onlookers would be gone well before any aircraft were aloft.

As years passed the airport got busier, and bigger, and when airplane hijacking became a real threat, security concerns were solved in part by limiting casual access. Which is to say, they put up a big fence. Sage grouse observations fell off to almost nothing.

Meg and I got the idea to revive strutting watches. We approached the Grand Teton National Park administration for help.

The airport lies within GTNP and there is a guarded cooperation between the two entities. With great reluctance—a stance we have encountered on, well, almost every occasion we've addressed bureaucrats—a park naturalist agreed to arrange a supervised visit to the airport lek. I won't mention his name, but I remember it. He bet us that no more than five people would attend, and if that was the case, we could forget bothering him ever again. About anything.

He underestimated the pent-up urges old-timers had to revisit that spectacle; the interest of a small bird club; and the power of a newspaper column alerting people to this opportunity.

So did we. As we drove to the airport (on what turned out to be a beautiful, calm morning) we were surprised at the volume of traffic passing us. Lots and lots of cars. We wondered where everyone was going at 5:15 a.m. It wasn't hunting season. Way too early for skiers. Slowly it occurred to us: People were going to look at birds.

And, they were. There were almost 70 people that morning. Lots of fun.

Oh, yes. By the very next Sunday the park had assumed authority over sage grouse observations. Personnel showed up in uniform, with red flashlights and for all I know, guns. They had a fancy hand-out for each attendee on the natural history of sage grouse. No mention, naturally, of anybody outside the park service. Ha! (That naturalist, by the way, used the entire affair to enhance his resumé and advance his career. He is stationed elsewhere now, probably where he doesn't have to get up so early.)

But, that incident wasn't on our minds this morning. We just watched the birds, enjoyed the sights and sounds, and trusted in another generation of sage grouse. As the sun crested Sleeping Indian Mountain, the grouse skipped away into the snowy sage flat. We believed we didn't influence the birds in their activity. Perhaps we even kept a coyote at a distance, but we don't know that for certain.

Time for breakfast. I'm not at all certain what grouse do aprés strut.

Rest, probably. Or smoke.

34

JACK WEBER'S CUTTHROAT ADVICE LASTS FOREVER (2006)

PAUL BRUUN (1944–)

Although Paul Bruun was born and raised in Miami Beach, Jackson Hole has a legitimate claim to him. Bruun has been a fishing guide on the Snake River (and elsewhere) for thirty-seven years. He also claims credentials as a newspaper owner (Jackson Hole Daily) *and journalist. For many years he has written a weekly column on fishing, saltwater as well as fresh.*

Bruun is a wonderful storyteller, and from this 2006 column published in the Jackson Hole News, *he entertains us with tales of guiding Jack Weber, an executive with Kaiser Steel and accomplished fly fisherman. Weber treasured fishing the Snake and his days with Bruun at the oars, so much so that when he passed on, his remains were returned to the place he loved to be.*

Good advice can take a while to penetrate a hard head. The absorption factor in this instance was at least a dozen years. But I will continue to treasure the lesson from Jack Weber for the rest of my life.

Jack paid Jackson Hole a visit last week and was joined by his family and friends. As always, his presence solidified September as the nicest month of the year. When we met in 1974 Jack was Kaiser Steel's midwest sales manager. He lived and worked out of Tulsa. Having grown up in the Butte-Anaconda area of Montana, Jack was partial to the West and he absolutely loved trout fishing. It was this fishing passion that helped him engineer one of the nicest corporate events this area will ever see.

Between 1966 until 1983 Kaiser Steel set up command headquarters in Jenny Lake Lodge after the facility closed to the public on Labor Day. For the next two weeks the steel division arm of the Oakland based parent, Kaiser Industries, would shuttle in the top brass of their best client companies. Little other than golf, sightseeing, relaxing, dining and fly fishing was on the menu.

As a host Jack Weber was without peer. Effortlessly he could assemble and preside over a flawless state dinner for visiting royalty and he just might squeeze out an extra million tons of metal sales over desserts.

The annual Kaiser visit was legendary for several reasons. First, it allowed a collection of accomplished and successful corporate chiefs to enjoy fall in the Tetons—one of the nation's most beautiful natural environments—during its best season. Secondly, the extra two weeks of post season work was eagerly anticipated by over a dozen young men whose careers back then and almost forever would be inextricably entwined with fly fishing and guiding on the Snake River. The Kaiser event was a post graduate education for everyone involved.

Almost all raft and fly rod owners in Jackson wanted to guide for Kaiser. Johnny Becker, then the head wrangler at the Lodge Company Moose Tackle Store (formerly the Bob Carmichael Fly Shop), handpicked his guide crew. I backed into four trips in the fall of 1974 when I was trying to get started taking fishermen on the Snake. That was pure luck and only because an unfortunate "part-timer" sank a raft in the then notorious Spruce Ditch.

I was teamed with Charlie Sands for a two-raft afternoon fishing trip on about September 10. Jack Weber in his familiar plaid flannel shirt, eager grin and big brown western hat with the lower crown hidden by giant streamers met me at the fly shop. "You're the new guy aren't you?" Jack warmly announced. "I look forward to getting to know you. You'll enjoy our group, too," he waved and was off for an afternoon float with one of the regular guides like Kirby Williams, John Simms, Jerry Amadon, the late Carson Hubbard or Becker.

"Who's that guy," I asked Charlie.

"He's the big boss of this shindig. Jack Ashby is the president of Kaiser Steel but Jack Weber runs this show," Charlie explained. "And he *can* fish, too!" Big Chuck added with a wink.

I became friendly with Bert and the other guys in the fly shop who kept gear, shuttles and assignments straight. I also got to know another legend—John "Cookie" Cooke—who was always available for counsel and a batch of funny stories. Niels Peak and Don Keirn were Jack's loyal lieutenants. Before each outing one of them would pull me aside for final instructions about the captains of industry I was about meet.

I soon discovered that Jack Weber frowned on my fishing style after he learned that I favored wet flies over patterns that spent most of their time floating on the surface. Niels and Don reported that Jack never let any of them fish "wet" when he was around.

I eagerly anticipated my Moose Tackle Shop meetings with the Kaiser entourage. How could I not? Here were the bosses of Campbell Soup, Del Monte, Continental Can, Ameron, international pipeline outfits, CITCO, Fisher Body and General Motors acting like schoolboys on a class picnic. Jack resembled a baseball manager on the steps of the dugout, giving final fishing orders and strategy every day before his team took to the water. It was an amazing assemblage of talent from all over the country. I loved the atmosphere as much as the fishing.

I got separated from Charlie on that first float trip and consequently took the only route I knew downstream between Deadman's Bar and Moose. This involved rocketing through the speedy but extra narrow Bar BC Channel that twisted like a wet luge course beside the tall moraine and through head high willows. My first client was a well-traveled outdoorsman and corporate vice president of the giant Texas based Brown and Root construction firm.

Things were going moderately well until I spotted a set of dark antler palms attached to a gigantic moose that was getting to his feet about 200 feet ahead. Trying to sound casual, I asked my fisherman, "How close you been to a bull moose?"

"Oh, about 150 yards to the last one I got in Canada," he responded.

If that moose were to take one stride forward he would have blocked the channel. That would have resulted in complete annihilation of Mr. Brown and Root, Becker's rookie guide and Jay Buchner's borrowed Rubber Fabricators raft.

"You're gonna be a lot closer than 150 yards to this one!" I had time to blurt as we hurtled under the hefty moose's nose, just like a Bullwinkle cartoon scene.

Whew!

"You run a mighty excitin' float trip, young man," the old Texan smiled after we ended up safely at Moose. He even caught a couple of little cutthroat on a fly his son had tied for him.

After a few seasons I "graduated" and began to get better anglers in my boat during the Kaiser event. Pat Daugherty, the Fontana, California steel plant manager, was excellent as were Don Keirn and Niels also came along because they wanted to fish some wet flies like the Woolly Worms and Muddler Minnows I frequently used. We had great fun. One morning a Kaiser guest questioned why I always folded a red shop rag in between the rear hatch and roof of my Blazer. I abruptly explained that due to a poorly fitting design, the rag reduced rattles and excluded rain and dust.

"Oh, I see," he said stiffly and walked away.

"Congratulations, Paul," Jack later announced with his challenging smile. "You have successfully told off the head of the General Motors Fisher Body Division. We're trying to entertain customers here, not get rid of them!"

Because of the hat with all the giant Sculpin, Muddler and Spruce Fly streamers, I finally asked Jack why he appeared so against wet fly fishing. Patiently he took off his venerable trademark and pointed to the giant fuzzy patterns. "Paul, these are for big brown trout in Montana. I love streamers and wet flies but the Snake River is different. This cutthroat trout is such a wonderful creature and rises so eagerly and beautifully to dry flies that it's a shame not to showcase that great trait of this fish!"

Jack never suggested that I not toss Muddlers but he made his point so clearly that I began using more dry flies, even with fishermen who would be challenged to keep a life vest afloat let alone a fly of hair and feathers.

The full impact of Jack's tribute to the Snake River Cutthroat took a few more years to penetrate the tough skull I mentioned earlier. But he was so right.

I couldn't get enough dry fly fishing when I began fishing the West frequently in the early 1960s. Later I became enthused about wet flies. But

I've gotten over that attitude as far as our cutthroat are concerned. This fish is too classy to torment with gigantic bunny streamers or split shot and tungsten beadhead nymphs bounced under bright bobber indicators. This stuff works but what's the point? So does Clorox and car batteries.

Whenever I see a handsome cutthroat performing its gentle, slow motion rise or refusal to a fly, I happily recall Jack Weber's lesson about this special fish and its affectionate surface habits.

Jackie and Val, Jack's daughters, and a granddaughter joined Don, Niels and other retired Kaiser operatives at Moose last week with Bob Dornan, Becker and some of the old guides from the Moose Tackle Shop stable. Jack Weber was there too, not for the last time but forever, as friends returned his remains to the place he always loved to be.

So long, Jack, and thanks for the fine memories and unique education.

35

ARE WE PAYING ATTENTION? (2006)

TODD WILKINSON (1962–)

Todd Wilkinson needs no introduction to people who care about the Greater Yellowstone Ecosystem. For over thirty years he has written about and defended this land he loves. Wilkinson's work has appeared in publications ranging from The National Geographic *to* The Washington Post. *Closer to his Bozeman, Montana home, Wilkinson has published a popular, yet often controversial, column called* The New West *in Jackson Hole newspapers for three decades.*

There is more to Wilkinson's professional career. He has published three books that have received critical acclaim: Grizzlies of Pilgrim Creek, *with photographer Tom Mangelsen;* Last Stand: Ted Turner's Quest to Save a Troubled Planet; *and* Science Under Siege: The Politicians' War on Nature and Truth. *His writings challenge us to do the right thing for nature. In the following essay, Wilkinson asks his readers, "Are We Paying Attention?" As we move toward new issues in our national parks, we need to listen to such environmental defenders as Todd Wilkinson.*

Those of us mutually interested in environmental issues—whether as journalists, scientists, natural resources managers, professional conservationists, local planners, business people, recreationists or as interested citizens—have questions before us. One is are we paying attention? The second is if we are paying attention, what are we missing about things happening right before our eyes?

If you are reading these words while in Jackson Hole or the valley on the western side of the Tetons you know what sets Grand Teton National Park and the surrounding ecosystem apart, giving it special context. But deep in our guts, we know the forces of profound change are upon us and unless we think differently, the park and the Greater Yellowstone Ecosystem of today will be, in many ways, left unrecognizable to those who follow.

Will our descendants forgive us for capitulating to that inevitability?

It is human nature to cling to what we know, or to what we think we know. We choose information or details that are familiar over those which press us out of our comfort zones. We believe in facts that confirm our worldviews rather than those which challenge them. Finally, we embrace doing status quo things over and over again instead of short-term sacrifice in order to achieve long-term benefits.

Empires have risen and fallen across the arc of human history because of this failure.

On a blizzarding January night Dr. Susan Clark, founder of the Northern Rockies Conservation Cooperative, and I gathered with four dozen intrepid souls at St. John's Church in Jackson, every one a denizen of Grand Teton or the Greater Yellowstone region. I said something that I knew made people mad. I could read it on their faces. I suggested that we need to say "yes" to saying "no"; that the current wonders of the Greater Yellowstone ecosystem—the most distinctive being the region's wildlife—set it apart from every other in the Lower 48 and the world. They are the products of previous conservation efforts.

In blunt terms, it means that previous generations accepted limits on what we as humans do across the landscape. Today we have reaped the rewards.

The irony, of course, is that some of the biggest financial beneficiaries of the dividends of conservation are people who, for their own ideological and self-interest reasons, are opposed to limits.

Were we to do it all over again—to re-ratify the visionary actions of the past—they would likely be opposed to the creation of Yellowstone and Grand Teton national parks, the establishment of the National Forest and National Wildlife Refuge systems, the passage of environmental laws and prescriptions for protecting habitat against natural resource extraction. The truth is that there are no example on Earth where conservation, over time, has not generated huge ecological, economic, social, cultural, and spiritual benefits. Jackson Hole and Grand Teton parks are testament.

Yet we live in times when it is not fashionable to ever say no. There are many who believe that natural landscapes have no limits for the amount and intensity of human activity that can occur without serious ecological harm. We live in a time in which users of landscapes (for profit, recreation or lifestyle) conclude that unless they do not actually see direct impacts, they don't exist.

That put scientists in a difficult position. Often, society has used science in field monitoring—to gather data that speaks to changes as they happen or after they have already occurred. It means that we are constantly chasing solutions to problems that race ahead of us, only because we refuse to get out in front of them.

As a journalist writing about Greater Yellowstone and Grand Teton for more than 30 years, there are, as I see it, three major issues that desperately need to be acknowledged. Yet they are resisted, in part, because they involve each of us having to say yes to saying no.

The three difficult impact areas include, first, climate changes and what they portend. Second, the deepening inexorable impacts of human population growth, both tourists and people emigrating to live in the Greater Yellowstone region. Lastly, the inability or reluctance of land management agencies and city governments to see the clear writing on the wall.

Saving Greater Yellowstone necessarily demands that we come together and wrestle with these challenges. If we don't, this ecosystem will go the way of every other region where the fracturing effects of human presence have overwhelmed nature in ways unlikely to ever be reversed. There is no other ecosystem like Greater Yellowstone residing on the other side of the next mountain range. This is it; this, in the so-called Anthropocene, is as good as wild country is ever going to be. It is our national treasure.

How can we preserve this national treasure? In recent discussion on this question, the preponderance of the audience dealt with growth related issues; too many people doing too many things on a finite sweep of interconnected private and public land. We know that the 22.5-million-acre

Greater Yellowstone Ecosystem, vast as it seems, is actually pretty small. It may become smaller, squeezed by climate change threatening its ecological carrying capacity and a doubling or tripling of the human population likely to occur in just two human generations.

If we don't get this "human growth" component of Greater Yellowstone addressed, it won't matter how fond we are of thinking about natural processes playing out at the landscape level. Species like grizzly bears, wolverines and elk need habitat free of intensive human intrusion.

How do we address such crucial issues? I find current discussions about process to be exercises in eye-glazing-over drudgery. I've seen countless meetings where the assertion is "if we only talked and respected each other more and exchanged more bear hugs"—the lingua franca of "collaboration" and "compromise"—then we would save the environment and all be able to pursue our own interests, living happily ever after. Which, of course, is a fairy tale. Who would argue with the notion that having respect and listening to each other are good things?

But where things of real consequence are in play, such as safeguarding undisturbed subalpine snowfields for wolverines, or elk winter range, "compromise" that results in 50 percent more human incursion upon wildlife will not work. We know what the outcome will be. It is writ large in landscapes everywhere. Places where wildlife abundance is depleted, and where only weedy species such as whitetail deer, coyotes, skunks, raccoons and magpies make a living.

Here, right now, there still remains every major mammal and avian species that existed prior to the arrival of Europeans on the North American continent. It even includes black-footed ferrets, a remnant population of which was miraculously discovered near Meteetsee on the eastern edge of Greater Yellowstone.

In Greater Yellowstone, there are no new wild lands being created to offset the ones being fragmented. The challenge is holding the line. Perhaps a major breakthrough in thinking is necessary, but before that is even possible, we have to make visible to the masses what is presently unseen.

The Greater Yellowstone of today only endures because people in the past not only exhibited self-restraint, they set aside lands and passed laws that paid their ethic of conservation forward. They believed that we, too, would see the light. However, the only way that the remarkable wild assets of the ecosystem are going to survive—especially in the face of climate change and inundation by more people—is if we protect as much of the remaining undeveloped lands as possible, both public and private.

By the middle of this century, less than one lifespan from now, Susan Clark notes, the Earth's human population is expected to climb to 10 billion from the current 7 billion—or by nearly 40 percent.

Demographers and planners often hold forth about growth in the abstract and they discuss things like the carrying capacity of human infrastructure. So often lacking are discussions of cumulative ecological impacts, both of how macro decisions play out on the landscape and combined effects of a zillion little incremental ones.

Margaret E. "Mardy" Murie, the late conservationist who made her home in Moose—inside Grand Teton National Park—had been called "the grandmother of the modern conservation movement." Between her and her husband Olaus, Olaus' brother Adolph, and her sister, Louise (Mardy and Louise, being sisters, married the Murie brothers), her clan wore their conservation ethic on their sleeve. Their surviving family members say they don't deserve to be, nor would they have wanted, to be treated as environmental heroes. Nevertheless, Mrs. Murie was awarded the Presidential Medal of Freedom.

Mardy told me something once on her front doorstep in Grand Teton that is undeniable: "There are just too many people, each one wanting to have his own piece of wild country. That doesn't leave a lot of room for the animals, some of them having no other place to go." Will we humans make an accommodation for wildlife?

Before I conclude here, let me offer a little anecdote about human growth trends in the Greater Yellowstone as we approach the 2020s. Randy Carpenter, a demographer with Future West, a think-tank in Bozeman, not long ago brought up the rule of 72 with me, which is you divide the population growth rate of a local place into 72 and you derive the number of years it will take to double.

Greater Yellowstone has more than 600,000 residents today. Imagine that number doubling or tripling in a relatively short time. Gallatin County, Montana, which encompasses Bozeman and represents the northern tier of

Greater Yellowstone, currently has about 100,000 residents. At a conservative 3 percent growth rate, it will double to 200,000 by the year 2031 and will hold a city the size of Minneapolis proper by 2067.

Think about how the megalopolises of Greater Salt Lake along the Wasatch or Denver along the Front Range of the Colorado Rockies have compromised—no, make that devastated—the once wild feel of that glorious wild country, where recreationists now battle each other over trail access. It's all about me-me-me—what makes me feel better in the moment—and not what enhances the essence of Mother Nature who is our muse. There is little regard given to wildlife, save for only the weedy species that can still persist amongst so much landscape fragmentation.

Greater Yellowstone is also facing a paradox. Its wildlife and the character of its wild lands may eventually lead to its undoing because of the sheer numbers of people drawn to it. And there is a frightening wild card. Many say the region could be swamped under by more people—well beyond projections—if environmental refugees, caused by climate change, leave the hot desert Southwest or people in low lying areas start fleeing coastal areas.

On top of this, imagine Teton Valley, Idaho, fueled by spillover from Teton County, Wyoming, becoming as large as Bozeman is today in another generation; the same for Cody, Livingston, and Red Lodge-Columbus. Imagine Jackson Hole at full build out. Imagine recreation trails with twice or three times as many users. Can the wildlife values persist? And can Grand Teton National Park offer the experience it does today?

Not long ago, both Yellowstone and Grand Teton national parks reported that 2016 was another record year of visitation. How many more people can the parks and forest reserves absorb without their essence being lost?

The role of biological and social scientists is more important than ever before if we are going to navigate our way forward to address the impacts of growth and serious issues that will determine the future of Greater Yellowstone.

GRAND TETON TIMELINE

Circa 10,000–12,000 BCE: First human inhabitants settle in Jackson Hole.

1300–1800: Shoshone, Arapaho, Crow, and possibly the Gros Ventre Indians visit and live in Jackson Hole in the summers, mainly on the shores of Jackson Lake.

1807: John Colter enters Jackson Hole, having left the returning Lewis and Clark Expedition.

1818: Donald Mackenzie of the British North West Company visits Jackson Hole in search of beaver pelts.

1860: Captain William F. Raynolds explores Jackson Hole, the first US-sponsored government expedition.

1872: Ferdinand Hayden explores Yellowstone National Park, supported by a Congressional appropriation. With his assistant, James Stevenson, they go south to the Teton Mountains. Photographer William Henry Jackson takes the first photographs of the Tetons.

1882: General Philip Sheridan recommends extension of Yellowstone National Park south to Jackson Lake to protect wildlife.

1883: President Chester Arthur and his party explore Jackson Hole with General Philip Sheridan.

1885: The first homesteader settles on Mormon Row.

1897: Teton Forest Reserve established, guaranteeing that much of the northern Jackson Hole area will remain public land.

1897: Colonel S.B.M. Young, Acting Superintendent of Yellowstone National Park, recommends that Yellowstone authority be extended to Jackson Hole regarding wildlife.

1898: Charles Wolcott, head of the US Geological Survey, advocates creation of Teton National Park.

1908: Teton National Forest established, expanding the reserve to over 1.9 million acres, including northern Jackson Hole.

1915: Stephen Mather, soon-to-be director of the national parks, and his assistant, Horace Albright, first view the Teton Range. They are determined that it should be part of the national park system.

1916: National Park Service established.

1918–1919: Congressman Frank Mondell of Wyoming introduces bills to extend the boundaries of Yellowstone National Park south to include the Teton Range, Jackson Lake, and some of the smaller lakes. The US Forest Service continues to manage the range and northern Jackson Hole. The bills fail to pass.

1923: Meeting at Maude Noble's cabin to discuss how to guard against unsightly development of northern Jackson Hole.

1926: Horace Albright brings John D. Rockefeller Jr. and Rockefeller's wife to Jackson Hole. Rockefeller is impressed and agrees to purchase private land on both sides of the Snake River to preserve for a national park.

1927: The Snake River Land Company begins to quietly purchase land with the idea of including it in a national park. The intent is secret, although Struthers Burt and a few other locals know of the Rockefeller/Albright plan.

1929: Grand Teton National Park is established. It includes only the mountains and some of the western shores of the glacial lakes.

1930: The intent of the 33,000-acre Snake River land purchase for a national park is made public. There is fear and resentment among some locals and opposition immediately forms.

1931: The *Grand Teton* newspaper, opposed to the Rockefeller/NPS park proposal, begins publication.

1932: US Senate Resolution 226 passed to investigate the activities of the Snake River Land Company. After extensive hearings, the committee concludes it was no more that "a tempest in a teapot."

1934: US Senate Bill 3705 introduced to enlarge Grand Teton National Park by incorporating 221,000 acres of Forest Service land and private land owned by the Snake River Land Company. The bill fails to pass.

1938: The National Park Service and Rockefeller again try to pass a bill enlarging Grand Teton National Park. They are again defeated.

1939–1941: The pro-enlargement faction considers using the Antiquities Act of 1906 to create a national monument.

1943: President Franklin Roosevelt signs Executive Order 2578 proclaiming Jackson Hole National Monument. 221,610 acres of Forest Service and other public lands, as well as 32,117 acres of Rockefeller land, come under the jurisdiction of the National Park Service. Many local and state officials are outraged.

1943–1948: All legislative and judicial efforts to abolish the Jackson Hole National Monument fail.

1950: The pro-park and anti-park factions finally put aside their differences. In September 1950, President Harry Truman signs a bill that extinguishes the Jackson Hole National Monument and creates a greatly enlarged Grand Teton National Park. It is the park we have today.

1950–1962: The National Park Service makes major effort to purchase private lands within Grand Teton National Park.

1950–2000: Cattle graze in Grand Teton National Park as grazing leases are preserved, meaning less grass for wildlife. Today, the park has greatly reduced grazing, with only one rancher allowed to graze cattle in the northern area of the park.

1950–2004: Throughout the park's history, superintendents have thought differently regarding the Grand Teton National Park landscape. Most have considered the park to be a natural area, and, as such, have believed that human artifacts (e.g., ranches, buildings, etc.) should be removed. After 2004, policy changes preserve historic sites and structures.

1950–2004: The Jackson Hole elk herd continues to expand. The park, in conjunction with the National Elk Reserve, seeks to keep the winter herd numbers to about 8,000. After 1950, the park initiates an annual elk hunt, which it calls the "elk reduction plan." It is controversial, and still is today.

1970–1985: The Jackson Hole Airport continues to expand, becoming a jetport by 1980. It is the only commercial airport located within a national park. For a time, it appeared that the airport would be relocated, but no longer due to pressure from local businesses and the ski industry. Noise is a constant intrusion, and the park has been permanently compromised.

1993–2011: Visitation to Grand Teton National Park steadily increases. From 1993 to 2011, around 3.8 million visitors come during the summer season. Since 2011, the summer season numbers have increased to over 4 million.

FURTHER READING

Albright, Horace M. *The Birth of the National Park Service*. Salt Lake City: Howe Brothers, 1985.

Bonney, Orrin and Lorraine. *The Grand Controversy*. New York: American Alpine Club, 2000.

Burt, Katherine. *Hidden Creek*. New York: Signet Classics, 1979.

Burt, Nathaniel. *Jackson Hole Journal*. Norman: University of Oklahoma Press, 1983.

Burt, Struthers. *The Delectable Mountains*. New York, NY: Charles Scribner's Sons, 1937.

Calkins, Frank. *Jackson Hole*. New York: Alfred A. Knopf, 1973.

Daugherty, John. *A Place Called Jackson Hole*. Moose, WY: Grand Teton National Park, 1999.

Diem, Kenneth L. and Lenore L. *A Tale of Dough Gods, Bear Grease, Cantaloupe, and Sucker Oil*. Laramie: University of Wyoming/National Park Research Center, 1986.

Everhart, William C. *The National Park Service*. New York: Praeger, 1973.

Fabian, Josephine C. *Jackson Hole: How to Discover and Enjoy It*. Salt Lake City: Grand Teton Lodge Co, 1949.

Fosdick, Raymond B. *John D. Rockefeller, Jr.: A Portrait*. New York: Harper & Brothers, 1956.

Frome, Michael. *Battle for the Wilderness*. New York: Praeger, 1974.

Futrell, J. William. *Our Common Land: Defending the National Parks*. Washington, DC: Island Press, 1988.

Keiter, Robert B. *To Conserve Unimpaired: The Evolution of the National Park Idea*. Washington, DC: Island Press, 2013.

Kreps, Bonnie. *Windows to the Past: Early Settlers in Jackson Hole*. Jackson, WY: Jackson Hole Historical Society and Museum, 2006.

Larson, T. A. *History of Wyoming*. Lincoln: University of Nebraska Press, 1965.

Louv, Richard. *Last Child in the Woods*. Chapel Hill, NC: Algonquin Books, 2008.

Murie, Olaus. *The Elk of North America*. Harrisburg, PA: Wildlife Management Institute, 1951.

Ortenberger, Leigh. *A Climber's Guide to the Teton Range*. San Francisco: Sierra Club, 1965.

Rettie, Dwight. *Our National Park System*. Urbana: University of Illinois Press, 1995.

Righter, Robert W. *Peaks, Politics and Passion: Grand Teton National Park Comes of Age*. Moose, WY: Grand Teton Association, 2014.

Runte, Alfred. *National Parks: The American Experience*. Lincoln: University of Nebraska Press, 1979.

Saylor, David J. *Jackson Hole*. Norman: University of Oklahoma Press, 1970.

Sellers, Richard W. *Preserving Nature in the National Parks*. New Haven, CT: Yale University Press, 1997.

Swain, Donald. *Wilderness Defender: Horace M. Albright and Conservation*. Chicago: University of Chicago Press, 1970.

Tweed, William C. *Uncertain Path: A Search for the Future of National Parks*. Berkeley: University of California Press, 2010.

Wirth, Conrad. *Parks, Politics, and the People*. Norman: University of Oklahoma Press, 1980.

SOURCES

Associated Press. "Journey Through the Yellowstone National Park and Northwestern Wyoming, 1883." Associated Press dispatches. Yale University Library.

Baillie-Grohman, William A. "Camps in the Teton Basin." In *Camps in the Rockies*. New York: Charles Scribner's Sons, 1882.

Betts, Robert B. "The Firstcomers." In *Along the Ramparts of the Tetons: The Saga of Jackson Hole, Wyoming*. Boulder: University Press of Colorado, 1978. Used with permission.

Bruun, Paul. "Jack Weber's Cutthroat Advice Lasts Forever." *Jackson Hole News*, September 20, 2006. Courtesy of Paul Bruun.

Burt, Struthers. *The Diary of a Dude-Wrangler*. New York: Charles Scribner's Sons, 1924.

Craighead, Frank C., Jr. *For Everything There Is a Season: The Sequence of Natural Events in the Grand Teton-Yellowstone Area*. Helena, MT: Falcon Press, 1994. Used with permission of Rowman & Littlefield Publishing Group. All rights reserved.

Dalebout, Lyn. "7 Stars for 7 Bears: A Praise Poem of Grand Teton Grizzlies," "Cross Fire," and "Antelope Dreaming." Courtesy of Lyn Dalebout.

Exum, Glenn. Selections from *Never a Bad Word or a Twisted Rope*. Edited by Charley Craighead. Moose, WY: Grand Teton Association, 1998. Used with permission.

Fryxell, Fritiof. "Teton Clouds and Shadows." In *The Tetons: Interpretations of a Mountain Landscape*, 1938. Moose, WY: Grand Teton Association, 1984. Used with permission.

Grinnell, George Bird. "Through Two Ocean Pass, 1884." Unpublished diary excerpts, volume 1, 41–61. Used with permission by Autry Museum, Los Angeles.

Jones, J.R. "The Bet I Made With Uncle Sam." In *Preserving the Game: Gambling, Mining, Hunting & Conservation in the Vanishing West*. Edited by Reade Dornan. Boise, ID: Hemingway Western Studies Center, Boise State University, 1989. Used with permission.

Judge, Frances. "Vital Laughter." *The Atlantic Monthly*, July 1954.

Langford, Nathaniel. "The Ascent of Mount Hayden." *Scribner's Magazine*, June 1873.

Leek, Stephen. "The Starving Elk of Wyoming." *Outdoor Life*, May 1911.

Murie, Margaret and Olaus. "Valley In Discord." In *Wapiti Wilderness*. Boulder: Colorado Associated University Press, 1965. Used with permission by University Press of Colorado.

Owen, William O. "The Matterhorn of America." *Frank Leslie's Weekly*, May 19, 1892.

Price, Rose Lambert. *A Summer on the Rockies*. London: Sampson, Low, Marston & Co., Ltd., 1898.

Raynes, Bert. *Valley So Sweet.* Wilson, WY: White Willow Publishers, 1995. Used with permission.

Reynolds, William F. In *Up the Winds and Over the Tetons.* Edited by Dan and Marlene Merrill. Albuquerque: University of New Mexico Press, 2012. Used with permission.

Righter, Robert W. *Crucible for Conservation: The Struggle for Grand Teton National Park.* Boulder: University Press of Colorado, 1982. Used with permission.

Roosevelt, Theodore. "An Elk-Hunt at Two-Ocean Pass." *Century Magazine* 44 (September 1892): 713–19.

Sanborn, Margaret. *The Grand Tetons: The Story of the Men Who Tamed the Wilderness.* New York: Putnam, 1978.

Seton-Thompson, Grace Gallatin. "Outfit and Advice for The-Woman-Who-Goes-Hunting-With-Her-Husband." In *A Woman Tenderfoot.* New York: Doubleday, Page & Co., 1900.

Sinclair, Pete. *We Aspired: The Last Innocent Americans.* Salt Lake City: University of Utah Press, 2017. Used with permission.

Smith, Robert B., and Lee J. Siegel. "The Broken Earth: Why the Tetons Are Grand." In *Windows into the Earth: The Geologic Story of Yellowstone and Grand Teton National Parks.* New York: Oxford University Press, 2000. Used with permission.

Smith, Sherry L. "A Woman's Life in the Teton Country: Geraldine L. Lucas." *Montana: The Magazine of Western History* 44 (Summer 1994): 18–33. Used with permission.

Thom, Laine. "The Origins of the Snake and Yellowstone Rivers." Courtesy of Laine Thom.

Turner, Jack. *The Abstract Wild.* Tucson: University of Arizona Press, 1996. Used with permission.

Van Dyke, Henry. "Rivers, Ranches, and Reservations." In *The Travel Diary of an Angler.* New York: The Derrydale Press, 1929.

Wilkinson, Todd. "Are We Paying Attention?" Courtesy of Todd Wilkinson.

Williams, Terry Tempest, and Edward Riddell. *The Range of Memory.* Livingston, MT: Clark City Press, 2005. Used with permission.

Wilson, Elijah Nichols. "The Crows." In *The White Indian Boy and its sequel The Return of the White Indian Boy.* Salt Lake City: University of Utah Press, 2005.

Wister, Fanny Kemble. "Introduction." In *Owen Wister Out West.* Chicago: University of Chicago Press, 1958. Used with permission.

Wister, Owen. "Great God! I've Just Killed a Bear." In *Owen Wister Out West.* Edited by Fanny Kemble Wister. Chicago: University of Chicago Press, 1958. Used with permission.

Woolsey, Elizabeth D. *Off the Beaten Track.* Wilson, WY: Wilson Bench Press, 1984. Used with permission.